De-Stressing WITHOUT DRUGS!

HAPPINESS

In Quantum Leaps

2.0

Aura McClain

Library of Congress Control Number: 2024927098

ISBN
978-1-964488-45-5 (Paperback)
978-1-964488-46-2 (eBook)
978-1-964488-47-9 (Hardcover)

Dedication

Dedicated to God and all of God's lost souls—the ones who need love the most, those who need a hug, and those who are searching for answers. I especially dedicate this book to those whom, I'm sorry to say, I unknowingly drove to hell and back but, at the same time, taught me the most about unconditional love—my husband, Thomas, and my daughters, Grace and Lauren—my superheroes. It was through my struggles with them and in my search for mental peace, love, happiness, and joy that brought me to my awakening and oneness with God. Thank you all. I am forever indebted to you for all the life lessons you have taught me and for bringing me to my highest self and closer to the Light. It is my prayer that this book will do the same for all of you.

In addition, I am grateful to all the people I have never met before, working behind the scenes to make this book possible. I thank you all for being part of the process. Special thanks to my editor Peter Lundell, for all his professional input.

To all my readers, know that God loves you, has always loved you, and will always love you unconditionally, no matter what. I pray that this book will help you get closer to the Light within, help you achieve mental peace, and help you reach your happiness goals.

Namaste!
(Meaning, I bow to you and the divine spirit in you.)

DISCLAIMER: This is only for educational purposes.

Table of Contents

PART III (+) Body "Taking Action in Creating Miracles"

Acknowledgments

Thank you, God, for using me as your vessel for this book. Even when I kicked and screamed to please pick somebody else, you believed in me anyway. Thank you for trusting me and having faith in me, as I have faith in you for leading me throughout the process. To repeat what Jesus said when he was done with his life's mission.

"It is finished!" (John 19:28-30 -NKJV)

Introduction

According to Learning Mind, in their article, "The Psychology of **Nature's Number One Killer: Stress**," they say, "It's so much worse than anyone could've imagined, and that's why researchers worldwide are advocating stress-relieving exercises such as meditation and mindfulness so vehemently. Because both your body and brain are at risk of a serious chemical imbalance that will last a lifetime." Then they go on to say, "Researchers at the University of California, Berkeley, discovered that chronic stress during your developmental years significantly impacts the brain's anatomy and physiology in adulthood.

Also, in the article "Chronic Stress" by the American Psychological Association (APA), they say that prolonged chronic mental stress causes wear and tear on your body making it more difficult for your body to recover from the various illnesses that your negative thinking creates in your **body**. It is estimated that mental stress costs the US $193.2 billion in lost earnings per year, according to the National Alliance on Mental Illness (NAMI) in their article "Consequences of Lack of Treatment." What makes mental stress more dangerous is that when it is left untreated, not only is the risk of chronic medical conditions increased, but also suicide, especially among kids.

NAMI states that suicide is the tenth leading cause of death in the United States, the third leading cause of death for people ages ten to fourteen, and the second leading cause of death for people between ages fifteen and twenty-four. They estimate that eighteen to twenty-two veterans die each day by suicide. In addition, the journal *Lancet Psychiatry* attributes 41,148 suicides in 2007 and 46,131 deaths in 2009 to the stress of unemployment worldwide. Therefore, we are killing ourselves into early graves. On top of this, about 50 percent of all marriages in the United States end up in divorce, which adds to the stress level for both parents and children.

The problem of mental stress is nothing new. This is part of what the Bible calls "man's generational curse." According to the Bible, this has been around since Adam and Eve, caused by their original sin when they decided to **mentally** separate from God and thought they no longer needed God in their lives. So began man's mental focus on the self, and only in the world of objects that they can see and touch as their only reality. In Genesis 2, God warned them to not eat *[don't focus]* from the tree of Knowledge *[your mind]* of Good and Evil *[the material world of objects that we're constantly judging as good or evil]* in the Garden of Eden *[the world of objects]*, or you will surely die *[of an early death of suicide or diseases]*.

THIS IS THE PROBLEM WE NEED TO FIX AND REVERSE NOW, so we can help save lives! I believe this is the answer to healing people from mental stress because what our scientists and educators are teaching our kids today is obviously not working because so many people are still mentally suffering.

According to the APA, mental stress and negative thinking are actually **treatable** problems, and research shows how a test group with coronary heart disease actually dropped by 22 percent simply by changing their state of mind through positive thinking and feelings of happiness, joy, peace, and enthusiasm. The trick is: **How do we think positively and achieve and maintain happiness, joy, and peace long term naturally, without drugs? That's what this book is all about.**

However, because most of the time we use temporary fixes to try to stop our automatic thinking, such as legal and/or illegal drugs, alcohol, or sex. The problem keeps coming back in the form of depression, some form of illness, or worse. For people who commit suicide, it's altogether too late. It was too late for my friend who killed himself at the age of twenty-eight, and too late for my friend's son who killed himself at the age of sixteen, and too late for many others, as you probably know someone who took their own life. My own cousin died of cancer due to mental stress. When the economy dropped, so did her income as a realtor and her ability to provide for her family. After her chemo, she insisted on going back to work right away since she thought she was okay; two weeks later she passed away. She was only thirty-nine years old.

Now is the time to save ourselves from an early grave. And now is the time to help our family and friends before it's too late. What I offer as a solution is not a temporary fix but a permanent one. That is, we must reverse Adam and Eve's original sin in us by learning to **mentally** reconnect to God's energy flow that exists inside all things and learn how to work and control this invisible energy/spiritual force field inside us that physicists say is constantly moving. What I offer is a potentially abundant long life, the way God in the Bible intended all of us to live to the ripe old age of 100 to 120. I believe Jesus came to teach us how to *naturally control our own minds* so that we think less, think more positively, and do so without drugs, as we learn to reconnect and use God's spiritual energy level more efficiently. This is so that we can learn to de-stress ourselves and all live longer lives when he said, "I have come that they might have life and that they might have it more **abundantly** *[longer life]*" John 10:10, KJV. *[Throughout this book all emphases in brackets are mine.]*

The Centaurian website states in their article "Commonalities Among Centaurians" that most of those who have lived a hundred years or more have an innate ability to deal with mental stress and are strong spiritual believers of God. Similarly, this book teaches both: (1) How to mentally de-stress ourselves naturally by learning how to control and reduce our thinking and how to shift from negative thinking to positive thinking. (2) How to connect with the spiritual energy of God—what it is scientifically and how to work with it and use it more effectively so that we can all live longer, happier, and more peaceful lives.

To fix our sin problem (our **mental** separation from God and His love), we all must learn what God is at 100 percent. We all must learn to control our thoughts, learn to build a strong relationship with God, learn to ask Him for help when we need it, and learn to rest our minds in Him on a daily basis and not solely on ourselves to overcome our problems. We must learn to love and forgive ourselves and our enemies so that we can walk away from anger. And finally, we can learn to identify what's causing our mental stress so we can eliminate or reduce its mental and physical effects on us.

Most importantly, we all must learn the **natural process of how our body, mind, and energy/spirit** *(that physicists say everything is made of)* **work best together in positive alignment as ONE unit** to help us successfully create our happiness goals more effectively. So it's the *natural* process of how our body parts work **TOGETHER** best when we understand that they are connected as **ONE whole unit** that we all need to focus on learning. Our lack of knowledge in this area is what's missing in our science and education. And it's why so many people suffer mentally and feel broken because we are taught in school that these are **SEPARATE entities** *(not connected as one whole unit and how they actually work together best as one).* **Healing can only happen once we understand and learn to master our connection and our ONENESS with God the Universe, at 100 percent, so we can fix our separation anxiety and sickness.**

Even though we live in the land of opportunity, this country is full of very sick and unhappy, miserable people. So I want to teach you how you can stop the cycle of depression, divorce, and lack of love, joy, and happiness so we can stop passing these terrible habits on to our children generation after generation by starting with you.

The goal of this book is to teach you how you can turn your life around 180 degrees by using your own hidden powers. I want to teach you how, within three years, I healed myself of a brain tumor that I was told I would have for the rest of my life—and I did it without taking any drugs prescribed by my doctors. I want to teach you how I pulled myself out of my very own hellhole from depression and brink of divorce to living a wonderful, happy, loving, and peaceful life within one year—again, without any drugs or expensive therapy—once I learned this natural process. I want to teach you how to be happy, have mental peace, and how to love again. I want to teach you how to reach your highest self and your highest potential so that you can co-create the grandest life you can possibly imagine yourself to have. I want to teach you how you can have perfect mental peace even when you are in the middle of a storm of chaos and struggle going on around you.

Initially, part of my determination to change my life was because I wanted to learn to help my daughter go through the growing pains of her teen years and get out of her own depression. The purpose was to write a simplified version about spiritual growth that she could learn from. In trying to help her, I helped myself. I also use this book as part of my coaching tool for my family and friends to help them attain love, peace of mind, and success in their own chaotic lives.

My Rock Bottom

My own transformation started when I was at the end of my rope after fifteen years in a miserable marriage. My husband and I were fighting all the time, and it got worse when he quit his job to play golf and the stock market. He would play golf all day, and then he would still expect me to cook and clean the house after I had just worked eight hours, picked up the kids from school, taken them to their after-school activities, helped them with their homework, and gotten them ready for bed. I got so jealous and enraged that I wanted him out of my life. I was thinking, "If I'm doing all this by myself, why do I need him?"

In my crazy mind, in the world of misery and hell that I created for myself in my head, I really hated him and hated myself. It was terrible. On top of this, I became vindictive, and I made sure his life was just as miserable as mine was. I wanted to divorce him so badly, but I did not want our kids to go through the pains that I had gone through myself at a young age when my parents divorced.

I was miserable, depressed, and inactive when I reached my bottom. In addition, I was miserable at work. I hated my job, and I was having problems with people at work. I was tired of fighting and being afraid of everything and everybody. I just wanted love and peace at home, at work, and in me, which was foremost.

For help, I was going to various Christian churches, but I still couldn't find permanent love and peace in my life that worked for me. I also didn't want to go to years of psychiatry because I'd been there and done that, and I didn't want to waste my money. Besides, all they would do was prescribe drugs, and that was not what I wanted to do. Neither one of these methods worked to make any permanent change in my life. At this time, I drastically wanted change in my life. I was going crazy in my mind. I even had thoughts of killing my husband—it was terrible!

But that wasn't my bottom, I reached my bottom when I heard my then twelve-year-old daughter crying in her bedroom one day. When I asked her what was wrong, she said "Mom, I want to kill myself," but she wouldn't tell me why. What she said hurt my heart so badly that it woke me up from my mental trance of self-pity, self-destruction, and selfishness. This was my rude awakening, my bottom. The hellhole I had created for myself that I was surely negatively influencing everybody I loved who was around me. But this was also the beginning of my transformation and my resurrection from the dead. The negative path I was on clearly wasn't working for me or my family. For my daughter's sake and for my family, I chose a different direction than divorce.

In my desperation to help save my family, I realized I needed to save myself from my own mental hell first, so I prayed as I never prayed before. I said, "God, help me! My life is falling apart. My life is out of control, and I can't do this anymore. I'm trying to do it by myself (which was one of the problems), but it's not working, and I don't know how to fix it. Please help me keep it together!"

That night on PBS, I watched Dr. Wayne Dyer talk about "The Power of Intention," so I took it as a sign. I was so impressed with what he had to say that, as a last resort, I bought everything he had to offer. As soon as I got his books and CDs in the mail, I bombarded my mind with his messages. I was so determined to change my life that I would listen to his CDs in the car, I read his books during gym and at night, and I watched his videos over and over until I learned and internalized his messages. In one of his books, he said that all around us we are surrounded with negativity—the news, the TV shows we watch, the books we read, and the music we listen to. There are lots of hateful and angry people out there. He said you need to turn everything off and learn the language of **love**, which most of us do not know. Schools fail us and our children because they themselves do not know the importance of learning about love as a way to heal ourselves, our relationships, and society as a whole. I didn't even know there was such a "language," and I grew up as a Christian, attending various churches.

So, for an entire year, I did what he said. I stopped watching negative news. I stopped listening to talk radio and to music. I stopped reading murder mystery books and just read nothing but positive-thinking books like the ones by Eckhart Tolle, Deepak Chopra, Neale Donald Walsch, Gary R. Renard, and Stuart Wilde. When I combined what I learned from these experts with my engineering background and the little bit of physics I knew, I learned forgiveness, unconditional love, and peace of mind that worked for me. This is what I call the *physics of human engineering*. By combining all the pieces of the puzzle together, along with science and religion, is what healed and saved me and my family once I figured it all out. Since we're not taught this in school, because mainstream science has not figured this out yet.

By learning about myself and examining and changing my mental beliefs that were not working for me, I was able to put the pieces of the puzzle together by trying to make sense of everything I had created in my life. When I learned to put it all together in my mind and learned how we are to interact with God's universe as a whole, as **one unit**— that was when I found the unimaginable peace, love, and joy I had been searching for all my life. So that no matter what was happening in the physical world of objects that we're always judging as good or evil, it didn't matter to me anymore. I knew where to find peace and love in an instant. It was just a matter of a mental switch I needed to learn to turn on.

What healed me and my family was changing my negative thoughts to positive thoughts, understanding who I am as spirit/energy, learning to be one with God or the universe, and making God my life partner in everything I wanted to create in my life. After learning about the natural process of alignment in body, mind, and energy/spirit, balancing the various areas of my life became much easier for me. I was able to move forward and do more with less time because I learned to remove the *mental and physical distractions* in my life. I wasn't struggling anymore. My life became much easier to deal with so that no matter what chaos the world of objects threw at me, good or bad, I was able to handle more, with little to no stress in my mind, and still feel God's unconditional love, peace, and joy inside me.

As a result, my body became automatically healthier. For example, I healed myself of a brain tumor without drugs. I rarely get depressed anymore; if I do, something extremely major has to happen in our family to get me to that stage. You see, I refuse to allow myself to get mentally stuck too long in those negative mental states and negative emotional feelings because I've learned to be conscious and be in control of my own thoughts.

Even when I do get sick, it's usually for minor stuff like a cold or the flu that doesn't require doctor visits, and it doesn't stay for very long. In other words, because I've learned to stop the craziness in my head and learned to manage and control my thoughts and keeping them silent, my physical body has become healthier as a result and is able to heal itself faster from mental and physical sickness caused by mental stress. I am able to create what some people call miracles in my life that would otherwise take years to heal. I even healed my own marriage without having to hire a family counselor, which would have cost us a lot of money and years of family therapy, or worse, we could have been another statistic in divorce like my parents.

The reason I share this is that ever since I changed my mental beliefs and attitudes, I have had so much more energy than I have ever had before. By changing my comfort zone, I am able to do far more and grander projects in a shorter amount of time. This is what I want to teach you in this book so you can do the same. I want to teach you how to love and find happiness in your life, no matter where you find yourself or how messed up you think you are, so you can make quantum-leap changes in your life. Because nobody should have to read hundreds of books and spend thousands of dollars on seminars or be an engineer to learn how our body parts (*body, mind, and energy/spirit that everything is made of*) work best together as ONE whole unit in God's universe—as I did. We are not taught this because our education and science have not yet discovered this, is the problem.

Beware . . . This Does Not Work For Everyone

I will be honest with you. This book does not work for everyone. It only works for people who are searching for answers, those who are looking for a different path because whatever they're doing isn't working, and those who are 100 percent serious about wanting to change their own lives. It works for those who are looking for mental peace, love, and joy, who are determined to change their life, and who are willing to look in the mirror and ask themselves, **"What am I doing to mess up my own life, and how can I change it?"**

I just know that if I can heal my marriage, my family, and my body from sickness due to mental stress, without drugs, that anybody can. This is what I call my own miracles. You too can create your own miracles once you understand and actually do the process because you are the only one in control of your own mind; nobody else is. Even when the people around you don't believe in this stuff, only you have to believe in it in order for it to work. Our scientists and educators don't seem to know that the natural processes of how our body parts (body, mind, energy/spirit) work best together as one whole unit. Our body parts are not separate entities as our educators currently teach in schools. Only when you change and learn the concepts in this book, can you change others around you because we are all connected as one invisible energy force field or spirit of God that everything in the universe is made of, which will be explained more in Part I.

Simply, this book is similar to physical exercise, but this is doing mental exercises that we all need to learn to do and implement to make it useful for ourselves; otherwise, it's just a waste of time. For example, we all know that exercising our body is good for our health, but how many of us actually do it? I myself don't. It's my fault because I'm too lazy. It's not that exercise doesn't work. It doesn't work for *me* because I refuse to do it, even though I know it's good for me. Well, this book works the same way. In other words, this book only works on people who actually want and are willing to do the mental exercises because we are the only ones in control of our own minds, nobody else.

In a book titled *A Course in Miracles*, by Helen Schucman *[an ex-atheist]* and William Thetford, professors of medical psychology at Columbia University's College of Physicians and Surgeons in New York City, they say, "Nothing **real** *[in reference to invisible energy]* can be threatened. Nothing **unreal** exists *[in reference to the 8 billion human mental perspectives]*. Herein lies the peace of God." Then they go on to say, "This is how *A Course in Miracles* begins. It makes a fundamental distinction between the real and the unreal, between knowledge and perception *[8 billion mental universes]*. Knowledge is truth under one law, the law of love or God. Truth is unalterable, eternal, and unambiguous *[in reference to the invisible energy or spirit that everything is made of inside]*. It can be unrecognized *[since it is invisible]*, but it cannot be changed *[since it is eternal energy/spirit]*. It applies to everything that God created and only what He created *[the invisible spiritual energy, not the 8 billion human mental perspectives]* is real. It is beyond learning because it is beyond time and process. It has no opposite *[invisible level]*, no beginning, and no end *[conservation of energy in physics states that energy can never be created or destroyed]*. It merely is."

The Problem With Mainstream Science

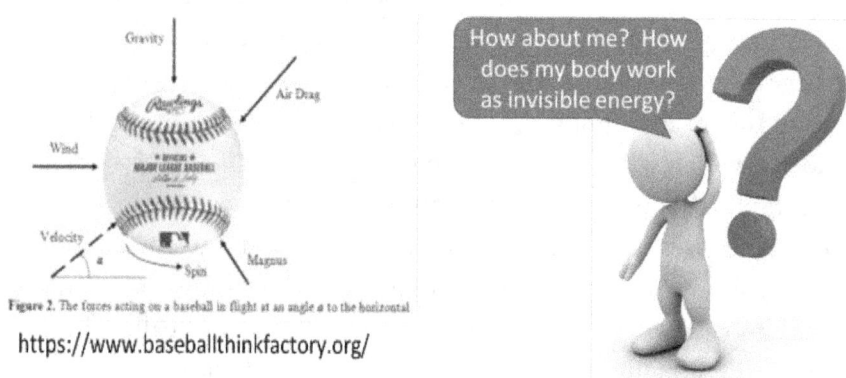

Figure 2. The forces acting on a baseball in flight at an angle *a* to the horizontal

https://www.baseballthinkfactory.org/

So let's be honest. To me, physics is nothing more than the science of the invisible realm that everything in the universe is made of, called energy that can move in different directions but cannot be seen. However, because it is invisible, it is also one of the most difficult subjects to learn in school. For example, one of the first assignments I had to learn in high school physics was to calculate the distance a baseball travels when it is hit by a bat. The solution to the problem was to add up all the invisible forces acting on the ball, like the kinetic energy force from the bat hitting the ball, the negative pull down of invisible gravity, the spin, the velocity of the ball, and finally, the negative or positive direction of invisible friction caused by wind energy.

Yet we never studied how the invisible energy of the human body worked with its environment in physics or engineering, even though they teach that ***everything** in the universe is made out of (invisible) energy.* Like, how does our body parts *(body, mind, and energy)* work together best within the invisible realm, similar to a baseball physics problem? This is because scientists haven't figured out this problem yet. But I will attempt to do so in this book.

Here are additional problems with science as it pertains to basic human engineering today: Because scientists have not yet discovered that the mental **thoughts** we generate exist and are just another form of energy type that we can learn to control, they therefore cannot teach us how to manage our thoughts more efficiently even though physicists say everything in the universe is made out of *[invisible]* energy.

Also, mainstream science has not figured out yet and discovered that there is actually a **major difference** between the **one physical** universe versus the **8 billion mental** universes or perspectives of realities that exist today, as another reason why so many people are fighting with each other. These are just some of the reasons why there are currently no educational courses available on these topics at any level, and why so many people are suffering mentally, and why anti-depressant drugs (used to control our minds from thinking thoughts) prescribed by psychiatrists are a multi-billion-dollar industry. This will be explained more extensively in the section "Types of Energy." Learning to manage and control our thoughts naturally and more efficiently is different than taking a psychology class in college, which is the study and treatment (usually by drugs) of mental illness, emotional disturbance, and abnormal behavior.

Another major problem with science is that they are not really interested in doing any research on how the trilogy of how our body, mind, and energy/spirit work best together as one whole unit in terms of systems and processes (from an engineering point of view) to improve human engineering. This is because, like the field of medicine, they only operate with *body (e.g., primary care physician) and mind (e.g., psychiatrist) levels as **separate** entities;* and without even considering the effects of our inner invisible energy force field or spirit that is inside all things. This is because science and engineering have not yet learned or discovered how our inner invisible energy field, which according to physics we are all made of inside, affects and works with our physical body and mind so that we are more effective and efficient human beings when our body parts are working together as **one whole unit since all three are actually connected as ONE**. *If you are made of something, then obviously you are together as ONE with it.*

I believe that once science figures this out, and they begin to actually start teaching, as part of our regular educational curriculum, the natural process of how our three major body parts (body, mind, and energy) work best together as one unit when they are in positive alignment and in sync, where we all learn to think and work with our invisible energy force field more efficiently, then managing our thoughts and healing our mental stress in this manner will just be a natural behavior for everybody, not just for some. When we get to this point is where the "miracles" stop happening because if everybody were doing it, and not just a few, it wouldn't be such a surprise anymore.

When science catches up with religion, maybe in another 2,000 years, religion will remain important because religious leaders are the only ones currently trying to teach this connection we all have with our inner energy level or spirit, is what they call it. Until then, religion and science will continue to butt heads on these important topics. So the end of the world as you know it will cease once you learn to refocus your mind's eye on the invisible energy or spiritual side of who you really are inside yourself. The process I teach in this book is just the natural part of human engineering simplified.

It's through my own spiritual transformation that I found my life purpose by helping others heal themselves spiritually and mentally so they feel whole, by teaching them where to find unconditional love and peace in their own chaotic lives. You just have to do the work and believe you can do it. So if you feel you have reached your bottom and don't know how to get out of it, if you feel your life is out of control, and you can't stop the crazy thoughts in your head, if you've tried therapy, religion, drinking, illegal and/or prescription drugs, and they are not helping you have mental peace, then perhaps this book can help you make sense of all the chaos and confusion being taught out there.

Do Not Get Easily Offended

Before you start, I just want to tell you that this book is meant for everybody. Originally, there were no Bible verses referenced, as I don't personally like to read the Bible myself because of the language, and most of the stories are too confusing and even contradictory to me. I much prefer to listen to somebody else interpret it for me. The Bible verses throughout were actually added as an afterthought because as I was sharing my book with some of my Christian friends, I noticed they had a hard time with what I was saying, and supposedly they read the Bible. For example, I made a comment to a friend and said, "God is Love" (1 John 4:8, 16). This person insisted that he read the entire Bible, and he was sure that statement was nowhere in the Bible, but it is. To another friend, I said, "God is everywhere" (Colossians 1:17), and she too insisted that is not in the Bible, but it is.

So the verses were added for those who are Christians, and there are many in this country, to help ease their mind that I'm not saying anything new and that what I am saying is supported by the Bible. In fact, once I was able to use science to connect and prove some of the Bible teachings, the natural process of how we are to work with God's universe made more sense to me. I believe that the messages are basics to all religions and to life itself—universal laws, if you will, that unfortunately our scientists and educators have not yet discovered is the problem and why we are not taught these concepts in school.

However, this book is really meant to help enhance the life of everyone who reads it, not just a few. It's not to replace anything but to build from what you are already familiar with, no matter what your religious background. So if you are not a Christian, please do not let the Bible verses offend you; just ignore them if they do. For me, the Bible verses actually showed me proof of how much more advanced religion was than science on how we can be more efficient human beings when we learn how to use our body parts more efficiently together as one unit, not as separate entities as currently being taught in schools and practiced by our medical experts. So basically, this book attempts to simplify and bring out what unites all the various religions and sciences together, and at the same time remove some of the contradictions and confusion that make it so difficult for us to understand and believe what they are trying to teach us as truth—all of which makes it difficult for us all to love one another and to live in peace.

HOW CAN THIS BOOK HELP YOU?

This is a self-help book to help you learn to control your own thoughts so you don't go crazy and blame others for your misery, or worse, hurt others or yourself along the way. It will help you to know ahead of time some of your own personal thoughts and prejudices that are keeping you mentally stuck, unhappy, and stressed in your life. So if you do the following exercises, you will get more out of the book. But they will only work for you if you are honest and diligent in answering them upfront because these questions will bring you awareness of your own negative thoughts that are not working for you.

The Checklist

1. Are you in love unconditionally and at peace mentally with yourself and with everybody else? **Yes No**

If not, who are you not at peace with? These are people you are angry with, hate, or are jealous of. Maybe it's your spouse, exes, or other family members like your parents. Maybe it's people you work with or people of other religions, races, political parties, etc. Maybe you're angry with yourself. Be honest with yourself. List them all.

_____

_____

_____

_____

_____

_____

_____

_____

_____

_____

Solution: Learn forgiveness and acceptance. This book can help heal your anger and hatred and will provide you with the love and peace you are seeking—if that's what you are looking for.

2. Are you happy about your family, work, money, health, or future? **Yes No**

If not, what are you not happy about? Be honest. List them all.

_____

_____

_____

_____

_____

_____

_____

_____

_____

_____

Solution: Learn to master positive body, mind, and spirit/energy alignment so that you can improve in any one of these areas and create your dream world. Then this book can help you.

3. Do you know what you are made of inside at the invisible level and everything else in the universe? Do you have a personal relationship with this invisible spiritual energy field of God's universe and know how to work with it? **Yes No**

If you answered yes, then write below what you think you are made of. As you read the book, it will either be in agreement with you or not. If you answered no, the book will teach you what it is you are made of so that you will know what you are and will be conscious of it.

_____

_____

_____

_____

_____

_____

_____

_____

_____

_____

Solution: Either way, you need to learn what you are made of inside and how to use it and work with it. Because schools fail to teach us these basic concepts for living a happy life, most of us are inefficient and ineffective in using this thing that we are all made of inside and applying its universal laws of eternal love, peace, joy, and happiness in all areas of our lives.

If you answered no to any of the questions above, then this book can help you, but only if you decide to choose to change your mental beliefs. Choose to learn about the power of love, forgiveness, and your spirit so that you may have peace and a life of abundance. You have to want to change your own mind to make it happen. Nobody else can do it for you, and you have to start with you. The answers are not outside of you; they are inside of you—it has to begin with changing your mindset and some of your strong belief systems that are not working for you or the people around you. Sure, you can blame others for your problems, but you will find neither peace nor a solution. It's your own set of personal belief systems that are keeping you stuck from having mental peace. Your mind is the doorway to the spiritual dimension of limitless love, peace, happiness, joy, and abundant blessings. Like a door, you need to be open to these possibilities; otherwise, your life will remain limited to only what living in a three-dimensional physical world of objects can offer, which is based on limits and conditions.

Attaining world peace is done one person at a time. Each one of us can make a difference if we choose love and peace in our own personal lives. We can all work together to change the world. Coca-Cola's success is selling one bottle at a time all over the world. We can all do the same thing. By practicing love and peace one person at a time, we can affect others.

This Book Can Help Answer These Questions

How do I have more love, joy, and peace of mind? What is God? Where is God in relation to where I am? Is God real? How come some people claim to hear God talk, but I can't? How do I talk to God? What is unconditional love, and how do I get it? How do I become more like God and be one with Him? How can I improve my relationship with others? What is my spiritual purpose in life?

Choosing love and peace over fear, pain, and chaos involves the following:

- Changing one's current mental beliefs and perspective
- Honest self-assessments
- Spiritual understanding and development

Read this book as a process to help improve yourself so you can move your overall life toward **mental wholeness**, which is what's missing for most of us. It teaches spiritual and mental healing by helping you find your center. In Appendix A, I have included a partial list of books I have read on spiritual growth to help you in your own path to spiritual development. I pray that this book will help guide you closer to your **oneness with God** or the universe so that you may have love, peace, joy, and happiness in all areas of your life, no matter where you find yourself in life's chaotic existence.

LIFE IS A NEVER – ENDING EVOLUTION OF ITSELF
(Your Life and the Universe Together as ONE)

Another word for evolution is growth. For a seed to grow and reach its potential, its highest level, it must first break through its hard shell, and then the seedling has to break through all the dirt and manure. Then it goes through day and night in light and darkness, growing during the day in the light, always reaching for the light, and remaining dormant at night in the dark. At its highest level, it will produce and give off oxygen and fruit for you and me to nourish us and help us grow. This is how it serves us. This is its purpose.

Everything has a purpose; even you have a purpose. Growing in knowledge and understanding about who you are as energy/spirit will help you find your purpose. It will also help you to lighten up your mind's load of negative thoughts and create space in your mind so that life will be easier. That's why it is important to be open to new knowledge that produces positivity in your life, which helps to increase your energy level so you can reach your highest self.

Knowledge = Light

We all grow and learn by going through a similar process as the seed. Until you open up and break through the hard-core beliefs that you have been accepting since you were a child—beliefs that are not working for you—it will be impossible for you to grow and change. Then you have to break through all the manure and the garbage—the negative beliefs and thoughts you have put in your mind. Only by growing and reaching for the light through understanding can you grow to reach your highest self of *unconditional love and spiritual energy level*. So always learn from others who can help you to get out of the hellhole you created for yourself, someone who can help you learn self-control through spiritual understanding and mental control.

Taking responsibility for your own mental and spiritual growth is the first step to creating a successful life of unconditional love, peace, joy, and happiness. Never stop learning to grow. Instead, stop watching negative TV, stop reading books that don't teach, and stop complaining and blaming. You need to push yourself to increase your own energy level by growing in mind, body, and spirit at the energy level. When you do, you will have so much more time for creating miracles in your life in quantum leaps that your excuses will simply disappear.

> *Never stop growing. Instead, reach for your highest energy level, towards God's UNCONDITIONAL LOVE for ALL, so you can create miracles in your own life, your own Garden of Eden.*

Life would be so much easier if you could look at it as an experiment or a game of trial and error instead of looking at it as winning or losing, right or wrong. To me, we are here to play and have fun, and our playground in which we learn to grow and evolve together is the entire universe.

Most people see only with their physical eyes, which is very limiting. We actually see with our minds first with labels we are familiar with that are already in our mental database. Then our minds try to associate the label with the object our physical eyes see. Certain words or knowledge help us see the universe differently, depending on our area of focus or expertise or language we are already familiar with. For example, if I were in a room full of doctors and nurses, looking at a body that is opened up for surgery, the doctors and nurses, because of their special medical knowledge, would be able to mentally and physically see the body differently than I would, even though we are all looking at the same thing. In this scenario, I would only see blood and gore, then throw up. That's what I would do. On the other hand, the medical personnel would probably see the heart, the lungs, the intestines, and the nerves, and because of their special knowledge, they would know how to help the person be better. The common knowledge and words used in the medical field in this example is the language that allows them to converse and coordinate action toward a common goal. Placing an engineer like me, who does not know the language of the medical field, and therefore, cannot make certain distinctions, to assist a surgeon is doomed for failure. On the other hand, if you put a medical doctor in the middle of an engineering project like developing a rocket to launch into space because the doctor would not know the language of that particular domain, they would be in the dark. So someone who does not know something simply means that person is in a kind of darkness, as the Bible calls it.

The point of all this is that if you want to see and experience a different world than what you are used to, it's important to learn new knowledge, new words, and new distinctions that will allow you to see and create a new world for yourself. You can't keep using and recycling the same negative words and beliefs in your mind that are not working and hope that something new will be created out of the same crap because all you get is mixed-up crap, but still crap nonetheless.

> *Insanity is doing the same thing over and over again*
> *and expecting different results.*
> –Albert Einstein

So if you currently live in a negative world that you are not happy with, and you want to change your life so that it is more positive, then you will need to learn a new language so that you can create a more loving, peaceful world of your own. Remember, this is a mental exercise, so you can do this from anywhere. This book and the books listed in the Appendix will help you learn this new language of inspiration for love. The language itself has been around for centuries, mainly in religion and spiritual teachings by field experts, but it may be just new to you if you have never been exposed to the concepts since most of us are not taught this in school. Like learning anything new, it takes awareness, commitment, practice, concentration, and time from you. You just have to promise yourself to commit yourself to reading this book at least two or three times until you get it. But once you get it, I promise you a life of peace and love you cannot have ever imagined, regardless of where you find yourself. After all, isn't this what we all want and are seeking?

THE POWER OF ALIGNMENT

Making Changes Through Positive Alignment

If you want to make big changes in your life in quantum leaps, you need to learn to increase your energy level by aligning your mind, body, and spirit/energy in the same positive direction so you can propel yourself to successfully create what you want in all areas of your life faster. Aligning your mind, body, and spirit pushes you to a higher energy level so that you can make improvements that will move you faster toward a more balanced life in health, God, family, marriage, career, money, or whatever you seek.

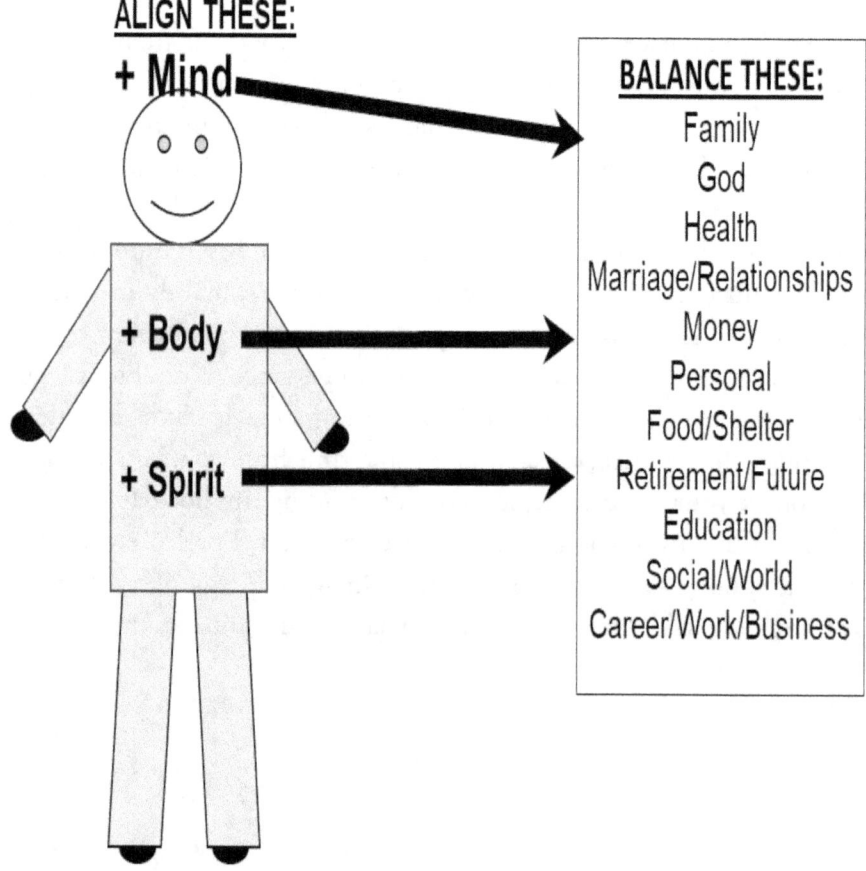

Being in Balance

To reach your highest energy level, you need to aim for totality and wholeness in your life by taking care of all areas of your concerns until you are satisfied with and feel good about, all of them, not just some of them. For example, if you hate your job or your family, that would be a good indication that you need to make changes in one or both of those areas. Sometimes, as we will discuss later, simply changing your own mental perspective helps a great deal. You can even make some problems disappear simply by changing or refocusing your perspective. Your family, God, money, career, health, and the world are all interrelated, so if you are not taking care of one, you will create a breakdown in the other areas of your life.

When my husband and I were arguing all the time, one day I asked him how he was doing in golf. He replied, "My putting is awful because I keep thinking of you complaining when I come home!" The point is, that he could not play golf as well as he could have because he wasn't taking care of his family and his spirit as well as he could have. His own internal voice was telling him that, but he wasn't listening. Even though he was reading all the right books, like *Mental Rules for Golf, Zen Golf, Mastering the Mental Game, Think Like Tiger, Be the Ball, A Golf Instruction Book for the Mind*, until he took care of what was really in his mind, he would continue to be terrible at golf.

The books were all great, but they only focused on golf. So it didn't matter how many of these books he read because he was restricting his mind game only to golf and not taking care of the problems at home, which were taking up space in his mind. The solution to his problem was to expand his love of golf, to his love of the family. It didn't have to be one or the other; he could love both and be happy in both by taking care of both. But by limiting his love to only golf, he was creating a breakdown in his family, and he ended up struggling and being miserable in both. This is because he was thinking in terms of limits, not of abundance thinking.

You are one whole being with only one mind, one spirit/energy, and one body, which are all connected together as one whole unit within God's universe, and it will not allow you to separate your life into separate entities in your mind. It's all connected as ONE!

The key is learning how they all work best together as one whole unit by taking care of and balancing all your projects with God so you can co-create abundance in your life. This way, you can reach your happiness goals faster by learning to love all as one through the understanding of unconditional love for all.

Here's another example. I have a dear friend who had a heart attack at work. This happened because he wasn't taking care of his health and was overworking; he also didn't know how to deal with people and took everything personally, and he smoked. His being out of work for a few weeks affected other areas of his life as well—his marriage, his family, his health, and his ability to earn money. As a result, he had to take an early retirement. You need to take care of all parts of your life so you can be at your highest energy level, or like a domino effect, you will create breakdowns in your life.

Being in balance does not mean equal time for everything. It just means you need to take care of and put some time into all the various areas of your life that are important to you. Don't just put all your time into work, for example, because most workaholics end up divorced. It's okay to spend time with your work, but you also need to spend time with your family; you also need to take care of your health, and you need to take time to learn to work with your spiritual energy. They are all interrelated, and only you know where your breakdowns are. These breakdowns in your life are good starting points for areas of improvement in your life through body, mind, and spirit/energy alignment.

Being In Alignment or The Law of Attraction

Success in life is easy when your mind, body, and spirit/energy are all going in the same positive alignment.

Un-magnetized (disordered)

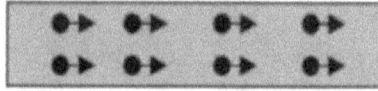

Magnetized (aligned)

In an article in ThoughtCo., "The Science of How Magnets Work" (September 5, 2019), by Anne Marie Helmenstine, Ph.D., states, *"A strong magnetic field is produced when the electron magnetic moments of a material are **aligned**. When they are **disordered,** the material is neither strongly attracted nor repelled by a magnetic field."* So for magnets to work, the electrons inside of them **all have to be going in the same direction, and they have to be in positive alignment;** otherwise, they cannot work to attract other metals. As humans, according to science, we too are made of energy and electrons and protons, just like everything else in the universe. And like a magnet, we can repel or attract things toward ourselves based on the negative or positive direction of our energy from our thoughts, attitudes, behaviors, and our perception of the environment or world we interact with. The results or creations of our lives are, therefore, dependent on how well we are in positive alignment with our mind, body, and spirit/energy working together as one unit with God's universe as a whole. This is because energy or spirit is always moving and going in different directions. That is why, if we want to create an abundance of love and peace in our lives, we must learn to control the direction of the various parts of ourselves at the invisible spiritual energy level.

To speed up success in creating anything in our lives, what some people call miracles, there has to be a positive ALIGNMENT of our body parts MIND, BODY, and SPIRIT/ENERGY together as one whole unit. The more these three areas are aligned and in sync, going in the same positive direction, like a magnet, the more natural and easy the flow of our lives will be. It might help to think of these as math problems with positive or negative values. You know that when you add three negative numbers, the results are guaranteed to be another negative number. When you add three positive numbers, the results are guaranteed to be positive, but when you add mixed numbers, the results will always be mixed. With mixed values, you may or may not get a positive result depending on which variable is larger or stronger.

Life is very similar. If, for example, I drop one hundred people in the middle of the ocean, the ones who will naturally drown are the ones who are negative in all three areas of mind, body, and spirit/energy. If a person's mind is negative, the conversation in his mind might go something like this: "I'm going to drown! I'm going to drown! I'm going to drown!" A person's body is negative if he or she never took lessons to learn to swim so they don't know what to do with their body. A person's spirit is negative if he or she lacks the understanding of how his or her own spirit/energy and surrounding energy (the ocean in this case) work and flow together to help create the desired outcome. In fact, if these people knew how to float, they would know that the ocean could lift them up without much physical effort on their part.

The people who would easily survive this scenario would be the people who are in positive alignment in the three areas of mind, body, and spirit/energy. My brother, for example, is an avid surfer, and he is in positive alignment with all three areas when it comes to swimming in the ocean. His mind is extremely positive because, in his mind, he **loves** the ocean. His body is very positive because he took lessons and learned how to swim at the local pool, and he's always practicing in the ocean. He also has great respect and understanding of how the oceans' wave energy works, so he uses its energy flow to his advantage to have fun by going in the same directional flow instead of swimming against the current and fighting it, so surfing and swimming in the ocean for him is very easy.

On the other hand, if I were in the ocean, I would probably drown because I'm mixed in body, mind, and spirit or energy. Physically, I know how to swim because I've taken lessons at a pool, and I understand how the universe's ocean waves work, but when it comes to my mind, I **hate** the ocean. I'm too negative, scared, and fearful because my mind is too focused on the sharks, monsters, and giant waves that the outcome would be drowning for me. This is why I do not like swimming in the ocean. I absolutely hate it! Knowing how my mind works in this domain if I were in the ocean, I would probably have a panic attack and a heart attack at the same time just thinking about the ocean monsters.

This is why you want to focus on learning to improve doing the things you **love** or want to do. Part of making life easy is learning to flow in the same positive direction as the universal energy. Remember, misalignment in any of the three areas (mind, body, and spirit/energy) constricts that energy flow and slows or stops your ability to successfully create what it is you want in the specific area you are trying to focus on creating for yourself.

SUCCESS FLOW = + MIND + BODY + SPIRIT/ENERGY
(*Focused Energy*)

By changing my thoughts from negative to positive, in seven months I went from almost being divorced to having a wonderful marriage once I understood this formula. Remember, with God the Universe, all things are possible when you are working together as one unit with Him in His presence, in the energy level at this moment, in the NOW!

The following three sections of the book will help you to understand and live in full (+) positive alignment so that your spiritual energy is focused in a controlled direction.

PART I

(+) **GOD/UNIVERSE:** *"Thinking Big, Thinking God"* is about understanding your **Spirit/Energy** and the universe in a positive light that allows you to be in a state of alignment with it all as one. This section also teaches the difference between looking at visible material objects as separate forms on the **outside**, versus imagining what those objects are made of on the **inside** (*at the invisible energy level*) and why it is important to do so. This section explains the God Factor, what it is, how it relates to us as individuals, and how to work with it.

PART II

(+) **MIND:** *"Garbage In, Garbage Out"* is about *mind* management. This section helps you to clear and silence your mind so that you can have mental peace. It discusses how you need to align your mind vertically with your body by keeping your thoughts in the *present moment* instead of aligning them horizontally by living in the *past* and creating stress about the *future*. This section also discusses the alignment of your subconscious and conscious mind and the importance of keeping them in the same directional flow. If, for example, you consciously (+) want to create a multimillion-dollar company, but subconsciously, you are (–) afraid of people, your success rate will drop dramatically because your subconscious is going in the opposite direction of what you are consciously telling yourself you want. Essentially, they are canceling each other out. This is like basic math.

PART III

(+) **BODY:** *"Creating Miracles"* is about the secrets to creating whatever it is you want in your life by learning to work your body in conjunction with positive thinking and your spiritual energy level so that all three are in sync. It covers things to do with your *body* to help create what you want. It explains writing goals and daily-to-do lists, praying, meditating, and following through on your projects so that you keep focused on the things you want to create in your universe.

By being in positive alignment in body, mind, and spirit, you can have it all without needing to sacrifice anybody along the way by learning how to work and create your own perspective of your own universe by *applying God's LAWS OF ABUNDANCE and RULES OF LOVE.* Simply choose to change your playing position and your **mental** strategy for playing the game of life if you are seeking long-lasting happiness, love, and peace in your life. After all, according to the Bible, man's original sin *(the belief that we are only body and mind)* was just a **mental** separation from God, the Universe. But because we have control over our own mental thoughts, we can change our minds just as easily. So breaking the spell of the original sin is just a matter of acknowledging and re-learning and having a personal relationship with our true inner selves, that we are made of God's invisible spiritual energy force field.

However, by **mentally** acknowledging that we only exist as body and mind, we limit the knowing of ourselves only to the object level of things we can only see with our eyes as good or evil and death, which is the cause of most of our suffering. We miss working in a deeper dimension of who we truly are when we refuse to acknowledge and learn to work with the eternal energy part of what we are all made of inside all things, the source of everything. Thus, we continue our mental suffering and, for some, physical suffering as well. This is because we are mentally disconnected from the invisible energy force of God, the Universe, when we don't know how to use our body parts more efficiently, since we are not taught in school.

Choose the easy way to create what you want instead of the hard way. True freedom comes from choosing not to fight the God of the universe anymore because it's not necessary. Stop fighting and swimming against God's energy flow of love; instead, learn to go in the same directional flow as His current so you can succeed in riding the fifty-foot wave of life.

PART I

(+) God/Universe
"Thinking Big, Thinking God"

1

Being Spiritual

Being Religious vs. Being Spiritual

In his book *Tomorrow's God: Our Greatest Spiritual Challenge*, Neale Donald Walsh states the need to redesign God so that it works for all of us. New Thought Spiritualist belief is that God *(made of **invisible** spirit)* and the universe *(made of **invisible** energy)* are ultimately one and the same. This book supports this idea and merges the two disciplines.

If science, technology, history, medicine, and even the dictionary are updated regularly, shouldn't we be updating our religious ideas also? After all, the Bible, the Koran, the Torah, etc., were all written centuries ago. Can you imagine going to a medicine man for brain surgery today? I can't. We forget that these books were written at a time when things were very different. For one thing, slavery was more prominent; unfortunately, some countries still have some form of slavery, especially children being sold as sex slaves. In those times and even today, some major religions still instill fear and abuse when they teach their followers that God is going to punish them if they sin.

I grew up in a religion believing in and fearing God, so I was always afraid to do anything wrong, fearing His wrath, and that women had to be subservient to their husbands. If their God hates gays, then their followers will think it's okay to hate gays too. If their books teach that God hates nonbelievers or infidels, then their followers will also believe they should hate them too. It's a shame because this teaching of hate in some major religions is what's turning a lot of people away from God because they see how people who follow these negative belief systems behave when the people considering them are just searching for something better in their lives. I don't think this form of negative thinking helps.

As I got older, I found later that there were churches out there that actually taught the opposite, which is God's unconditional love for everybody equally. They do not teach and perpetuate hate; instead, they teach that we are all to follow and practice God's unconditional love for each other. During the Bible years, almost everywhere, women then were treated as second-class citizens; even today, some countries still treat women as second-class, thanks to these books that were written thousands of years ago by men for control. The point is that we need to look at each of these books and investigate what about them works and what about them no longer works so that we can update our ideas to this century so that they work for the benefit of all, including women. For example, many religions to this day still will not allow women to lead services. They perpetuate inequality, religious prejudice, religious wars, sexual prejudice, fear, hatred, and separation because these religions, like most people, are stuck on the object level that only you can see and touch. They lack the understanding of working with their invisible spiritual level or the God level at 100 percent.

I once had a conversation with a coworker about God, and his interpretation of the Bible was that God only loved Christians. To him, God hates everybody except those who believe in Jesus, and he believes that it's okay for God to kill people who don't believe in Jesus. What kind of sick thinking is this? This kind of belief is hatred to the core. This kind of belief is no different from that of Osama Bin Laden, who believed his religion was the only true religion and that, according to Allah, it was okay to kill non-Muslims. In both cases, they miss the entire goal of religion; **it's about God** or Allah, not the religion itself. Whether it be Christianity, Islam, Judaism, Buddhism, or whatever religion, it is just a different path to God or Allah. If you only focus on the path, then you will never have peace. God or Allah is about loving *all* because He is in *all*! It's like loving all of yourself versus only parts of yourself. All these religious wars we have today and have had in the past are caused by our misinterpretation of the religious books we follow. We continue to teach our children that it's okay to hate other religions, have wars over them, and treat women as a second class; or worse, we teach them to continue slavery and instill in them the mentality that men are better than women.

If we ever hope to have world peace, for our children's sake, a massive change has to start within all religions. All religious leaders have the responsibility to stand up against hate and separation and start standing up for the loving of *All*—the belief in one God/Universe/Allah or whatever you call the *All*. We all need to start thinking big—thinking God—regardless of what we choose to call the *All!* The point is, that we need to learn to accept all other religions if we ever hope to have world peace. You don't need to believe in what they believe and do what they do. You just need to accept them so that we can stop the fighting.

Religious people tend to follow only one path—their chosen path, whatever that may be (Christianity, Islam, Hinduism, Judaism, etc.). To them, they are right, and everybody else outside their religious circle is wrong. This is the practice of separatism, and all are stuck in the object-level ego. Spiritual people, on the other hand, believe that because we are all part of God's universe, all religions are acceptable. The path for us is not important, only the goal, which is God is the focus. How you get to know God at the invisible level is immaterial as long as you get there.

For example, let's say you want to go to New York from Los Angeles. Wouldn't you agree that there are many paths, literally hundreds of ways, to get to the goal, which is New York? Well, it's the same with learning to know God, which is the goal; there are unlimited paths to know and understand Him. It's not true that there is only one way—there are many ways. Don't believe this crap! The underlying message of this kind of belief system is that your religion is better than the rest—love only us, but don't love them. A subliminal message like this is very harmful to our society because it only teaches and encourages people to hate others who are not like them. You can never achieve mental peace this way. So ask yourself, what kind of negative beliefs have you bought into from your religion that teach hate and separatism? How big and expansive is your circle of love? Is it *all* God-encompassing or not?

Being spiritual is the practice of *oneness*—the unity of *all* under **one God or universe.** It doesn't matter what your religious beliefs or preferences, color, race, or sex are. To spiritualists, everybody is equal, and all religions are equal. No one religion or person is better than another, and we can learn something from all of them. In the universe or God, everything and everyone is made of the same *invisible* spiritual energy, which connects us all together as *ONE because, at this level, nothing can be destroyed according to physics.*

This is what the New Thought movements' focus and teaching is all about, getting us all to understand the invisible side of who we really ALL are. In fact, what I have found with spiritual centers is that they tend to reference and mix different ancient religious books, quantum physics, and current spiritual books to teach people about how to understand and reach our oneness with God, the Universe. It's wonderful how these various disciplines work great together to help life be more meaningful for all of us. Agape in Los Angeles and Unity of Tustin are examples of spiritual centers that promote nondenominational services. They teach *oneness* and to love *all unconditionally.* There are many others in the country if you want to join one. In any case, if you feel that you are not growing spiritually, simply choose another. If you are not learning to love **all** but instead are learning hate, anger, and separateness toward others, then choose another. If you are not learning about peace for all but rather confusion, choose another. Use your power to choose.

Another difference between traditional religion and New Thought is our perspective of God. New Thought practitioners believe that God is pure love and that as part of God, having been created in his image, we as individuals have the power to create abundantly what we want. Our perspective of God does not punish us and make us go to hell if we screw up; although, I believe we, as humans, create our own mental hell because of our own twisted perspective of this world when we insist on living without God's love in our lives and that we are only bodies and minds.

So always ask yourself what is best for the whole (*God/Universe*) or for everybody (*since He's everything and everywhere*), not just for the part (*for only you or for a small group of people, a club, or a religion*). Is your religion practicing God's wholeness or oneness with everybody and the loving of all unconditionally, or does their message state that they are right and everybody else is wrong, or their way is the only way?

People who believe that their God only loves their religion's adherents and nobody else's are practicing religious prejudice, all stuck in the object-level ego. Osama bin Laden who was the mastermind behind the September 11, 2001, attacks in New York City, is a good example of this, and you know the destruction he had caused that killed 2,977 people.

When you belong to a hate club like this, it alienates those who are outside the club, and those who belong inside think they are better than everybody else. If God is everywhere and in everything, why would God hate parts of himself? It would be like loving yourself except for your arms. Doesn't it make more sense that if God is unconditional love and is everywhere that He loves everything and everybody, including all the various forms of religions that are a part of Him? I think God loves us all so much and is so very patient with us because it's taking man so long to figure out who we are in God in relation to Him and how we are supposed to work with Him because of all the different belief systems coming in from various religions, different religious sects, and science—all adding to mass confusion. It's no wonder we are all going mentally crazy trying to make sense out of everything.

Peace is in learning to be like God, which is to love everything and everybody unconditionally as one, no matter what! This is the goal of reaching your highest level of energy or spirituality. This is the whole point of striving for our godliness—by being like God! Remember:

"God is love." –1 John 4:8, KJV

Self & God-Realization

Self-realization is realizing that you are part of this universal invisible spiritual energy system—what religious people call God and what scientists call the universe, everything ALL connected together as ONE unit. So part of the goal of this book is to help you learn about who you really are and what you are made of inside, as well as to help you learn to develop the invisible part of yourself—your spirituality or your energy level. It will teach you how to reach your highest energy level by learning how to live moment by moment, by thinking positively, by creating abundantly, and by talking to God *(the universe)* on a regular basis. Like learning anything new, it takes time, discipline, and most importantly, it takes a conscious choice from you to make the changes permanent until they become new habits.

Self-realization will help you find peace, love, and success in your chaotic life. I encourage you to read other books on spiritual growth, as there are many great teachers out there, and this is only my perspective. You can't read one book on this subject and think you understand it. Repetition is the key to changing your body at the molecular level and subconscious level so that the change is permanent. That is why affirmations are a powerful part of this process. Once you get going, you want to make sure to keep your momentum going so you don't revert back to your old ways. Appendix A lists recommended books on similar topics for you to explore.

As you learn more about who you really are, as an **invisible spirit or energy,** learn to work with it so you will become enlightened. As you bring your mental focus to yourself at the invisible energy level, inside yourself, you will no longer be in the dark because you will have brought your spirit or energy level and your divinity forward to your mental awareness. This is what being enlightened means or being awakened by being conscious of it. It's about being able to imagine yourself and everybody else, as what they are made of inside at the invisible spiritual energy level, versus only what they look like on the outside as separate objects. When you first begin to learn about your spirit, at the invisible energy level, and how to work with it, everything will seem brand new to you. Some spiritual books call this process of spiritual learning being **reborn,** but it's not a physical birthing, only a mental learning of how to use your spiritual energy level. It's like being a baby where everything is brand-new, and you have to learn how to use your body parts. However, this is just learning how to use the spiritual part of what you are made of inside.

This is basically a learning process. Actually, for most of us, it's simply remembering what we were taught in school physics—that everything in the universe is made of invisible energy. The main difference regarding spirituality is that we all need to start imagining all objects as such. We need to eliminate the thought that we are all just separate objects—because we're not; we're more than that. We are, in fact, all made of God's **invisible** spiritual energy that can never be created or destroyed. Therefore, we are all eternal inside our bodies, according to both religion and science.

2

What Is God?

The Best Explanation Of God I've Come Across:

*For by Him [**God**] all things were created that are in heaven and that are on earth, 1)**VISIBLE** and 2)**INVISIBLE**, whether thrones or dominions or principalities or powers. **ALL things were created through Him and for Him**.*
                    –Colossians 1:16, KJV

*The **universe** is defined as (a): the whole body of things and phenomena observed [**visible**] or postulated: cosmos: as a: a systematic whole held to arise by and persist through the direct intervention of divine power [**God's invisible spirit**] (b): the world of human experience (c): the entire celestial cosmos.*
            –Merriam-Webster's Online Dictionary

*The **universe** is **everything**. It includes **all** of space, and **all** the matter [**visible**] and energy [**invisible**] that space contains. It even includes time itself and, of course, it **includes YOU**.*
—NASA (Exoplanet Exploration)

Science without religion is lame; religion without science is blind.
—Albert Einstein (Nobel Prize, Physics)

***Reality is merely an illusion**, albeit a very persistent one.*
—Albert Einstein (Nobel Prize, Physics)

The GOD FACTOR:

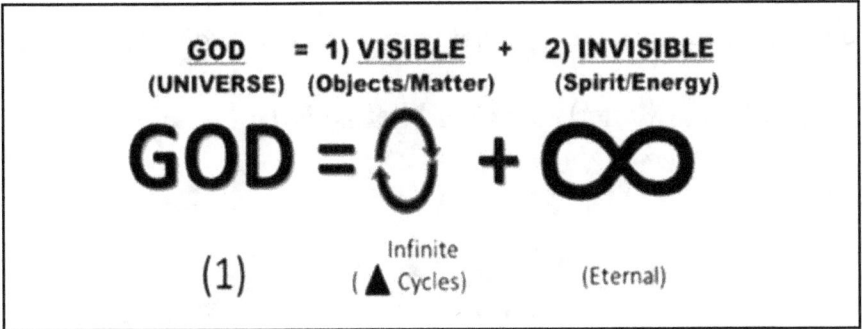

NOTES: ◯ *This is my symbol for nature's cyclical process.*

∞ *This is the math symbol for infinity or eternity.*

In an article written by Anne Marie Helmenstine, Ph.D. for ThoughtCo., "Why Light and Heat Aren't Matter," she states that the universe is actually made up of **both (1) [VISIBLE] matter and (2) [INVISIBLE] energy**. The Law of Conservation of Energy in Physics states that the total amount of ***matter (visible objects) plus (invisible) energy is constant***, but that ***matter may change forms***, which means they are just temporary shapes of objects that we can see and touch. And according to Clara Moskowitz in her article "Fact or Fiction? *Energy Can Neither Be Created Nor Destroyed,*" (*Scientific American*, August 5, 2014), conservation of energy is an *absolute law.*

According to physics, the **universe** itself is actually a ***closed system,*** so the total amount of *(2) **invisible energy** in existence has always been the same since it cannot be destroyed; but the different (1) **visible forms of matter*** that energy takes ***are constantly changing.*** In other words, all matter is just temporary forms of objects that you can see with your eyes because they are constantly changing according to the laws of physics. However, the energy that all matter is made of inside, is the opposite. It is ***invisible*** and it ***can never be created or destroyed***, which means it has always existed. Therefore, it is eternal—as religion has been teaching all along. This closed system is what religions call the spirit of God, and this is what everything inside all objects is made of. This is also what connects us all together as **ONE** unit in God's invisible universe of energy since it cannot be destroyed, according to physics.

1. VISIBLE (Matter) - The World of Objects:
(Your temporary body—the ILLUSION)

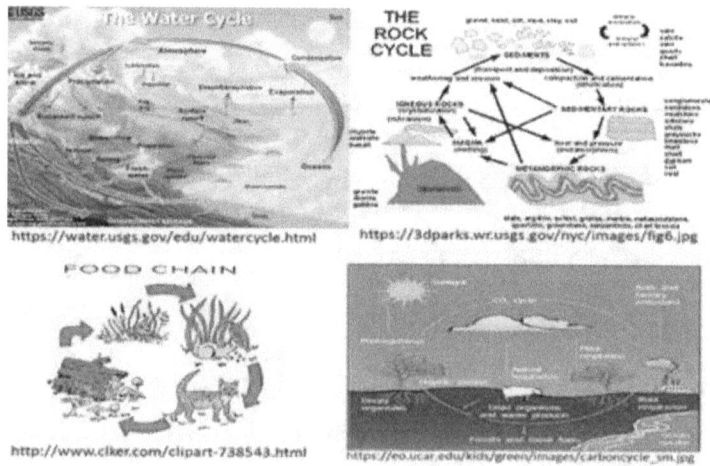

https://water.usgs.gov/edu/watercycle.html

https://3dparks.wr.usgs.gov/nyc/images/fig6.jpg

http://www.cker.com/clipart-738543.html

https://eo.ucar.edu/kids/green/images/carboncycle_sm.jpg

The biggest issue most people have is the fear of death because they focus too much on the visible world of objects, only that which they can see, touch, or feel—like people, cars, houses, money, things, and their jobs. They only see the outside parts of themselves—what their egos and senses are telling them is their only reality. They only see the world as separate objects. However, if you can imagine looking very closely at what you're made of, inside yourself, beyond the subatomic level, you will see that there are no boundaries between your body and whatever it is touching, whether it be air, dirt, a chair, or anything. At that level, there are no boundaries! We have forgotten that in reality we are all made of what physicists call energy or what religious people call spirit, which I call the invisible spiritual energy of God because you can't see it. Therefore, we are both visible and invisible at the same time, depending on the distance you are from the object being viewed. We are not one or the other; we are actually both at the same time. However, one is more real or eternal (*because energy cannot be destroyed*) than the other one, which is just temporary forms or shapes of objects, what science calls matter.

The visible world of objects that you can see and touch, which includes our bodies, is what physicist Albert Einstein calls the illusion because it's only temporary and because of the never-ending life cycle process of forms constantly changing and being recreated into new forms as taught in school science; it is persistent at the same time. Every form of object that you see in the material world eventually changes to another form or shape based on the Law of Conservation of Energy in physics—or it dies, for lack of a better word—and comes back to life and gets *recreated* and resurrects or reincarnates into another form. However, what all objects are made of inside never really disappears because all material objects are really made of invisible spirit or energy that physicists say can never be created or destroyed. Therefore, it is eternal, as religions have been teaching all along for centuries, even long before scientists figured this out.

God *(the Universe)* **Has a Thousand Names**

We need to stop being petty and stop fighting over silly names. They are just words after all. Too often we fight over nomenclature even though we are talking about the same thing but just using different words to describe the same phenomenon, just to prove how right we are. We let our egos get in the way. You can call **it** whatever you want. Whatever **ALL** is for you, and you need to accept whatever other people decide to call the **ALL**. This is no different than my having multiple names. I'm Mom or Mommy to my children, Honey to my husband, Aura to my friends, Manang ("auntie") to others, Mrs. McClain, Ma'am, or Miss to some, yet I answer to all of them. When my brothers and sisters fight, we even call each other names that are not in the dictionary, which I will not repeat here. Heck, even our dog, Trappy, has at least ten names. He doesn't care what we call him. He just knows we all love him by how we relate to him and by the way we talk to him and cuddle him all the time. In fact, I don't know anybody who's got just one name.

I once had a conversation with a Christian friend and was surprised when he said, "Muslims do not believe in God; they believe in Allah." But they do; Allah is just a different *name* they use for God, but it doesn't mean they do not believe in God, since they too have multiple names in their Quran for God.

> *"Allah" is the* **name** *which* **God** *has chosen for Himself, as stated in ayah 9 of Surah Al-Naml (chapter 27) and in ayah 14 of surah 20 of the Holy Quran.*

A Muslim friend once told me that they have a saying that God has a thousand names. Even the Bible has multiple names for God. Depending on which websites you search for the various names for God in the Bible, they list anywhere from six hundred to nine hundred names for God in the King James Version alone. The various names of God I've heard used by the various Christian services I've gone to are Jesus, Christ, Lord, Father, the Almighty Father, Light, Love, Peace,

Yahweh, He, Him, the Creator, and Jehovah—these are just the ones I remember. Then if you count all the various language translations of the Bible around the world, there are literally hundreds of names for God. For example, Father in English is Padre in Spanish translation, so now we're talking about thousands of names that God has to contend with when we are all praying while using different names and translations. In fact, some religions actually refer to God as a female and sometimes use the pronoun "She" instead of "He" because the act of birthing or creating a child is done through women, and most women have that maternal instinct of wanting to care for and love their children the way God loves us.

Then there's the scientist who calls the All, the Universe. What's important here is not the name, but that we each have a personal relationship with God, the invisible universe, and He/She doesn't care what we call Him/Her. People who are so sensitive that they get so hung up on God's name and who are mentally stuck in their name preference as the only right name are the same people who, in their personal life, you will find very controlling of others and therefore very dangerous. These are typically the radical people that exist in all religions initiating and fighting religious wars in the name of God, Allah, or whatever their choice of name—all stuck in the object-level ego! These are Christian and Islamic terrorist groups that exist today who are petty, petty, small-minded people.

They limit God to believing that God only loves them. We all need to use our brains and avoid these very dangerous people. We can love them but love them from a distance, far, far away. We can accept them without believing what they believe in. Please, **stay away from them**! This is why we need to stop fighting and having wars about who's got the right name because nobody has a monopoly on naming and labeling God's universe of ALL.

> *Have we not **all ONE father [God/Universe]**? Hath not **ONE God created us**? Why do we deal treacherously every man against his brother, by profaning the covenant of our fathers?*
> –Malachi 2:10, KJV

2. INVISIBLE – Spiritual Energy of GOD:
(The eternal and your mind's thoughts – the real you.)

> For **God created (all) man to be immortal,** *and* **made him to be an image of his own eternity.**
> –Wisdom of Solomon 2:23, KJV

> *Conservation of energy in physics states that* **everything in the universe is made from invisible energy.** *Energy can change from one form to another, but* **energy can never be created or destroyed (eternal).**

> *Definition of ETERNAL: 1a) having* **infinite** *duration, EVERLASTING, 1b) of or relating to eternity; 1c) characterized by abiding fellowship with God*
> *–Merriam-Webster's Online Dictionary*

The basic law of physics states that **"everything in the universe is made out of *(invisible)* energy,** but that **energy can never be created or destroyed; it just *changes forms.*"** To illustrate, if you put a whole bunch of colored marbles (*representing science's atoms*) into a box (*representing the universe of energy, since according to science, it's a closed system*) and you keep shaking this box (*according to science, energy and atoms are always moving*), you will see different shapes appear to form. But you will notice that these shapes are temporary and disappear to create new ones.

Our bodies work just like this box of marbles. Our true nature is to change forms. When forms break apart, we call it death. We forget that when we die, our energy or spirit is simply going through a transition phase from one form to another form, according to both physics and religion. Something new will be created and formed out of our energy or spirit because that is our true nature. This is why some religions call God the Universe, the Creator, since according to physics, energy is always just changing and creating new forms of itself.

Since invisible energy can **never be created or destroyed**, according to the laws of physics, that means it is **eternal**, which according to the Bible, is God! Therefore, since science says that we are all made of invisible energy, which the Bible calls God's spirit, the real you inside is also eternal and has no boundaries or limitations. You can't even be destroyed at this level because you are made of invisible energy, according to physics. This is true for everybody, even though some religions claim that only their followers will have eternal life or that only a few elite people will live eternally. In religion, they say God is everywhere and that we (*our bodies or forms*) are all part of the whole (*the one invisible universal energy of God that is eternal, the divine power*). If you think about it, both science and religion are talking about the same thing but just calling them different names.

everything in the Universe is Energy = God is *everywhere* as Spirit
INVISIBLE *Energy* = INVISIBLE *Spirit*
(*can never be created or destroyed*) = (*eternal*)

Transitive Property in Math: *If two qualities are equal to the third quantity, then we can say that all the quantities are equal to each other.*

If **everything** in the universe is made out of energy and God is **everywhere,** that means both the universe (*made of invisible energy*), and God (*made of invisible spirit*), are taking up the same space. Therefore, they are one and the same. Essentially, God the Universe is made out of invisible energy or spirit, just like you are. They are both saying that while brown people, black people, white people, aliens, and rocks on the surface appear in form to be different on the surface, in reality, they are all made of the same invisible energy that is between the electrons and protons. You can't see it because it is invisible energy, yet that is what everything is really made of. It is what we all have in common. It is how we are all connected. You can think of this invisible material as just one big universe of energy, a living organism. This is what religious people call God; it is what scientific people call the universe. God's universal energy or spirit, as the Bible calls it, is what binds us all together as *ONE unit since this invisible level cannot be destroyed according to the laws of physics.*

Therefore, we are all part of this universe as **one**, not as separate beings or objects *(what Einstein calls the illusion)*. Jesus knew this when He was being asked who He was and He said, *"I and my Father (God/Universe) are (together as)* **one***" (John 10:30, KJV)*. However, because most Christians are taught that this only applies to Jesus, it is really difficult for them to understand that they too, are together as one in God's universe since we are all made of His invisible spiritual energy. This is part of the confusion that's being taught out there by some religions since some religions actually teach that we are also separate from God. However, this separation is only a **mental** separation *(which we can correct)*, not a physical separation since it is impossible to exist without God's energy or spirit that everything is made of and is inside all things.

This is the reason why some religions say you cannot live without God because everything is made out of His spiritual energy; therefore, it is impossible to be *physically* separated from Him! This is also the reason why some religions teach that God knows everything about you and what you are thinking because you and everything else around you, that you can see as an object, are all made of God's invisible eternal energy or spirit, and therefore, are physically together as one. So I ask you: *"Do you know who you are in God the Universe?"* I hope you answered the same as Jesus, that you too are together as ONE with God.

> For by Him were **ALL** things created that are in heaven *[invisible level]*, and that are on earth *[visible object level]*, **VISIBLE and INVISIBLE**, *whether they be thrones, or dominions, or principalities, or powers:* **all** *things were* **created by him**, *and* **for him***: And he is before all things, and* **by him ALL things consist**.
> –Colossians 1:16–17, KJV

As stated above (Colossians 1:16–17) from the Bible, *God created ALL things (VISIBLE objects),* which can be supported by the law of physics of energy, which states that *energy is just continuously changing forms (VISIBLE objects)*. Since the universe of God is in all or everything as invisible energy/spirit, creation is nothing more than energy changing and manifesting itself into various forms of itself, according to physics.

So it makes sense that God the Universe created *all* forms of objects or things that you can observe and see with your eyes, since He is in all as invisible energy/spirit, always just changing into different forms of itself.

This concept is illustrated when an artist creates objects by stippling, which is a method of using tiny dots on a canvas. The objects are nothing without the canvas, the space, and together they make the complete picture as **ONE**. It's the canvas that makes the objects possible, and what is created on the canvas unites all objects. So without the canvas, the objects or the illusion cannot exist. When you stand far from the picture, you can see the illusion of the objects; however, if you stand really close to the same picture, you will see nothing but dots with no boundaries or shapes. The objects actually disappear from view when you look at them closely. You can think of our universe—which is made of invisible energy or what the Bible calls spirit—as a canvas. We are all parts, as temporary forms of objects, of the whole universe, which is all connected through God's invisible spiritual energy as the canvas. Can you imagine that we are all somehow connected as ONE invisible energy, like a canvas?

In the invisible universal energy of God, there are no boundaries. It's just unlimited! And each of us is a part of the unlimited energy of God, the canvas, or whatever you choose to call it. This connection we all have with the universal God allows us to draw from it an unlimited source of energy. This concept is extremely important to understand and accept if peace and abundance are what you are seeking in your life. You are not just limited to the body that your energy took as a temporary form in the material world. You are more than that! Whether you choose to believe it or not, you are an invisible spiritual energy that is eternal. You need to accept that you are part of the body of God's universe. Because we are made in God's image, in a sense, we are **mini** gods, here to create our own perspective of our own universe or our own Garden of Eden, like God our Father. Since we are all His children, according to the Bible, we are supposed to be able to mimic His creative abilities, which will be discussed and explained more later.

Your body is not just a temporary shape or form that your spiritual energy took. And contrary to most religions, having eternal life energy (spirit) doesn't require membership. However, it does require you to know this: know how to use it, or work with it, that is why having a personal loving relationship with it is so important if you are searching for mental peace and stability. If you continue to ignore what you are made of inside and continue to believe that you are just a separate object that you see in the visible world of objects (the illusion), then you will continue to have chaos in your life and continue to live in a life full of *limits, boundaries,* and *conditions* instead of a life full of *peace, love, and abundance.* This is your choice.

> **They** *[includes you]* **are not** *[made]* **of the world** *[of objects]* **even as I** *[Jesus speaking]* **am not** *[made]* **of the world** *[of objects].*
>
> –John 17:16, KJV

Universe of God

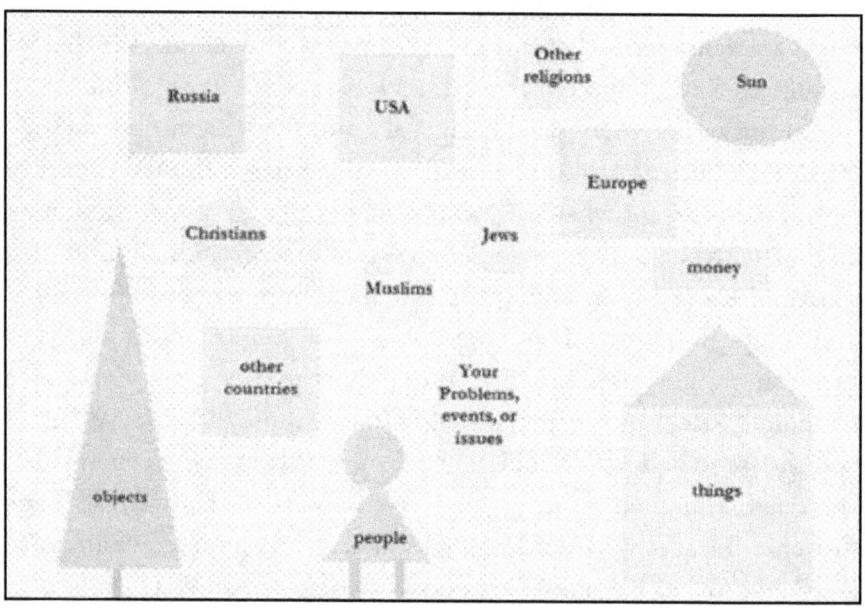

This is an example of computer-generated stippling, which is the art of creating objects on a canvas using tiny dots. Even though everything in the picture is made out of dots *(representing atoms),* the objects are just part of the whole picture or canvas *(representing* God's universe). *See how they are all connected together as* **ONE** *unit, both the canvas and*

all images on the picture, which can easily be made out because of the concentrations of the dots that form the shapes. This is what Einstein calls the illusion. It's not real. The real you is what you are made of inside. This is also how images from televisions and computers work, by using tiny dots called pixels. However, the dots are so concentrated and so small that the images appear as two- or three-dimensional objects that are familiar to us so that we can see the different scenes that are always changing on the screen. They seem real even though they are only temporary forms or shapes, the illusion. Can you see that the illusion of the objects exists because of the space, the screen, or the canvas? Without the canvas or screen, the objects cannot exist because they **ALL** exist together as **ONE** whole unit.

God's universal canvas is eternal. Since you are part of it, you are also eternal inside, since according to physics you cannot even be destroyed at this level. As I said, energy is constantly changing forms or objects that we can see and touch, yet the invisible canvas itself was never created and it cannot be destroyed according to physics, which means it has always existed. The different forms or shapes are simply concentrations of atoms that are temporarily attracted together by an invisible energy force whose atoms are moving slowly enough to appear solid so that they can be seen as objects.

The cyclic process of spiritual energy changing from one form into another form is what some religions like Hinduism, Buddhism, and Sikhism call reincarnation, a never-ending set of cycles that are similar to what is taught in school science today, like the water cycle, the rock cycle, the food chain, and CO_2 cycle, which are some examples of this natural process always going on all around us. The event, in which forms come back to life as another form, is what Christians call the resurrection. It's like a caterpillar that changes into a butterfly; at its core or center, it wasn't destroyed by any means, it just recreated itself into a new form or shape. This is why Einstein calls life an illusion, because of the constant changing of spiritual energy changing from one form to another form or shape according to physics' law of energy.

Why should it be thought incredible
by you that God raises the dead?
–Acts 26:8, NIV

I am just as sure as these people are that God
will raise from death everyone, good or evil.
–Acts 24:15, CEV

God is the greatest recycler in the universe. Therefore, death is nothing more than the ending of an illusion before another new illusion is created and formed into a new shape or form. According to physics' conservation of energy, the process in which we change into different forms is also eternal, which is part of God's perfect intelligent design for us. For example, in the food chain cycle, the small animals eat the grass, the middle size animals eat the small animals, the big animals eat the middle size animals, and when the big animals die, they decompose to feed the grass, and this cycle goes on and on. Again, our bodies that you see with your eyes are only temporary shapes, but our real selves, what we are all made of inside, the invisible spiritual energy field, is eternal. This is key. In terms of time, our physical body forms are just a blip on the eternal radar compared to the lives of our eternal energy, our spirit, or our divinity—however, you choose to call the invisible you inside.

*While we look **NOT at the things which are seen***
*[temporary objects, with 8 billion realities], but **at the***
***things which are NOT SEEN** [invisible energy/spirit]:*
for the things which are seen are temporal** [objects]; **but
***the things which are not seen** [invisible energy or spirit]*
***are eternal** [cannot be created or destroyed].*
–2 Corinthians 4:18, KJV

Eternal Life & Reincarnation

A large proportion of human suffering occurs because people think they only live once. When they become fully aware that the present life is only one point in the eternal flow of time, and that they have lived in the past and will live again in the future, they will understand that their future lives will depend on their present life and also that they can choose what kind of life they will live in the future.

–From the book *The Essence of Buddha*

THE TEN ENERGY TYPES
(*What Science Has Yet to Discover*)

In another ThoughtCo. article by, Anne Marie Helmenstine, Ph.D., "10 Types of Energy and Examples," she states that there are currently only ***ten types of (invisible) energy discovered by scientists so far:***

1. Mechanical
2. Thermal
3. Nuclear
4. Chemical
5. Electromagnetic
6. Sonic
7. Gravitational
8. Kinetic
9. Potential
10. Ionization

However, you'll notice that "mental thoughts" are not listed as a form of energy type, even though the definition of energy in physics is that "***everything** in the universe is made out of [invisible] energy.*" Therefore, by default, you would think that thoughts we mentally generate would also be listed as a type of energy, but it's not. Do you see that? Thoughts are different than sonic or sound energy because most of our thoughts are silent, vibrational energy. We don't always speak our thoughts loudly, and our thoughts can be documented in digital formats or book formats, and most importantly, our thoughts can be controlled when we learn how to do it naturally without the drugs that some people use to control their thinking.

This is the difference between science and religion. ***Science has not yet discovered and does NOT consider our "thoughts" to be a type of energy we can learn to control*** like any other type of energy that we have learned to control for our use; whereas, ***religion has discovered that.*** Until our scientists and educators discover *thoughts* we generate in our minds as just another energy type, they cannot teach us how to use our minds to control it, how it works within God's universe as energy, how thought energy is related to God, and how we can learn to manage the thousands of thoughts we generate in our minds every day. Therefore, **the main focus of religion is nothing more than just teaching people what they consider the most powerful and important type of energy or spiritual force in the universe of God, which is "thought energy,"** that we all can and must learn to mentally control, or as the Buddhists say, ***"Control it [your thoughts] or IT will control you!"*** Because scientists have not yet discovered that thoughts are real and are just another form of energy type, as the reason learning to control our thoughts is not currently being taught in our educational system today, and this is also why many of them scoff at religion.

In fact, all the energy types that have been discovered by scientists so far began with **thought energy** first. If it weren't for the series of *thoughts* that the inventors, engineers, and scientists initially *thought* about, to begin with, the questions in their minds as to how things work, they would not have even come to discover the ten energy types. So without **"thought"** first and then words, none of these energy types would even have been discovered. In fact, the byproducts we all enjoy today as a result of their discoveries over time would not exist either. We would have no cars, no computers, no houses, no money, no electricity, and we would not even have books available for schools or universities without *thought* energy first that educators and scientists could *speak about or teach* about.

When I was an aerospace engineer working on various projects, whether it was making helicopters, rockets, missiles, or designing the inside of a building, **the beginning** is called the planning phase. They all required a lot of thinking, talking, communicating, and weeks of meetings between the various engineers, the different levels of management, manufacturing, accounting, finance, government, and more in order to create the projects. All shared communications, no matter what form, whether oral, digital, or printed, are all thought energy, and *all creation* begins first with using our **thought** energy.

In other words, the cars we drive, the houses we live in, electricity, and our computers, did not just magically in an instant just appear or randomly put themselves together, without thoughts or words first. In fact, you can't even have a party or get a job without mentally *thinking thoughts and words* about it first. Try to plan a party without using thought energy or try to go to college without thinking any thoughts or speaking any words to anyone or writing any words while signing up on college applications, see how far you can get. It's impossible!

How powerful is *thought* energy? Let's put it this way, according to Ashley Kirk in "How Many Nukes Are in The World and What Could They Destroy?" (*The Telegraph News*, October 11, 2017), there are around 15,000 nuclear warheads around the world. These are the most powerful weapons the world has today. If the US were to drop its largest arsenal, the B-83, it would kill about 1.4 million people in just the first twenty-four hours, and another 3.7 million people would be injured due to the thermal radiation radius at thirteen kilometers. However, if Russia dropped their largest bomb on New York City, because of the concentration of people there, they estimate it could kill around 7.6 million people and injure another 4.2 million due to the nuclear fallout. If you think about it, it is **thought** energy that began the creation of all the nukes. The nukes did not create themselves without somebody, *first thinking* about creating them and giving the order to make it so. It's only by the grace of all the world leaders' mental self-control since WWII that nobody has yet decided to give the order to push the button against their enemy.

In WWII, it was General Groves who drafted the **written order (*words*)** to use the atomic bomb against the Japanese cities, that then US President Truman approved. The *written* order was nothing but words and thoughts written on paper, and President Truman had to mentally decide to sign the order. He could have decided to say the word "no," but instead he chose the word or thought "yes." This is how powerful his "yes" was to the dropping of the atomic bomb: *90,000–146,000 people in Hiroshima and 39,000–80,000 people in Nagasaki died, almost half died on the first day alone.* You see, the **bombs did not drop by themselves without somebody first giving the *verbal or written* order to push the button. This is what is meant by the saying:**

> *The pen [written words] is mightier than the sword.*
> –Edward Bulwer-Lytton

THOUGHT Energy – Our Power to Create or Destroy (The missing link–the Eleventh Energy Type)

Our power is in the *thoughts or words we create in our minds,* and we can all choose to create positive thoughts of love, peace, joy, happiness, and forgiveness or negative thoughts of hate, anger, jealousy, vengeance, worry, or guilt in our minds since it is all under our mental control, and it is all invisible energy. So the question for you is, ***"How are you going to choose to describe and create your everyday life?"*** Will you choose to live in **love** every day, or will you choose to live in misery, fear, worry, or stress every day? Where do you choose to put your mental focus, in the temporary chaotic world of **visible** objects that we're constantly judging as good or bad, with everybody fighting with each other? Or, will you choose to focus your mind on the **invisible** spiritual energy of God's unconditional love, peace, and joy, where there is nothing to judge (*no good or bad, no rich or poor, no skinny or fat people, no males, females, or gays, no religions, no races, no sickness, no stress*)? The choice is yours since you are the only one in control of your own mind.

This is why religion teaches the importance of mental self-control because to them *thought energy/spirit* is the most important form of energy type. The Bible teaches this eloquently when it comes to creating anything, whether it is God doing the creating of the Garden of Eden (*the physical world of objects*), corporations full of professionals creating missiles, computers, or cars, or regular people doing the creating of their own perspective of their own Garden of Eden. The Bible states,

In the beginning was the WORD *[thoughts]*
–John 1:1, KJV

Therefore, **all creation starts with creating our *words* or *thought energy* first**. This is why ***thought energy is even more powerful*** than any of the ten energy types that scientists have discovered so far. Because without *thought* first, nothing else would exist, not even God's Garden of Eden, His creation of the material world of objects. ***This part of the creative process cannot be bypassed!***

In big corporate projects, to reduce cycle time in creating and manifesting anything at the object level, what works best is to form focused groups so that the thoughts generated are controlled conversations on one specific topic, not multiple topics. For example, you never want to mix missile builders with car builders; otherwise, it's a waste of time of too many distractions, unless the project calls for a missile to be built as part of the car. When I was an engineer, management created focused teams whose sole purpose was to solve a specific problem right away. This reduced cycle time in finding a solution to the problem at hand. All these focused teams, or *think tanks* as they are sometimes called, did was to create thoughts and ideas that would solve a specific problem immediately so that they could move forward toward creating whatever it was they were trying to create. All this required a lot of mental or thought data. These were controlled thoughts that were usually written down and entered into a computer to be digitized so that everybody knew their part of the puzzle and that it all worked together at the end.

For example, the electrical engineers would create their own sets of electrical data and instructions, the mechanical engineers also would create their own data and set of instructions, and the manufacturing engineers had their own set of documentation. Then somebody else put all the documents together to make sure they all worked together. So at the beginning of any project, reams and reams of data made up of instructions (words) and diagrams documenting the processes and materials list were all required to successfully create whatever it was the engineers or developers were trying to create; otherwise, the project would die and never materialize.

Merriam-Webster's definition of a **think tank** is *"an institute, corporation or group organized to study a particular subject (such as a policy issue or a scientific problem) and provide information, ideas, and advice."* The information, ideas, and advice generated are examples of controlled *thought, or energy forces* because think tanks are typically made up of experts in a particular field, to specifically *think thoughts* to solve a particular problem so that they can create whatever they are trying to create. If *thoughts* were not a powerful energy type, how come corporations, institutions, and governments spend so much time and money forming **think tanks** just to try to harness *ideas and thought energy from field experts* to try to solve a particular problem? If **thoughts** were not such a powerful energy force, why are psychiatrists prescribing thirty million Americans antidepressant drugs to control or stop their patients from thinking too much? *(See Global Research's online article, "Making Money from Addiction: 30 Million Americans On Antidepressants. Twenty Facts on America's Big Pharma Nightmare.")*

Going back to documentation as a form of written thought energy, religion does the same thing as engineers who document their project processes. Religious people believe ***thoughts*** are powerful invisible energy forces that we can all learn to control. *(Religion just happens to call energy "spirit").* The various religions have created their own sets of instruction books for people on how to be happy and live peacefully, how to control the thoughts that our minds generate, and how our body, mind, and spiritual energy work best together as one in positive alignment. The Christians have their Bible, the Muslims have their Quran, the Hindus have their book of Vedas, and the Jews have their Tanakh.

We have to remember that just because scientists *discovered* a particular type of energy at a particular time in our history, it does not mean these forms of energy *never existed before that time*. In fact, it's the opposite. All their discoveries just mean that up until that point in time, ***scientists were just not aware they existed***. They did not invent any of these types of energy; since they've always existed. The fact that scientists became **aware** of these various types of energy as existing in the universe today, just means ***they were there before they discovered them, otherwise, they would not have existed to be discovered***. It wasn't until scientists became aware that these energy types existed and learned ***how they worked and how to work with them and learned to control*** the various energy types did scientists, engineers, and entrepreneurs began to invent products for us to use.

For example, once scientists "discovered" how to use, work, and control nuclear energy, by releasing or combining the nuclei of an atom, they started figuring out ways to use it so our lives could be better or worse depending on your perspective. Initially, during 1939–1945, most of the development work in using nuclear energy was concentrated on creating atomic bombs, by splitting the nuclei of uranium atoms. But now the technology is being used to generate electricity, it's also being used in medicine, and space travel.

According to the World Nuclear Association's article, Outline History of Nuclear Energy, "Bohr soon proposed that fission was much more likely to occur in uranium-235 isotope than in U-238 and that fission would occur more effectively with slow-moving neutrons than with fast neutrons." *So why haven't scientists figured out yet why certain **words** we think about are more effective than others in creating a more loving, peaceful world, but they've figured out that certain invisible elements are better to use than other elements in creating nuclear fission?*

As I said previously, what's obviously missing for scientists is that they have not yet discovered that mental thoughts are just another form of energy type that humans can create and control. As a result, they cannot help people learn to use, work, or control them so we can be more effective in creating peace, love, joy, and happiness in our lives and be healthier as well. For example, scientists do not know how our minds processes mental data, how our thoughts affect our bodies, or how they affect others. Neither do they know why creating positive thoughts is better than negative thoughts; how to naturally control and reduce the 12,000 to 60,000 thoughts a day we generate without drugs; how our body, mind, and energy/spirit work best together in positive alignment as ONE unit; and finally, why it's necessary to learn to work with the source of God's energy itself so that we can improve how we interact with our environment as a whole, thereby improving our overall way of thinking and living.

To me, religion is nothing more than institutions for learning how to effectively control and process our thought energy. This is so that we can reduce our mental suffering and live happier, longer lives by thinking less and thinking positively versus negatively. Also, it is so that we don't hurt ourselves and others with our words and actions simply because we cannot control our constant mental babbling and negative thoughts of anger, hate, and overall stress.

This is where religion is more advanced than science because, to religion, thoughts are just another form of invisible spiritual energy that we all can and must learn to mentally control so we can end our mental suffering naturally, end hurting ourselves, and end the fighting amongst each other by creating "thoughts of love and being of service to others." So basically, religion is just trying to save us from creating our own hell hole and from destroying ourselves and each other to an early grave created by our negative thinking and not knowing how to use our brains more effectively.

You might ask, what exactly is religion trying to save us from?

Well, they are trying to save us from killing ourselves, destroying our relationships, and destroying others. Remember what I said at the beginning, that according to Learning Mind, in their article, "The Psychology of **Nature's Number One Killer: Stress**":

- 50 percent of all marriages in the US end up in divorce.
- Thirty million Americans are on antidepressants.
- According to NAMI (National Alliance on Mental Illness), in their article "Consequences of Lack of Treatment," **mental illness** costs the US $193.2 billion in lost earnings per year; suicide is the tenth leading cause of death for children between ages ten and fourteen; suicide is the second leading cause of death for kids between ages

fifteen to twenty-four, and each day it is estimated that there are eighteen-to-twenty-two veterans who commit suicide.

- In 2016, there were 44,965 recorded suicides in the United States, up from 42,773 in 2014, according to the CDC's National Center for Health Statistics (NCHS).

- There were 41,148 suicides in 2007 and 46,131 deaths in 2009 due to the **stress of unemployment alone** worldwide (Lancet Psychiatry).

These are God's lost souls. They are our loved ones, our children, our friends, and our families. They are all worth trying to save, don't you think? Since our scientists, educators, and doctors don't yet know how to help us stop our automatic thinking naturally, we should, therefore, all encourage a different method to our loved ones—methods that are more advanced in teaching mind control, like religion and the experts listed in the appendix. *(See also articles at the end Summary section titled: "US Antidepressant Use Jumps 65 Percent in 15 Years," "Recent Study Confirms That Antidepressants Increase Suicide Risk," "Exposed: Our Dangerous Dependency on Antidepressants"; and online: "Making Money from Addiction: 30 Million Americans On Antidepressants. Twenty Facts on America's Big Pharma Nightmare," End of the American Dream (2014); "The Half-Trillion-Dollar Depression," The New York Times Magazine; and "Money for Nothing," U.S. News.)*

Here are examples of Bible verses about positive thinking and mind control by placing our mental focus on God's invisible spiritual energy level (*where there is eternal peace, unconditional love, calm, and freedom from mental hell from objects*) instead of focusing on the temporary material world of objects that's very chaotic, uncontrollable, always changing, and with 8 billion different mental realities:

*For the Spirit [**invisible energy level**] God gave us does not make us timid, but **gives us power, love, and self-discipline.***
–2 Timothy 1:7, NIV

Finally, brothers and sisters, whatever is true, whatever is noble, whatever is right, whatever is pure, whatever is lovely, whatever is admirable — if anything is excellent or praiseworthy—think about such things [think positive].
–Philippians 4:8, NIV

You were taught, with regard to your former way of life, to put off your old self, which is being corrupted by its deceitful desires; **to be made new in the attitude of your minds[think positive]; and to put on the new self, created to be like God[which is unconditional love] in true righteousness and holiness. [wholeness]**

Therefore each of you must put off falsehood and speak truthfully to your neighbor, for **we are all members of ONE body [one God/universe].** *"In your anger do not sin": Do not let the sun go down while you are still angry, and do not give the devil a foothold. Anyone who has been stealing must steal no longer, but must work, doing something useful with their own hands, that they may have something to share with those in need.*

Do not let any unwholesome talk come out of your mouths[negative thinking], but only what is helpful for building others up according to their needs[positive thinking], that it may benefit those who listen. And do not grieve the Holy Spirit of God, with whom you were sealed for the day of redemption. Get rid of all bitterness, rage and anger, brawling and slander, along with every form of malice. Be kind and compassionate to one another, forgiving each other, just as in Christ God forgave you.
–Ephesians 4:22–32, NIV

What goes into someone's mouth does not defile them, but what comes out of their mouth, that is what defiles them.
–Matthew 15:11, NIV

*Set your minds on things above [**invisible level**], Not on earthly things [**visible object level**].*
–Colossians 3:2

The Universal Mind of God

As a man who has devoted his whole life to the most clear-headed science to the study of matter, I can tell you as the result of my research about atoms, there is no matter as such. All matter originates and exists only by virtue of a force which brings the particle of an atom to vibration and holds this most minute solar system of the atom together, **we must assume behind this force the existence of a conscious and intelligent mind. This mind is the matrix of all matter.**
–Max Planck (Nobel Prize in Physics)

GOD/UNIVERSE = **VISIBLE** *(objects/matter)* **+**
INVISIBLE *(energy+universal/collective Mind)*

Your mind, all your thoughts, and your imagination belong in the invisible part of you because thoughts are energy that cannot be seen or touched. Remember what physicists say, "**Everything** is made of invisible eternal energy that can never be created or destroyed"; this includes all thoughts, both negative and positive thoughts that people mentally generate, even though scientists have not yet discovered thought as an energy type. Your mind makes you and all humans and animals unique from other objects in the universe because God made us in His image. Rocks and trees, for example, do not have minds to allow them to think about who they are or what they are, and they cannot create. Thoughts are a form of eternal energy that come in different frequencies depending on how negative or positive a person's thoughts are being generated. This allows them to create and attract objects toward them or push them away.

Haven't we all experienced being around negative people? We just want to stay away from them and avoid them. This is one of the ways I create mental peace in my mind and in my life, by purposely staying away from negative thinking people, or at least I try to limit my time with them. This is the same thing as when parents tell their kids to stay away from gang members or druggies so that they themselves do not get easily influenced by the way these negative people think and behave. But as I said before, we do not need to hate them; we can still love them—but from far, far away.

> *Do not be yoked together with unbelievers. For what do righteousness and wickedness have in common? Or what fellowship can light have with darkness.*
> —2 Corinthians 6:14, NIV

However, I do believe in trying to help lost souls, but only if we are spiritually and mentally strong ourselves, and we put on our God-power shield and work with a spiritual team. The other side is very negative, and there are many all in need of help. Most don't even know it, since they are in automatic thinking and mentally out of control since we're not taught in school how to naturally control our minds. Currently, our experts can only offer drugs to help control their thinking. Until our scientists and educators discover that our thoughts are real, and they learn to control them naturally without drugs, and learn how thoughts work with the universe as just another form of energy, they really can't help and teach our children mind control—until perhaps another 2,000 years. Until then we need to try to educate our kids ourselves and bring them to church or synagogue. Also, there are many great organizations out there for you to join if you feel you have the calling to help others from their mental suffering through God's power.

The saying "We all stand on the shoulders of giants" explains this eloquently. What this means is that our status today in technology, science, medicine, religion, etc., is the result of many people and many minds from years and years before that got us to where we are today. This is true with everything. Essentially, everything is an accumulation of thousands of years' worth of intelligent thought. This is what some people call the universal mind of God or the collective mind. This is part of our mental evolution. If you could come back three hundred years from now, do you think the airplanes would be the same as they are now? Of course not. I know for a fact that businesses and engineers always need to make things faster or better, or else people will not buy their products. And making things a little bit better and faster requires billions of intelligent people using their minds to keep the ball rolling generation after generation. All this requires creativity, which starts collectively in the minds of billions of people through the centuries of human evolution. Do not ever think that we just got here in the snap of a finger. Everything you see today evolved in this world as a result of the collective mind or the universal mind of God, with the belief that all thoughts are invisible energy or spirit.

We were taught in school that the universe is made of electrons and protons and invisible forces of energy. While that is true, the concept of God is more than this; it also includes the collective thoughts of the universe as just another form of invisible energy that connects all humans together as one. It is this collective mind that has been accumulating over the centuries, and which physicists like Max Planck talk about, that distinguishes us from other forms of life. If we only believe in the universe as nothing more than protons and electrons without the mind in the equation, then we humans would be just like any other object, like a rock with no mind.

You see all knowledge in technology, medicine, science, etc., is built and accumulated from the history of people's past developments that originated from their minds and their imaginations—called the collective mind. You can think of it like the World Wide Web of the internet, but bigger and better. The internet has no intelligence behind it because it is essentially just a whole bunch of servers that are connected together that act like a giant memory bank that anybody who is connected has access to. When asked, for example, "Who was the US president in 1960?" a list will show which servers have the data that will answer that question. However, the invisible mind of God, because He is everywhere and is connected to everything as an invisible energy that by default can never be created or destroyed, is in you and in me.

Because we are all connected as *one*, this universal mind is simply the connection of all minds together as *one*, like the internet servers. But unlike internet servers, the universal or collective mind is better because everybody's got access to it, it's free, and it has intelligence. It is real and alive; it has spirit and soul, and it is a moving energy. It is your intelligence with everybody else's intelligence combined together as *one* universal mind, and everybody has access to its unlimited source to draw from.

The problem is that most of us do not know how to efficiently access this universal database. I have found that the most efficient way to access God's database is through quieting of the mind, meditation, and prayers, which is why religious monks do this and are so good at it. This will be discussed more in the next section on the best way to do this process because a lot of us are misguided by the churches we attend, that praying and meditating are the same, but they are not.

> ***If you BELIEVE**, you will receive whatever you ask for in prayer.*
> –Matthew 21:22, NIV

Here are some examples of how I've accessed and used this universal mind. When my kids were young, every morning during the week, I was always so busy trying to get my daughters ready for school and myself ready for work that most of the time I was rushing, and I found myself over and over again asking God to please get me to school on time, and He did. Because God is in me, as part of His spiritual energy, He actually knows what I need and want by the thoughts I generate. So when I ask for help in getting to school on time, unlike the internet that you need to ask specific questions to, He already knows which school I'm going to, which route I take, and which signal lights I need to be green to get me there on time because everything is connected as *one invisible energy field*. This is where God's intelligence comes in; computers and even GPS systems cannot get me to school on time. In fact, the GPS sometimes takes me to the wrong place or makes me go in circles. They can help, but learning to work with God's invisible spiritual energy level gives you that added advantage of working directly with the eternal source at the of energy level. Doing so will reduce cycle time in meeting your goals and reduce mental stress, thereby improving your health overall.

However, it doesn't work well when my mind is negative, and I'm angry or pissed. This is because it's like a PC with a virus—it doesn't work well. In fact, I call upon God to be my partner in all my problems and concerns with my husband, my kids, people at work, money, investments, love, and forgiveness—with everything, in short—and He answers. I simply need to ask Him for help on how to do something, and often He comes up with better solutions that I didn't even think about. This is why God is about abundance. His intelligence is not based on human intelligence that most of the time is only limited to the object-level viewpoints of limits and conditions.

Because I am always thinking big, thinking of abundant possibilities, and thinking of God now, I am no longer alone, thinking small and thinking limits. By putting Him in all my thoughts first and always, together we make everything work for me. Try it, it works! At first, it's kind of freaky how it all works, but you'll get used to it. You will see what I'm talking about; there's definitely a difference. However, this partnership works best when you are in full *positive* alignment in mind, body, and energy/spirit, as stated previously, and you've learned to control your mind so that it is silent so that you can hear His voice.

Accessing the internet requires a working PC, clean hardware, strong links, and the proper software. If the computer is infected with a virus, for example, its ability to access and retrieve data from the World Wide Web will be limited. Similarly, accessing the universal mind of God requires an open, clear, clean mind, a positive attitude, and a good, strong link or relationship to *all*, or God. So if you think of yourself and your mind only as a small being that is separate from the universe, then like a stand-alone computer that is not linked to the World Wide Web, you will produce life results that reflect your small thinking.

*Do you not know that **you are God's temple**
and that **God's Spirit [energy] dwells in you?***
–1 Corinthians 3:16, ESV

So, if you think you are alone or that nobody loves you, or that you have to do life by yourself, don't believe your own negative stories. For one thing, it's impossible for you to be alone because God is in you as an invisible energy/spirit, so you cannot be physically separated from Him; but you can only be *mentally separated* from Him by choosing not to believe in Him. God loves you so much, that He gave you free will to choose however you want to live your life, whether you want to believe and love Him or not.

Also, God loves you unconditionally, no matter what! He can never hate Himself as you because He is in you! God does not love us the way humans love each other, which is based on limits and conditions. Humans will love you only if you believe what they believe and do what they do. God's love for us is unconditional (*with no conditions*) and it's eternal. It is supernatural love, and it can never be destroyed (*according to physics*) even when we get angry with Him, blame Him, curse Him, or don't believe in Him, He loves us anyway. In addition, He will always be there for us when we ask Him for help with our projects or problems. This is His natural characteristic to want to help us if we just learn to love Him and learn how to work with Him, much like a loving parent who wants to always help their children.

There are many books written by successful people about thinking big. If you want success in your life, you can look them up on the internet. Even though most of these books were written in terms of creating a business or money, which is also energy, the same applies to all areas of your life: your family, all your relationships, your work, religion, politics, etc. In everything, think big and think God if you want success in all parts of your life. When I say success, I mean unlimited love, peace, and a long life of abundance. I discuss this in more detail in later sections. Remember, just because you can't see it doesn't mean it does not exist. Gravity, electricity, and magnetism are just a few examples of energy that is invisible, but you can sure see the results of their pulling power.

Take roller skates as an example of an accumulation of thought. Somebody invented the wheel (3500 BC), somebody else invented the shoes (cavemen), and somebody put the two together to invent roller skates (1700s). All creation requires a *collaboration* of thought and effort by many. Everything goes through this evolutionary process—a growing process, or a learning process if you will. All human creation starts with imagination in the mind, with the thought that the imaginer can do better and be better—or just create for the fun of it.

So ask yourself, what can you do better for yourself and your family, and what can you do to help serve others and God? The answer to this question is your purpose. It doesn't have to be earth-shattering; it could be anything. Most of us could start with ourselves by learning to love ourselves and our spouses unconditionally because we are all role models for our children. Our children copy our behaviors, and as I said previously, our behaviors stem from our minds and our beliefs. So we all have a great responsibility to teach our children—our future generation—about how to love and cooperate with one another so that we may have peace in the bedrooms, at home, at work, with our neighbors, with other countries, and with the world.

This is another great gift God has given us; because He is pure love, *He loves us all unconditionally.* Learn to be like God so that you can give love away to others unconditionally. This is not a minor task. Look at all the hate and the negativity in this world. We all need to learn to love ourselves first, and then we can give everybody else the overflow. Learn to expand your scope of love to encompass everything and everybody—*all* in the universe. This is how we become mentally one with God—by being like Him.

Who's the first scientist to discover that we are all made of INVISIBLE energy and that our body is together as ONE with this energy force field?

This is eternal [energy/spirit] life, that they may
know You [God], the only true God [the Universe].
–John 17:3, KJV

In Jesus' time, most religions were already teaching about God's "eternal" life, even though they used different words to describe what physicists currently teach in schools that we are all made of invisible energy that can never be created or destroyed. We can then think of religion as the first to discover this, not science. For example, John 17:3 is what Christians have been trying to teach their followers since Jesus' time, and the scientific concept of invisible energy wasn't even discovered until the early 1800s.

Although they don't credit this discovery to one person, according to historians, scientists' version of energy was discovered when Michael Faraday, 1791–1867, discovered electromagnetic energy; Benjamin Franklin discovered positive and negative electrical charges about the same time; and Julius Robert Mayer discovered conservation of energy in 1842. It took scientists almost two thousand years to discover what Jesus talked about, that we are all made of an invisible spiritual/energy force that is eternal. It's probably going to take scientists another two thousand years to discover that our body, mind, and eternal spiritual/ energy force field (*that everything is made of inside*) are all actually connected as one and that they work together more efficiently when viewed together as one whole unit—not as separate entities, which is very inefficient, as is currently taught in schools. If you don't believe me, ask your doctor if he can separate your physical body from the energy that is inside you that physicists say everything is made of. It's impossible because they are all together as ONE UNIT. Your body cannot exist without invisible energy.

According to the Bible, Jesus was trying to teach us that we are all together as one with God the Universe when He said, "*I and my Father are ONE*" (KJV), when He was being asked who He was. However, most Christians miss this most important lesson, that Jesus was also talking about every matter or material object, including themselves, as being also together as one with God the Universe. Their lack of understanding is caused by people's misinterpretation of this verse, that this only applies to Jesus. Then the Bible goes on to say that to achieve mental peace, we all need to learn to practice how our spiritual energy, mind, and body work best together as ***one whole unit,*** so that we don't feel as if something is missing or broken in our lives, but rather that we feel like a whole and complete person.

> *And the very **God of peace** sanctify you **wholly**, and I pray God **your whole spirit (energy) and soul (thoughts) and body** be preserved blameless unto the coming of our Lord Jesus Christ.*
>   −1 Thessalonians 5:23, KJV

Jesus could not save and heal everybody during His time. The only people whom He was actually able to help heal physically from their mental illness were only those who believed and understood His teachings of our oneness with God, the Universe, at 100 percent. Therefore, Jesus did not actually heal these people, the people healed themselves based on their belief system and level of understanding of His teachings. That is why, even today, **anybody can heal themselves, IF they only have faith, belief, and full understanding of God's natural process that is within themselves at 100 percent.** However, anything less than 100 percent understanding, may or may not work, because it all depends on the person's thinking.

> ***Your FAITH** [your belief in the invisible] **has made you well.***
>   −Matthew 9:22, ESV

This is why they called it a miracle because only a few people (and even today) really understand the concept that **we ALL exist naturally together as ONE whole unit in the universe as an invisible spiritual energy** that cannot be destroyed, according to physics. Therefore, we are all eternal inside since everything is made of it. This form of healing only works when people no longer think they only exist as separate beings in the temporary, visible world as broken objects, where chaos exists, and everybody is fighting with each other. This level is what Einstein calls the illusion.

Our scientists today could actually reduce their cycle time in discovering how humans work within God's universe as one unit if they would just investigate the various religious books for best practices to see what works and doesn't work, and then compare their findings on how to best use our minds to connect mentally to our invisible spiritual energy level, and also to compare how to best manage our thoughts to improve our behaviors naturally and achieve mental peace without drugs.

Wouldn't it be nice, though, if we could have all learned to use our body, mind, and energy together as one unit more efficiently at an early age so that this process would not be considered a miracle, experienced only by a few, but rather something we all practice naturally? However, we and our children will never learn this in school because scientists haven't even figured out yet that all three parts (body, mind, energy) are actually connected as one unit, as religion has been trying to teach for centuries, let alone how they work together to improve human efficiency.

I don't know about you, but I don't have another two thousand years to wait for science to discover this connection and how they work together, do you? This is why **some** religious people who are 100 percent believers of God's invisible spiritual energy and have learned how to mentally use it properly have experienced miracles as described in the Bible. Humans are here to learn to discover how God's universe works naturally as part of our evolution, and this is just one of those things we all have to eventually learn if we want an abundant long life of love and peace in our lives that is lasting. How do I know this? Because I've experienced this myself through trial and error in trying to learn what worked and what didn't work in naturally healing myself and my family from mental stress, without drugs or expensive therapy.

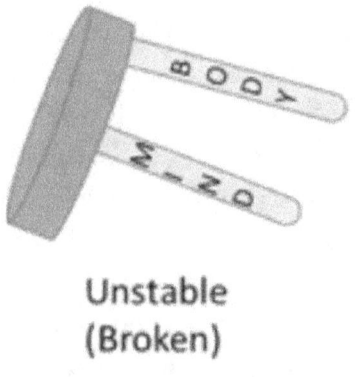

Unstable
(Broken)

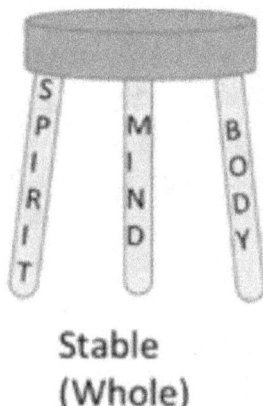

Stable
(Whole)

The simplest way I can explain why it's important for all of us to know how all three parts of ourselves work together best as one whole unit to make us better and more mentally stable is if you can imagine a three-legged stool, where each leg represents our body, mind, and spirit respectively. You can see from the picture above how the three-legged stool keeps it stable. However, if you cut one of the legs off the stool, it becomes a broken stool and not a very efficient form of a chair. Most people are like this. They become broken like the stool above when they only operate with their minds and bodies (only two legs), without learning how to work with their invisible spiritual energy force that everything is made of and is inside all things.

We become spiritually, mentally, and physically broken and handicapped because without believing in the invisible spiritual energy side of ourselves and not knowing how it works within ourselves, we have nowhere to release our pent-up negative thought energy of anger, jealousy, inadequacy, depression, loneliness, suicide, and guilty feelings other than taking it out on others so we hurt them—or keeping our negative thoughts bottled up and stuck in our minds only to make ourselves mentally crazy or physically sick as our body transforms these thoughts into sickness, such as cancer, autoimmune diseases, or heart attacks. This is because according to the laws of physics, energy changes into forms, and as the saying goes, "**thoughts become things**."

Our other option is to go to drug dealers and doctors to get drugs to try to help us control our minds from thinking too much. That often does not work, or we can learn to do it ourselves naturally without drugs. It's up to you since you are the only one in control of your own mind.

This is the emergency we have now! This is why the Bible asks all of us to learn this mental self-control process ourselves first, so we can then be disciples and help teach others this system of natural healing. Since schools refuse to do the educating, then we are all called to do the teaching ourselves, once we learn it for ourselves.

The increase in mental craziness and stress in our society is causing an increase in illegal and prescription drug use in our society and at the same time making doctors, drug dealers, pharmaceutical companies, and our government (in the form of taxes) billions and billions of dollars. Thus, there is no incentive for our scientists, doctors or the government to investigate and research this natural process of healing ourselves at all because it is a multi-billion-dollar industry. They just think that our body, mind, and energy/spirit working together is part of religion, which to them has no proof that God's universal energy even exists since it is invisible. This is why they want to remove God from our schools and government. All the while, our kids at younger and younger ages are getting addicted to either prescription or nonprescription drugs, and suicide rates are also on the rise as well as divorces.

I believe we can solve our society's mental craziness and most of the physical ailments people are experiencing that are associated with mental stress when we educate people on the following:

- How do we manage and control the thoughts we create in our minds?
- What invisible energy/spirit is, that everything is made of that is inside us?
- How do we effectively use and work with our spiritual energy so that it improves our lives?

This is so that we can all be more efficient and effective human beings and save ourselves from sickness caused by mental illness, save ourselves from drugs that do not work, save our relationships, and be able to help our family and friends as well. **If you understand this, PLEASE help me pass God's knowledge and process on to others.** Together we can all help heal the world from mental madness by telling your family and friends about this book. God is calling you to help!

3

Where Your Source Comes From

The day science begins to study non-physical phenomena, it will make more progress in one decade than in all the previous centuries of its existence.
—Nikola Tesla (inventor, engineer)

If you want to find the secrets of the universe, think in terms of energy [invisible spirit], frequency, and vibration.
—Nikola Tesla (inventor, engineer)

God created everything through him [as spiritual energy], and nothing was created except through him [in energy].
—John 1:3, KJV

Without me [in reference to God's spiritual energy that everything is made of] ye can do nothing.
—John 15:5, KJV

Feelings of lack have to do with the thought that you are separate and alone from the universe. This is a fallacy because you are together as one with God the Universe since you are made from its spiritual energy, which is limitless and boundless. Therefore, the possibilities of what you can think and create—when you believe in God's invisible spiritual energy level as your creative canvas—are endless as well. Yes, you are an endless possibility. The universe is your playground, not just the city you live in. You just have to believe it, trust it, and have faith in its fullness. When you are in full positive alignment with the universe, **it** will help you and guide you toward whatever it is you want to create. It will bring you all the people and things you need to help you manifest your projects, whatever that may be when you believe in and learn to work with God's invisible energy force field directly. You are part of its universal energy flow. You just have to learn to go with its energy flow of love. You can tell when you are going against God's love flow whenever you are fighting, struggling, and having difficulty and mental stress in your life. This is a sign you are doing the process wrong.

Your lack of long-life abundance of love, joy, health, and peace comes from your belief that your source of love, peace, and happiness comes from visible objects, such as specific people, institutions, corporations, drugs, sex, liquor, etc. This is very limiting. Your dependence on objects as your source and not knowing who you really are as part of God's invisible spiritual energy and how to work with it as ONE, at 100 percent, causes all your mental suffering. Your mental stress comes because these people whom you are so dependent on can only love you so much until they leave you, corporations can only pay you so much until they lay you off, and drugs, sex, and liquor eventually wear off. This is because physical objects are all temporary forms of spiritual energy and are constantly changing, according to physics. So, your shortages and limitations come from believing that you are just an object that has been separated from everything else and that your source of happiness, love, and peace comes from other objects.

> *Verily, verily, I say unto you,* **He** *that* **believeth** *on me* **(Jesus teachings),** *the works that I do shall he do also* **(you can do what I do)***; and greater works* **(teaching, healing, creating)** *than these shall he do* **(you can do better)***; because I go unto my Father.*
> –John 14:12, KJV

Let's take the creative *abundance* of God and compare that with what most of His children (that's you and me) have created for themselves. Look around you and really see what God or the universe has created for us. He created billions of stars, billions of people, billions of gallons of water, billions of trees, billions of animals, billions of bugs, billions of fish, billions of sand grains, and so on. It is His nature to create abundantly and effortlessly. But as his children, *made in his image,* we often don't project that same abundance. In fact, most of us project the opposite of abundance, which is lack. Most of us lack love, lack peace, lack money, lack health, and most of us seem to struggle at everything we try to create. Going in the opposite direction of the universe's *positive love* energy flow creates this lack. For example, most people in the world today live at the poverty level and are themselves struggling for love and peace. Even the United States, one of the richest countries in the world, struggles with its own poverty. Many people are depressed, many are on drugs or alcohol, many are struggling just to meet their day-to-day living, and we have high rates of suicide and divorce. In fact, this so-called rich country is really not so rich because most people, even those who appear rich, are in credit card debt up their yin-yang and are often dependent on drugs or alcohol or are extremely unhappy with themselves and are often mentally sick or physically sick, or both, from mental stress.

This is an opportunity for all of us to reduce this disconnect in our lives from living in lack to living in a long life of abundance in love, mental peace, happiness, and joy. So let's all get off our rear ends. Let's stop the pity parties and the victim mentality, and start taking responsibility for our own lives, and our own happiness so that we can make our own lives better; thereby making the universe better. Instead of supporting the drug and liquor companies by pumping ourselves with their products to make us feel better, let's pump our minds instead with positive thoughts of God's energy by learning how we are related to it, understanding that we are all made of His eternal energy of love, and by supporting those who teach these concepts. This is the only way to make permanent changes in our lives NATURALLY so that we can get out of being stuck in our own mental hellhole and have mental peace. Only by mentally and spiritually healing ourselves of this form of sickness of lack can we help others to do the same.

Some religious beliefs actually encourage lack and struggle such as believing that "the love of money is a sin, therefore having too much is a sin," even though evidence of God's universe shows otherwise as stated above. If God only creates in abundance, it doesn't make sense that He would create you in His image so that you would struggle and have very little in your life. If that were the case, then the Bible would be wrong in stating that you were made in his image.

An *image* is defined in *Websters' Dictionary* as "a representation of a person or thing" or "one exactly resembling another," "a copy," or "a likeness." As mentioned before, God's gift to us is creating us in his image by giving us our own minds to freely do and create whatever it is we want. The only catch is, you have the responsibility to choose to create what you want, but most of us choose to give that responsibility away by blaming others for our problems or by copying or following the wrong negative crowd, or by believing we don't deserve it or by living in fear.

When my oldest daughter was a teenager, for example, one day she was complaining because we refused to allow her to attend high school parties where drugs and liquor were being served. She stated that she would not do them, but she just wanted to hang out with the cool kids from school. You see, whenever you follow the wrong crowd, you will have a tendency to do what they do. Just like the saying, "Monkey see, monkey do." As adults, we do the same thing as the kids. We tend to follow the wrong crowd by following negative, depressed people who live in lack of love, peace, joy, and mental stability, and that is why we struggle ourselves and become like them. Again, this problem stems back from choosing to depend on people, objects, and things that are inherently limited by the shapes they take to follow rather than God the Universe, the Creator of abundance. This is following false idols.

> For *all the gods of the people are idols [visible objects]:*
> *but the* **LORD** *made the heavens [invisible dimension].*
> –1 Chronicles 16:26, KJV

> *All we like sheep have gone astray,*
> *no one seeks after God, no not one.*
> –Romans 3:10, KJV

In reality, there is no reason to struggle when we are in positive alignment with God's energy flow of love, because when we are in the same flow, He carries us though our struggles and He helps us get to where we want and need to be faster than if we were trying to meet our goals by ourselves. It's like being in the middle of the ocean, you can go with the flow of the current, or struggle and fight against it. Also, there is no reason for lack in our lives when we learn to copy and work with Him to create abundance such as love, joy, peace, and money because He is the universal source for all. When you want to learn something, it is always best to learn from the best. God is the master of creating abundance. We just have to learn to understand Him and ourselves. This allows us to work as one so that together we can co-create abundance in our own lives. By simply expanding our mental focus from objects (people, cars, houses, etc.) to encompass the entire universe as our canvas to do our creations, from visible to invisible, then abundance is possible for us.

> *The fruit of the Spirit is love, joy, peace, forbearance,*
> *kindness, goodness, faithfulness, gentleness, self-control.*
> –Galatians 5:22-23, NIV

> *"For I know the plans I have for you," declares the LORD,*
> *"plans to prosper you and not to harm you,*
> *plans to give you hope and a future."*
> –Jeremiah 29:11, NIV

As children, we were taught to rely on our parents for everything: money, love, toys, food, and shelter. When they kicked us out of their homes to be independent, we never really cut the cord entirely. Instead, we simply shifted our dependence on other people for love, and institutions for money and security. What we need to do is break our obsession and dependence on other objects—like people, drugs, alcohol, and institutions—as providers and solvers of our problems. The basis of this assumption is that things are created from other things; for example, you may believe that money and love should come from your spouse, and if you take enough drugs or drink enough liquor, your pain and problems will disappear. Actually, everything visible is created from the invisible spiritual energy of God—from nothing to something.

So when you want to create something, you first need to share or surrender your *thoughts* (invisible energy) to God, and He in turn will provide you with all the right people and things you need to manifest (make visible) whatever it is you want to create. Often these are people you have never met before or people you may not have even considered. Creation does not happen the other way around.

Most people make the mistake of trying to make things from something, and they can't figure out why sometimes it doesn't work or why they've pissed off people because they were using and manipulating people to get what they wanted. Before I understood this, I was trying to force my husband (from something) to create more money (to something), which failed drastically because he wanted to play golf, not make money. This was one of the major reasons we fought so much. In fact, the main reason most couples divorce is because of money fights, and often one of the partners tries to force the other person to work more or to change somehow. But this only causes strain in the relationship and causes people to fight even more.

For the longest time, I was angry at my dad because I thought he didn't love us. I couldn't imagine why he would otherwise allow himself to beat us and leave us. I kept thinking that I needed his love. However, as soon as I realized that God, who loves me unconditionally and always, was my true Father, (*the creator of all things*), I cut the cord between my dad and me. As soon as I did this, all the hate and anger toward my dad dissolved instantaneously. So, it wasn't my biological father's love that I needed, because his form of love for his wife and children was very limiting. It was rather a matter of mentally realizing that God was my source for unlimited love and happiness because He already loved me unconditionally and abundantly. This gave me the greatest peace of mind.

> *Do not call anyone on earth your "father," for you*
> *have one Father [God], and he is in heaven.*
> –Mathew 23:9, NIV

The same thing happened with my husband. As soon as I stopped relying on my husband as my source for money and started looking to God as my source, I stopped fighting with him, and I began to see opportunities for making money everywhere. This simple mental shift dissolved my money stress instantaneously. You see, all the opportunities had always been there, but because my mental focus was only on my husband as my source for money, I was limiting myself. I could not see anything else but what he could provide, which was very little to me. However, once I opened up and cleaned up my mind, and redirected my mental focus from my husband as my source to God, the universal possibility of abundance as my source, I was able to see and receive more of what was possible for me.

When you can see as God sees, that we are all connected as one invisible spiritual energy, then you can do as God does in creating your own abundant, long life of love, joy, peace, and happiness, RIGHT NOW! You can create your own unique perspective of your very own Garden of Eden because you are the only one who knows what you want to make you happy since you are the only one in control of your own mind, nobody else. So start using God's power, the spiritual energy that is within you, not your own power, because this is healing.

> *Yet for us there is [only] one **God**, the Father,*
> *Who is the **Source of all things**.*
> –1 Corinthians 8:6 (AMPC)

What makes us move and behave BADLY?

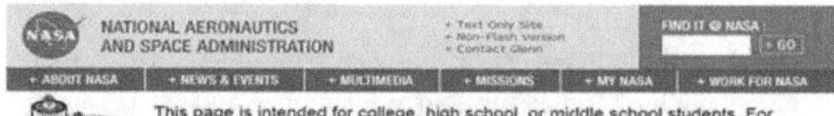

This page is intended for college, high school, or middle school students. For younger students, a simpler explanation of the information on this page is available on the Kid's Page.

Newton's Laws of Motion

Glenn
Research
Center

"Every object persists in its state of rest or uniform motion in a straight line unless it is compelled to change that state by forces impressed on it."

"Force is equal to the change in momentum (mV) per change in time. For a constant mass, force equals mass times acceleration."

F = m a

"For every action, there is an equal and opposite re-action."

Newton's Law of Motion, states that "for every action, there is an equal and opposite reaction," this is in reference to the invisible push or pull force on all objects in the universe and why they move and behave the way they do. I disagree that this law applies to **all** objects because this law only works on inanimate objects like rocks, cars, and books and does not really apply to humans or animals as objects within the universe because of our brains. For example, when my 100 lb. (45.35 kg) lab was five years old, if you had kicked him hard, he would not have kicked you back with equal force, he would have probably attacked you and bitten you. However, when he got older, same mass at fifteen years old, he could no longer stand up at that point. So, if you had kicked him hard with the same amount of force as before, he would have only barked at you.

Then there are humans who have what some religious people call a soul, which includes our thoughts, will, emotions, and conscience. Depending on a person's state of mind, they will behave differently given the same mass and same situation. This is because humans are able to generate thoughts verbally and silently. Scientists do not typically include thoughts (*our minds' invisible software*) that our brains (*the visible hardware*) generate as a form of invisible energy that affects how humans actually move or behave, even though physicists say that everything is made out of invisible energy.

For example, most of us have probably experienced being accidentally bumped by someone or someone's cart while at the grocery. In most cases, normal people will not hit back the other person with equal force. I myself, have never hit back another person with equal force whenever I've been accidently hit at the groceries and have always just apologized to the other person, even though I did not cause the accident. However, if you accidentally hit an angry gang member with the same mass at the grocery store, depending on his state of mind, he may not hit you back with equal force, but just shoot you if he has a gun. My father who used to physically hit us when we were kids, I would never think of retaliating and hit him back with equal force as Newton's Law says I should be doing, without thinking he was going to kill me if I did.

The saying "***the pen is mightier than a sword***" is defined in *Websters' Dictionary* as "writing [words or thoughts] is more effective than military power or violence [physical energy force]" when it comes to making changes in the world. Our forefathers knew how powerful our words, generated from our minds, can be. In fact, it is our thoughts that are the source of our behaviors because it's our positive or negative thoughts that tell our body what to do. People don't even need to physically touch in order to get a negative or positive reaction from them. It is our thinking and our belief system that is part of the invisible energy force field that motivates how we are going to react and behave in certain situations.

For example, in the *Washington Post*, there was an article about a twenty-three-year-old kid who was charged with murder, assault, and other charges, for shooting four people, and the shooting appears to have "stemmed from a road rage," according to a news release from the Westminster Police Department. This kid did not know any of the victims, and they never touched each other, not while driving and not even while he was shooting from outside their car. Here's another example of road rage where a teen in Grand Rapids, Michigan, was sentenced to a hundred years in prison after beating a sixty-four-year-old retiree to death. According to the news, even though the retiree was already lying on the ground, bleeding and not moving, the teen continued to kick and hit the older gentleman. The point I'm trying to make is that in this case, Newton's Law fails. Even though the older gentleman was being kicked, he did not respond back with equal force, as Newton's Law states he should be doing. However, in both cases, the road ragers let their emotions of anger take over their mind and body and went way out of control.

I myself almost mentally snapped from road rage as I was waiting for a parking space at the grocery store. I got there first, had my turn signal on to let the other cars know I was waiting for the space, and this person quickly took the space that I was clearly waiting for. I got so angry with this person, that I was ready to kill her, which was my first instinct. Fortunately for me and for the other person, I had enough mental sense and self-control to not do anything, but I was angry and fuming for a while. I was so enraged as I let my negative thinking take over my entire mind and body. I really wanted to beat the crap out of her! She was lucky I found God and learned to forgive the idiots that lived among us. I have to remember, that sometimes I'm that village idiot too, and will probably be in need of forgiveness from others at times.

NewsRoom

Nearly 80 Percent of Drivers Express Significant Anger, Aggression or Road Rage
An Estimated Eight Million Drivers Admit to More Extreme Behavior Says New AAA Foundation Research

WASHINGTON, D.C. (July 14, 2016)- Nearly 80 percent of drivers expressed significant anger, aggression or road rage behind the wheel at least once in the past year, according to a new study released today by the AAA Foundation for Traffic Safety. The most alarming findings suggest that approximately eight million U.S. drivers engaged in extreme examples of road rage, including purposefully ramming another vehicle or getting out of the car to confront another driver.

"Inconsiderate driving, bad traffic and the daily stresses of life can transform minor frustrations into dangerous road rage," said Jurek Grabowski, Director of Research for the AAA Foundation for Traffic Safety. "Far too many drivers are losing themselves in the heat of the moment and lashing out in ways that could turn deadly."

A significant number of U.S. drivers reported engaging in angry and aggressive behaviors over the past year, according to the study's estimates:

- Purposefully tailgating: 51 percent (104 million drivers)
- Yelling at another driver: 47 percent (95 million drivers)
- Honking to show annoyance or anger: 45 percent (91 million drivers)
- Making angry gestures: 33 percent (67 million drivers)
- Trying to block another vehicle from changing lanes: 24 percent (49 million drivers)
- Cutting off another vehicle on purpose: 12 percent (24 million drivers)
- Getting out of the vehicle to confront another driver: 4 percent (7.6 million drivers)
- Bumping or ramming another vehicle on purpose: 3 percent (5.7 million drivers)

Nearly 2 in 3 drivers believe that aggressive driving is a bigger problem today than three years ago, while nine out of ten believe aggressive drivers are a serious threat to their personal safety.

"It's completely normal for drivers to experience anger behind the wheel, but we must not let our emotions lead to destructive choices," said Jake Nelson, AAA's Director of Traffic Safety Advocacy and Research. "Don't risk escalating a frustrating situation because you never know what the other driver might do. Maintain a cool head, and focus on reaching your destination safely."

AAA offers these tips to help prevent road rage:

- **Don't Offend** Never cause another driver to change their speed or direction. That means not forcing another driver to use their brakes, or turn the steering wheel in response to something you have done.
- **Be Tolerant and Forgiving** The other driver may just be having a really bad day. Assume that it's not personal.
- **Do Not Respond** Avoid eye contact, don't make gestures, maintain space around your vehicle and contact 9-1-1 if needed.

The research report is available on the AAA Foundation's website and is part of the annual Traffic Safety Culture Index, which identifies attitudes and behaviors related to driver safety. The data was collected from a national survey of 2,705 licensed drivers ages 16 and older who reported driving in the past 30 days. The AAA Foundation issued its first Traffic Safety Culture Index in 2008.

According to an article from AAA *Newsroom*, "Nearly 80 Percent of Drivers Express Significant Anger, Aggression or Road Rage" (July 14, 2016), research done by AAA Foundation, says that there are about eight million American drivers involved in some kind of extreme road rage, including purposely ramming the other car or physically confronting the other driver. They say too many people are getting *angry* and losing it *mentally and physically* at the other drivers due to road rage that sometimes turns out deadly. AAA offers these three tips to avoid road rage, which I believe are biblical, so I've added verses to each tip. However, they do not offer drugs as a solution, because their mission is to save lives. This is a great example of how we can perhaps teach tolerance, forgiving, and treating people with love and kindness in our schools without being religious or preachy, since these characteristics are too religious for some atheists, politicians, educators, and scientists, so we can help reduce violence and bullying in the streets, at schools, and at home—and perhaps even save lives.

- **Don't Offend** – "We give no offense in anything" (2 Corinthians 6:3, NKJV).
- **Be Tolerant and Forgiving** – "Bear with each other and forgive one another if any of you have a grievance against someone. Forgive as the Lord forgave you. And over all these virtues put on love, which binds them all together in perfect unity." (Colossians 3:13-14, NIV).
- **Do Not Respond** – "Don't repay evil for evil. Don't retaliate with insults when people insult you. Instead, pay them back with a blessing [like silent prayer]. That is what God has called you to do, and he will grant you his blessing" (1 Peter 3:9, NLT).

The invisible thought energy of anger in our minds that sometimes consumes us, like a body snatcher, is what the Bible calls Satan or the Devil. In the field of psychiatry, they have hundreds of labels and categorizations of combinations and permutations of diagnosis (e.g., depression, ADD, ADHD, PSD, OCD, anxiety disorder, social anxiety disorder, personality disorder, psychosis, stress, psychological stress, mental disorder, schizophrenia, delusion, and more) depending on the various uncontrolled thoughts, feelings, and behaviors we might be experiencing. This is so that they can charge us more money and prescribe more cocktail drugs so we can stop the too-much thinking in our heads and what seems to be a body takeover by an invisible entity, because they do not know how to do it naturally. However, today most of us just call it negative thinking or stress.

The problem with science is that they do not think of our thoughts or words we generate as a strong enough force to reckon with, and I honestly don't think they know what to do with it. At least we are not there yet scientifically. Now with most religions, they teach that our words, written and verbal, are spiritual energy forces that we have power over. For example, Christianity teaches the power of love and mental self-control to its believers. They often describe thoughts we generate as having positive (good) or negative (evil) spiritual energy that we then manifest in the physical world through creation or destruction, whether the source was a positive thought or a negative thought.

In other words, to religious folks, our words are extremely important as a form of spiritual energy force that we all must learn to mentally control since it stems from there. But unlike science and psychiatry, they offer hope by teaching us that ***we have control over and can overcome our own thoughts, and they teach lessons on how to do it naturally without drugs***. They teach that if we immerse ourselves mentally in LOVE, as God loves us unconditionally, then we can ACT and behave lovingly to others, so we don't kill each other like in road rage cases. You see, people do not automatically learn and grow to be loving, because we get our cues from our environment, and our environment is extremely negative. Most of the digital games our children are exposed to and the movies we watch are with people trying to kill each other. Most music kids listen to today has violent themes to them and so does the news. Nothing but bad news of rape, kidnapping, killings, and schools teach a lot of violence in history classes too.

If the kids come from broken homes where parents are fighting and/ or abusing their kids, then most of these kids will have very little hope of exposure to love and forgiveness as another way of thinking and living. We had a neighbor once who adopted a twelve-year-old boy. The kid's background was that when he was five years old, his mother had left him and his two-year-old brother in the lobby of a hotel, telling them she would return, but she didn't. So he and his brother were living in the streets for five days, looking for food in the garbage, when someone found them and brought them to an orphanage. His little brother was adopted right away, but nobody wanted the older one until our neighbor took him in seven years later. The orphanage warned them to keep an eye on him because all he knew how to survive was to steal. Sure enough, he was found stealing at home and from other kids at school. The new parents couldn't deal with it, so they took him back to the orphanage. Here's an example of a child that his school could have helped, but failed to help him.

In the outside world, violence is the norm; that's why the subject of tolerance, forgiving one another, and loving one another has to be taught not only in churches and synagogues but it should also be taught in all schools. We have to learn to undo all the negative thinking that is stuck in our heads, so we can clear it and reformat its contents, as you would a computer hard drive that has been infected with a virus, and renew it. The Bible calls this process the renewal of our minds.

> *Do not be conformed to this world [of objects],*
> *but be transformed by the renewal of your MIND*
> *[change the way you think by loving God and all*
> *people unconditionally].*
> –Romans 12:2, ESV

Until scientists and educators start taking our *thoughts* more seriously, and discover it as just another form of invisible energy force that we all must learn to mentally control and teach, suicides among our kids will continue to increase and legal/illegal drugs to synthetically control our thoughts will continue to be used and abused. Also, school bullying, road rage, violence in schools, and abuses at home will continue to increase—what the Bible calls our **generational curse. This is because most of us are mentally stuck on the object level, operating in darkness, not knowing how to use our body parts more efficiently since we are not taught in school.**

The Power of Our Words

Here are some Bible verses on the power of our thoughts:

- Death and life are in the power of the tongue, and those who love it will eat its fruits (Proverbs 18:21, ESV).
- Let no corrupting talk come out of your mouths, but only such as is good for building up, as fits the occasion, that it may give grace to those who hear (Ephesians 4:29, ESV).
- There is one whose rash words are like sword thrusts, but the tongue of the wise brings healing (Proverbs 12:18, ESV).
- A soft answer turns away wrath, but a harsh word stirs up anger (Proverbs 15:1, ESV).
- Gracious words are like a honeycomb, sweetness to the soul and health to the body. (Proverbs 16:24 ESV).
- Whoever keeps his mouth and his tongue keeps himself out of trouble (Proverbs 21:23, ESV).
- Whoever guards his mouth preserves his life; he who opens wide his lips comes to ruin (Proverbs 13:3, ESV).
- A gentle tongue is a tree of life, but perverseness in it breaks the spirit (Proverbs 15:4, ESV).
- But what comes out of the mouth proceeds from the heart, and this defiles a person (Matthew 15:18, ESV).
- Let your speech always be gracious, seasoned with salt, so that you may know how you ought to answer each person (Colossians 4:6, ESV).
- But be doers of the word, and not hearers only, deceiving yourselves (James 1:22, ESV).
- The good person out of the good treasure of his heart produces good, and the evil person out of his evil treasure produces evil, for out of the abundance of the heart his mouth speaks (Luke 6:45, ESV).
- But now you must put them all away: anger, wrath, malice, slander, and obscene talk from your mouth (Colossians 3:8, ESV).
- It is the Spirit (energy) who gives life; the flesh is no help at all. The words that I have spoken to you are spirit and life (John 6:63, ESV).

The Importance of FAITH in the INVISIBLE Realm

Walk by FAITH, not by SIGHT.
–2 Corinthians 5:6-8, KJV

Just wondering, have you ever seen the balls of hydrogen atoms in water or the atoms of your body that scientists and educators keep telling us exist? Do you know what you are made of inside?

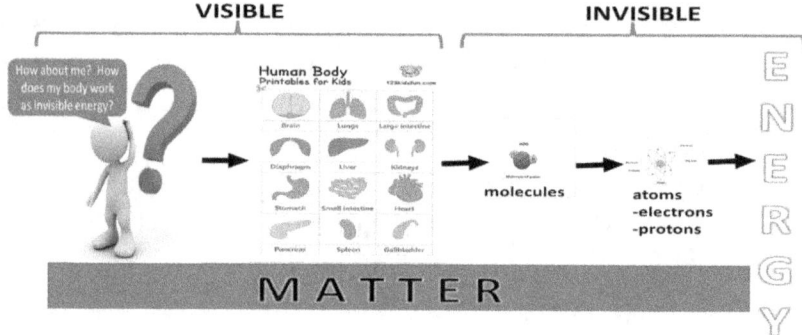

I personally have never seen molecules and atoms that scientists say all matter is made of, but it doesn't mean they do not exist. And I don't know anybody else who has ever seen them either because they exist only in the invisible realm. The fact that scientists and educators keep teaching our children that **if something is invisible, then it cannot exist,** is completely misguided. This is their way of trying to get students to not believe in an invisible God, or they're just plain ignorant of this fact. However, they contradict themselves because most of the topics taught in school science are in fact invisible to the naked eye and cannot actually be seen without using an extremely strong microscope just to even see **some** of them.

It wasn't even until 1590 when the microscope was invented, when scientists were actually able to see beyond what the naked eye can see. But without a strong microscope, viruses, bacteria, blood cells, yeast, etc. are still invisible to the naked eye. What was true 2000 years ago during Bible years, that they could not see these microbes, is still true today. We still cannot see them without a strong microscope. But then how many people in the world are actually walking around looking at the world through a microscope stuck to their eyeballs? Only those working in labs. So basically, microbes still belong in the invisible realm.

In an article on LiveScience.com by Lauren Cox titled, Who Invented the Microscope?, she says: "*For millennia, **the smallest thing humans could see was about as wide as a human hair**. When the microscope was invented around 1590, suddenly we saw a new world of living things in our water, in our food, and under our nose.*"

Then there are things like energy or gravity that can never be seen under any microscope no matter how strong it is. This is one of the ways science and educators try to keep people from believing in an invisible God, by teaching and repeating the same lies, that "unless you can see it, it cannot exist."

Learning to work with the invisible level requires using your imagination by refocusing your mind's eyes on the invisible realm, and it requires letting go of people, government, institutions, and objects as your source for love, joy, peace, happiness, and income. This frees them from the responsibility of having to take care of you and frees them from having to provide you with what you think they owe you.

Taking on the responsibility for your own life's creation is especially good for you because it develops your inner strength, and it gives you the freedom to play, create, and pull together whatever it is you want or need from the entire invisible energy field of the universe, which is boundless. This is where your creative canvas and your source and freedom from chaos come from. You can then use this universe as your playground rather than just pulling energy from your significant other or from your workplace because this is extremely constraining to them and to you. To actually believe in this at the invisible spiritual energy level—from the most religious to the most scientific person—requires a leap of faith, because you can't see it or touch it.

In school science whenever they tried to teach us about bacteria, viruses, molecules, atoms, electrons, protons, energy, and gravity, because they are all invisible to the naked eye, the science books always just used hand-drawn illustrations or digital drawings that were a million times bigger than they actually were to make us all believe they existed, even though I have never really met anyone who had actually seen them. So scientists, engineers, educators, and students all have to have **a leap of faith, and a lot of it**, in believing in the invisible things, just as religious people do. However, just because it's invisible doesn't mean it does not exist, like bacteria, viruses, blood cells, yeast, molecules, atoms, electrons, protons, quarks, gravity, magnetism, gas, energy, or thoughts. In fact, the ***invisible*** **spiritual** ***energy realm*** **that everything is made of is actually more powerful and eternal than the** ***temporary visible*** **world of objects** since this level cannot even be destroyed, according to physics.

Only the temporary visible object level can be destroyed, which is why we all need to be extremely careful how we talk to each other since we can hurt and destroy people when we speak to them negatively and unlovingly. Only positive thoughts of love can heal and unite people who are already hurting and broken inside.

When I was taking a class at UCLA at nineteen years old, I used to hang out with grad students in the physics department, and I had a friend who asked me, "So, do you still believe in the invisible God?" He was giving me a hard time because he knew I was a God believer, and I reluctantly said, "Yes." I felt like the little kid in Hans Christian Anderson's children's story, "The Emperor's New Clothes," who told the truth and said the emperor was walking around naked with no clothes, while the wise people were afraid to lose their jobs and not wanting to appear stupid or unfit for their important roles lied to the emperor how beautiful his clothes were.

Well, I was that kid, but in physics. I took several courses in physics in both high school and college, and I cannot, and have never, seen energy that they kept teaching that the universe was made of, that was supposed to be visible. I couldn't see it for some reason. The physics books never showed pictures of energy or gravity, only arrows, going this way or that way. Until I realized and finally accepted that it must all be invisible since I could not see it.

How about you? Can you see the energy that everything in the universe science says is made of, including you? How about gravity? Have you seen it? Try how Newton discovered gravity by dropping an apple. Does the apple fall to the ground? Do you see the entity, energy force called gravity, pulling down the apple to the ground? If you cannot see it, don't worry, you're not the only one. I cannot see it either because an energy force field, like gravity, is just one example of the invisible realm that exists in the universe that scientists refuse to accept is invisible, as religious people have been teaching for centuries.

It is amazing though how scientists are such hypocrites with their dogma about trying to get everybody to believe in their version of the truth as the only right version of the **invisible energy level** that the entire universe is supposed to be made of, that they say **can never be created or destroyed**, yet at the same time, they argue and mock the religious version of an **invisible spirit** of God that is **eternal** and that exists inside all things. However, in examining the two seemingly distinct perspectives, logic tells me they are both talking about the same thing, but just using different words to explain what the invisible universe is and what it's made of. We have to remember that scientists do not get paid for discovering something that repeats what religion has already discovered 2000 years ago. That is why they have to come up with new words when they "discover" something new *(e.g., invisible energy= invisible spirit, universe=God, matter=visible world of objects, etc.)* to sound really intelligent, new, and unique. But this just adds to the mass confusion people already have about how the universe operates, because now they have to figure out what the new words of scientific discoveries mean.

For this reason, the invisible world of God's energy for some is difficult to imagine because too often, they focus only on the temporary object that energy took as a visible form, only that which they can see and touch. However, many people give lip service to the invisible energy/spirit of God's Universe without really understanding how it lives within them and how it works, so they still struggle in their own lives because they have never figured out how to work with it as one, at the deeper level. **Their lack of understanding of how the process of positive alignment in Body, Mind and Spirit/Energy work best together in helping them be more efficient in creating love, peace, and joy in their lives, is the main cause of their mental suffering.** This is why, even some of the most spiritual people, get sick and sometimes die caused by some form of mental stress even though they go to church on a regular basis. This is because, for the most part, the various religions and their ancient books are hard to read and confusing for most people to follow.

For example, my cousin who died of cancer at the age of thirty-nine after she lost her job as a realtor when nobody was buying houses, was actually a very religious person following the Christian path. She attended church every Sunday, but she never learned to control her mental stress. Like most people, she mostly lived in the material world of objects as her mental focus. In her case, it was the love of money, and insisted that everything was from her efforts. In other words, even though she went to church and prayed, like most Christians, she did not trust and have faith and really understood how to use and work God's natural process at 100 percent, since she thought she was the source for money.

So if you were to ask your doctor what you are made of, he would say you are made of blood, bones, a heart, and the rest of the body parts. Then if you ask what your body parts are made of, he will say that all your body parts are made of cells and molecules, which are made of atoms and those are made of electrons and protons. Then if you ask a quantum physicist what those electrons and protons are made of, he will say that they are made of particles called quarks that are so small they seem to appear as a blur in space (*like a ghost*), and that's made of invisible energy. Therefore, in the two extremes, we are both VISIBLE on the outside and INVISIBLE on the inside at the same time, as religion has been teaching all along for thousands of years before scientists even figured this out.

The bottom line is that you are mainly made of space, of nothing. This is where you came from—nothing. This is what you are made of—nothing; and when your body is no longer the form you see, it's still going to be made of nothing. It never changes. You are made of the same stuff as everything and everybody else that is part of the **invisible** universe of nothingness called God or the Universe. **By simply refocusing your mental obsession from the world of visible objects** to the invisible spiritual energy of God, you will solve most of your problems because this is the only place where you can have mental peace and freedom from the 8 billion different mental realities, people constantly fighting over who's got the right reality, and chaos from objects constantly changing forms, which is healing. In the invisible realm, there is nothing to judge *(as good or bad, no rich or poor, no sickness, no right or wrong, no fat or skinny people, no males or females, no religions, no countries, no people, etc.).*

For me, a lot of the petty things that used to bother me and stress me out stopped bothering me once I learned to surrender my thoughts to God. It's having a strong faith and belief that God the Universe as invisible spiritual energy exists at 100 percent that spiritually and mentally healed me from being stuck in the world of object chaos. However, when I was only a 50 percent believer, I was always stressed, sick, afraid, and fighting with people all the time.

For example, I used to worry about my kids' health and safety all the time. My negative thoughts mentally consumed me all day long even while I was at work, and my thoughts became a distraction for me, making it difficult to concentrate. However, when I realized they were God's children anyway, as we all are, I started to pray every morning, surrendering my worries to God and asking Him to keep them safe and healthy since I couldn't physically be with them twenty-four hours a day. I figured since He was more powerful than I was, He could do a better job than I could in taking care of them. This is how I've kept my sanity and mental peace—by having a strong belief and faith in the invisible universe of God's spiritual energy level that we are all made of, that we are all connected as one, and that God answers my prayers.

Focusing on objects is a problem because of their inherent limits as objects, which are bounded by their temporary shapes. For example, H_2O, water molecules in the form of an ice cube are limited by their shape; they cannot move. The particles are so compacted together that there is very little space between them for anything to get through. However, if you take that same H_2O and energize it by adding heat, you get water vapor that is unbounded and becomes one with the cosmos. The molecules seem to disappear from our field of vision because the particles are vibrating so much faster that there is greater space between the particles to allow this integration to happen.

Like heat that energizes the ice molecules into invisible water vapor, learning unconditional love for all energizes us and makes us **mentally one** with God's **thought energy** that vibrates at a higher-level frequency of love. This is **not a physical change in our *body***, since we are all one with God physically already as energy. This is a ***mental* change** in us. If we learn it, it allows us to communicate with God in a one-on-one when we learn to vibrate at the higher frequency level. We have to learn to vibrate at a higher level of unconditional love to meet Him; He doesn't come down to our mental low-level negativity. This is part of the mental process that is missing for most people.

What we need is to learn to change our mental focus from visible objects to imagine seeing all things at the invisible level, as God sees. Focus on the perfect invisible energy level that connects us all as one universal energy so you can learn to access His eternal peace, His joy, His unconditional love without having to do anything but be mentally quiet, by learning not to think so much, through the practice of meditation. This can be done anywhere and anytime by anybody, where there is no religious membership requirement.

Who's the Chosen One?

You are! According to the Bible, God chose ***all of us*** to be fruitful because we are automatically part of his spiritual kingdom.

> *You did not choose Me but **I chose you** and appointed you*
> *to go and bear fruit – fruit that will last.*
> –John 15:16, NAS

Most Christians are brought up to believe that God's chosen people are only the Jewish people, as taught by most churches, which oftentimes makes the rest of us feel "un-chosen," as the not-so-favored child in God's family of objects. I know for me, for years I have always felt that the Jewish people were better than the rest of us since we're not the chosen ones, but that the rest of us were born a nuisance. I think this kind of negative thinking and teaching puts the Jewish people at risk of other people being jealous and is one of the reasons they are persecuted so much. We all need to stop thinking that they are the only ones chosen, for as the Bible says, we are all chosen specifically created to work with God himself for his glory and purpose. Whatever that may be, each of us just needs to get together with God to find out His purpose for us and ask him, "God, what's your purpose for me? What can I help you with?"

Yes, the Jewish people were chosen specifically to know God's teachings of wholeness (holiness), and Jesus was a Jewish man specifically chosen by God to teach the spiritual workings of God's universe, as it pertains to human engineering at that time. However, so was the Buddha, the spiritual teacher for the Buddhist followers, and Mohammed, the spiritual teacher for the Muslim followers. Then there's Helen Schucman and William Thetford, professors of medical psychology at Columbia University's College of Physicians and Surgeons in New York City. They were specifically chosen and called by God to write their book *A Course in Miracles*, as I was called and chosen to write this book and many others like the many preachers on TV. Millions of people throughout history were all chosen and called to teach about how God's invisible spiritual energy works within us.

However, we all have to remember that learning how God's universe works, at the invisible spiritual energy level, is just a matter of our human mental evolution. We hope that each generation gets more and more knowledgeable. For example, when scientists finally discovered that everything in the universe was made of invisible energy that can never be created or destroyed, 2000 years *after* Jesus and all the other religions had already been teaching the same thing about how to work with God's invisible eternal spirit that exists inside us. The next evolution for science, I believe, is when they discover that ***thought energy*** actually exists. As Jesus says in John 14:12 (ESV), "Truly, truly, I say to you, whoever believes in me will also do the works that I do (*in reference to his teachings and healings*); and greater works than these will he do (*due to our mental evolution over time, we can all do better if we understood God's process*), because I am going to the Father."

God has chosen all of us to be His disciples (*as teachers, writers, or preachers*) of the invisible spiritual energy level—once we learn it for ourselves. Therefore, we are all supposed to disseminate the information to as many people as possible, so that others will know Him and understand how to work with Him naturally, so we can all help stop society's mental suffering. *(NOTE: Please no letters, emails or phone calls that I'm a Jewish hater because I'm not. It is my prayer and hope that those who hate them stop hating them. If only those who bear hate knew that the God of abundance loves them too, just as much as God loves the Jewish people, and that they too are chosen as everybody is chosen. It's when people put limits on* **God's love** *that we get ourselves into trouble.)*

The fact you exist today means that God purposely created you from His own eternal spirit or energy and that He loved you from the beginning because He specifically chose you to be part of His kingdom as already perfect energy. So God only sees you as Himself, perfect already in Him as invisible energy/spirit, even if you are not so perfect as a temporary object person. He is aware that we are all evolving as humans and just trying to grow up toward our highest form of being and living in unconditional love for all and our ONENESS with God's universe.

Understand that you cannot possibly do anything wrong that can ever, ever sever God's eternal, unconditional love for you since He is inside of you. Absolutely nothing! We are all one with God's energy. God created you out of His love for you because He has a plan specifically for you that is greater than your own personal plan. This is your purpose in life, and you have to get with God yourself and ask Him what that is for you, so you can figure it out together and decide whether you want to do it or not.

Only **you** as an individual can separate your **mental** ties with God by refusing to believe in the truth that (1) the God of the universe exists as invisible spiritual energy and that (2) He exists inside of you as such. When you consciously choose **not** to believe and follow Him, what you are doing is essentially closing the door on His face and telling Him you don't need Him because you can do life all by yourself. If that is the case, I ask you, how is that working for you?

Are you one of the 50 percent of couples that are now divorced or are about to get divorced? Or are you so messed up in the head and out of control, like a water hose out of control, that you need drugs every day just to keep yourself barely alive, or worse, maybe you are seriously thinking of taking your own life? Thirty million Americans are on anti-depressants, and these are just the legal drugs; this does not even include the millions of people on illegal drugs. Or maybe you have been so traumatized from your past, maybe from abuse, or you've seen too many deaths, maybe from being in the military, and you don't know how to have mental peace from that. You can choose to do your life all alone, by yourself. Or you can choose to experience and learn to have God's unconditional love, unimaginable peace, and joy right now, from anywhere. It's your choice, you're in control of your mind. You can do your own life the hard way by yourself, or the easy way with God's love and peace that exist inside you and all around you already. It's up to you.

What Was the Original Sin, and How Can We Undo It?

The original sin was just Adam and Eve's **mental** separation from God, this was their disobedience, thinking they did not need God in their lives, wanting to focus only on the object level that they could see and touch. Thus came the generational curse we all inherited, which causes endless mental suffering from not knowing how to manage and control our thinking and how to work with the invisible God to naturally end our mental suffering. God gave us free will to mentally make our own individual choice to believe in Him as invisible spiritual energy or not, and whether we want to have a personal relationship with him or not, to help us deal with our problems. It's our choice to believe or not believe.

So, if you want to keep believing and living a lie that you are not part of God's invisible universal energy, and you want to keep being stuck with all your mental craziness in your brain and keep your suffering bottled up inside of you so that you have nowhere to release all your pent-up negative thoughts; and if you want to keep being mentally stuck in the superficial physical world of objects by hurting others or yourself or allowing all your mental pains and stress to manifest as cancer or disease in your body, then just keep doing what you're doing. All your negative thoughts and feelings of anger, hate, jealousy, betrayal, bitterness, loneliness, insecurity, revenge, guilt, fear, and abandonment have to move somewhere since thoughts are forms of energy. According to the laws of physics, energy is always moving and changing forms. You can either have your negative thought energy stuck, contained in your mind like an ice cube in a container, or you can pray and release them to God to deal with.

When you learn to release your thoughts to the cosmos, you are essentially freeing your mind from mental chaos and stress from pent-up thought energy so that mental peace is possible. It's like an ice cube that is heated up so the molecules vibrate faster to become free to be one with the cosmos to become invisible water vapor. It's up to you since you are in control of your own mind and the thoughts you generate. It's your choice.

I am not talking about a physical separation from God because that is impossible since everything is all made out of His spiritual energy. But a *mental* separation is causing your mental craziness inside of you, causing some people suicidal thoughts, stress, physical sickness, or acting out their mental madness on others by hurting them verbally or physically. When my husband and I first got married, I had all these negative thoughts bottled up inside my mind of how much I hated men. All I knew about relationships was the constant fighting I learned from my parents, as they were my role models. This was my generational curse.

But I hated men so much because of the physical abuse and trauma I got from my father when I was young. I did not even realize I had so much pent-up anger and hate for men inside of me because, like most people, my mind was on automatic pilot. But I was picking fights with my husband all the time, even though I do not even remember what we fought about. Once I remember trying to beat him up by kicking and trying to punch him anywhere and everywhere. I remember being so angry all the time, and I was ready to really kill him! Here are our stats: he's five feet ten inches, and I'm five feet one inch, he weighed at least 175 lbs., and I was 102 lbs. He's a Marine trained to be a killing machine, and here's me with no prior fighting experience or training, a super nerd trying to beat the crap out of him. What was I thinking? But I wasn't thinking; that is the point. I was this mad-crazy person, and I couldn't think! Again, we are not taught in school how to think and use our minds properly.

My husband could have easily killed me with his bare hands because that's what he was trained to do, but to this day I thank God that he never fought back. What he did do I consider so loving. He picked me up and hugged me tightly from the back so I wouldn't hurt myself as I was trying to kick him and hit him as hard as I could. He just let me get it all out, all the pent-up anger and hate inside of me. All the years of wanting to get back at my father, I took it out on him—or tried to anyway. He said, "Are you done yet?" I have to admit, that exercise was so mentally therapeutic for me as it allowed me to release so much pent-up negative energy inside of me; it was like releasing the evil demons out of me! After that, I never had the negative energy to get that angry ever again.

Besides, if it did, I knew he would just hug me tight again. He would never let me hit him anyway, and I know my husband, he loves me so much, I knew he would never hit me back no matter how angry I got. I knew then that my relationship with him would not be like my parents' relationship of constant fighting. This is how I knew: We stopped the cycle of physical abuse in my family, our generational curse. When my kids were born later, I made sure we never laid a hand on either of our kids, even though at times, as they got to their late teens and early twenties, when the older one was acting up, there were times when I saw my husband get angry, wanting to slap her across the face, but he didn't. I have to say that my husband has a lot of mental self-control.

For those who have a lot of pent-up anger and hate inside of them, like I did from trauma, God is trying to reach all of us to release the anger and hate stuck inside our heads and to just give it to Him. If we could all just believe. It might help to imagine God hugging us tightly from the back, like a giant Marine, and saying to us, **"I've got your back. I will always love you unconditionally, no matter what. I know what you've been through because I was there with you. I will never leave you or forsake you. It's time to let it all go. I'm always here for you, to hear and help you with your problems. Give it all to me, so I can help you!"**

By only operating at the object level, you can never reach your full potential in God. You can only reach what the Christians call heaven on earth, and what Buddhism calls nirvana, when you are able to mentally understand this concept and are able to control your mind so your mental focus is mostly on Him, at the invisible spiritual energy level, instead of your own limited version of yourself as only a temporary physical object that dies.

> **Seek ye first the kingdom of God** *and his righteousness*
> *and all these things shall be added unto you.*
> –Matthew 6:33, KJV

All solutions and creations come from God's universe of energy as the source for everything. Learning to work with it, so that you can attract and create what you want easily is just a matter of shifting and refocusing your mind's eye from **visible** objects to **invisible** God energy, from problems to solutions, and from fear of other objects to love of God. When you get this, it will energize you and bring you closer to your higher self, God's light and truth that is inside all things, because this is who you really are.

Your true freedom from object-level chaos and madness comes from knowing that you are invisible spiritual energy at 100 percent. This is where there is no chaos and no objects to judge, knowing how to manage your thoughts so that they are clear and positive, knowing that you are the creator of your own universal perspective, and knowing how to use your power to create by getting in the flow of God's love energy. If you want to make quantum leaps (*not baby steps*) in the money flow, for example, it is required that you be in full positive alignment in mind, body, and spirit/energy. It's the three together as one unit, going in the same positive directional flow that will push you toward meeting your happiness goals faster.

Looking at the universe in terms of separate objects is extremely limiting. It creates chaos and struggles for those who follow this belief only because they lack the knowledge and understanding of who they really are, what they are really made of inside, and how they fit into the big picture I frame as the *universal energy of God*. I use the term universal energy of God as an inclusive term to unite science and all religions together as one.

You see, each has a piece of the puzzle, and they are both separately trying to solve the same problem of who we are as spiritual energy. If only they would work and play together, they would see that the pieces of the puzzle that they each have fit together beautifully, and that each of them is important in solving the same puzzle of one God—one universe. Instead of trying to solve the puzzle separately because they actually complement each other. I think if they all focus on what they have already found in common—religions' best practices and using science for testing and verification—to discover the universe's inherent laws in how God's universe works best, especially in the invisible realm, then science could reduce their cycle time into our next evolution to improve human effectiveness.

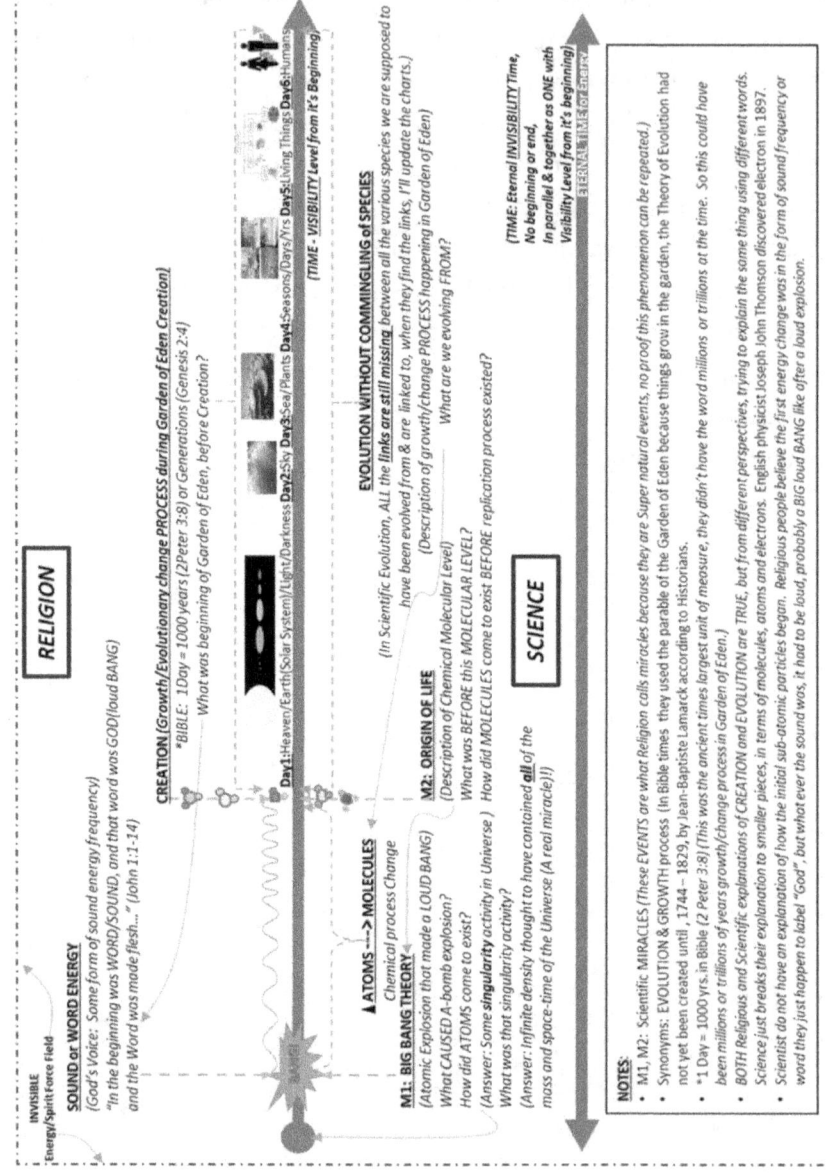

CREATION (Event) vs. EVOLUTION (Growth Process)

The argument between creation and evolution does not make sense to me at all because both to me are right—the manifestation process of matter or objects. They just happen to be coming from different perspectives and describing different time frames of the entire process. For example, you can look at a car and describe it as one unit or you can describe the parts and say something like, "A car is made of a chassis, the engine, the interior seats, etc." Does describing a car as one unit or by parts make one more right than the other? Would the car care either way? I think regardless of how the car is described, as one unit or an amalgam of multiple units, the car will still be a car; both descriptions will be right, and the car doesn't care.

Case in point, the hot topic of our creation is a good example of this clash of opinions between the religious who believe that we were **created** intelligently, designed by God the Universe, and the scientists on the other hand who believe in **evolution**. The answer is not either-or but both theories actually work better when they are viewed together as one, not as separate. Genesis 1 and 2 provide all the clues for both theories to occur at the same time.

> *In the **beginning** [event in time—*
> ***The Big Bang Theory**]*
> *God created the heaven and the earth.*
> –Genesis 1:1, KJV

It is stated in the Bible that it's only in the *beginning* that God created the objects, but after the initial creation of things, evolution or growth took over. *After the beginning,* God just goes through a never-ending evolution or growth process of itself. It's kind of like when OB-GYN doctors monitor a baby's birthing process. The doctors will always tell the new mom the approximate conception date of the baby; this is the **event** in which the baby began its creation. This beginning date is extremely important for the doctor and the mom because babies typically take nine months to grow and evolve during the gestation period to a full term in the mother's uterus before the baby's birth. So there's the beginning of CREATION, the BIG BANG, then evolution or growth process took over God's Garden of Eden, which is what happens with all gardens. They all grow and evolve from seeds to mature plants and trees to produce flowers, fruits, and vegetables.

Evolution is defined as:
*1: a **process** of continuous change from a lower, simpler, or worse to a higher, more complex, or better state: **GROWTH**.*
—Merriam-Webster's Online Dictionary

What is the Big Bang Theory and How Does it Correlate to the Bible?

*[**INVISIBLE** - ETERNAL (energy/spirit)]:*

"I am the Alpha [beginning] and the Omega [end] [like an eternal loop like a rubber band, both occurring at the same time]," says the Lord God, "who is, and who was, and who is to come, the Almighty."
—Revelation 1:8, KJV)

*[**VISIBLE** - TEMPORARY MATERIAL (matter/objects)]:*

In the beginning God created the heaven and the earth. And the earth was without form, and void; and darkness was upon the face of the deep. And the Spirit of God moved upon the face of the waters. And God said, Let there be light: and there was light. And God saw the light, that it was good: and God divided the light from the darkness. And God called the light Day, and the darkness he called Night. And the evening and the morning were the first day.
—Genesis 1:1–5, KJV

Remember, *there are two parts to God or the universe*, the ***invisible*** spiritual energy level is the eternal part of the universe. This is what the Bible refers to as the Alpha (beginning) and the Omega (end), which means it just goes on eternally forever. As physicists say, this energy level was never created, and it cannot be destroyed, so it's always been there eternally, forever. The other part of the universe is the ***visible*** material world of objects, or what scientists call matter, and what the Bible refers to as the Garden of Eden. Again, they're just using different words to describe the same phenomenon. The Big Bang Theory is the scientific explanation of how the ***visible*** part of the universe began.

According to Space.com, the universe's visible material started from a "small singularity," but they don't explain what exactly that singularity is. The Bible explains this beginning "singularity" as a word or some type of sound ("In the beginning was the Word" John1:1). Remember that words are energy types that come in different frequencies; some are loud *sounds,* and some are silent. Science, on the other hand, describes this initial LOUD frequency sound as a form of explosion, the "Big Bang (*sound vibration*) Theory." So one is describing the sound, while the other is describing the explosive event that occurs in any kind of explosion. This is similar to a firing of a gun. Most people never see the actual explosion, but they will typically hear the sound, even if they are a mile away because the sound vibration lasts longer than the actual explosion itself.

In addition, both agree that light came later into being, according to the Bible, which correlates to the rest of the article on the Big Bang Theory about how light came to be in existence in the universe. So really the Big Bang Theory can be used to prove how the cosmos in God's universe began since both agree there was a (1) loud sounding explosion in the beginning, The Big Bang, then (2) there was light.

INTELLIGENT DESIGN by God the Universe

> *We have already considered with disfavor the possibility*
> *of the universe having been planned by a biologist or an*
> *engineer; from the intrinsic evidence of his creation, the*

Great Architect of the Universe now begins to appear as a pure mathematician.
–Sir James Jeans (physicist, astronomer, mathematician)

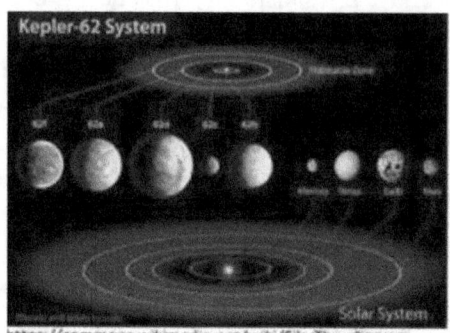

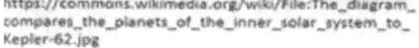

https://commons.wikimedia.org/wiki/File:The_diagram_
compares_the_planets_of_the_inner_solar_system_to_
Kepler-62.jpg

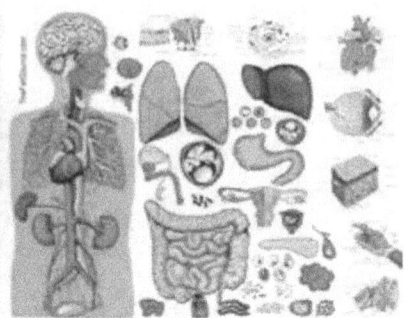

http://clipart-library.com/clipart/1996728.htm
Human Anatomy Cliparts #2475454

Intelligent is defined as:
*1: having or indicating a high or satisfactory
degree of **intelligence** and mental capacity
2: revealing or **reflecting good judgment**
or sound thought: **skillful**.*
–*Merriam-Webster's Online Dictionary*

To begin with, where do we get our arrogance anyway that we as humans are so intelligent? Why we need to discuss why some humans think they are more intelligent than the Creator of the universe is beyond my understanding, but here we are. I realize that we have all been taught in elementary school that humans are the **most intelligent mammals** in the world, so I get how some people can get big egos on this matter. But then some seem to expand the notion that, therefore, we are also more intelligent than the Creator of the universe. However, as compared to monkeys, yes, humans are more intelligent. But compared to whatever created all the objects in the universe—the solar systems, the planets, the oceans, plants, people, and animals . . . it's obvious to me and to a lot of people that there is no comparison. But as far as I can see, the most intelligent thing humans can make for now is "**artificial**" intelligence (AI), in terms of complexity, and that doesn't even come close.

So if we can call humans intelligent, and the only intelligent thing we can come up with is AI, copying what God the Universe created, then the obvious question for me is, how much more intelligent can the original Creator be? Or we can just as easily assess that compared to monkeys, people are more intelligent, but compared to the Creator of the universe, humans are all dummies since we can't yet make our own solar systems, animals, oceans, or people. Or God must be super intelligent as compared to human intelligence. These are some of the ways of looking at it from an **intelligence** point of view, and we can also look at it from the **design** point of view.

> **Design** is defined as:
> 1: ***to create***, *fashion, execute, or **construct*** ***according to plan***.
> 2: a: *to conceive and **plan out in the mind***.
> b: ***to have as a purpose: INTEND***.
> c: *to devise for a **specific function** or end.*
> —*Merriam-Webster's Online Dictionary*

For intelligent design to happen, you first have to believe that you have a mind that creates thoughts and that others do too, and that they all exist together as a collective mind, connected as one as just another form of energy, which I have explained as God's intelligence. Remember what physics says: **Everything** is made out of invisible energy that can *never* be created or *destroyed*; **it just changes forms**, including thought forms.

Sometimes, science to me is very confusing and contradictory. On one hand, they teach that for something to exist it has to be **repeatable** for it to be true. But at the same time, they teach that we were created through **random selection** in evolution, which is **not repeatable**. Then they say that if God is invisible, then it cannot be real, then they turn around and teach that everything in the universe is made of energy, which is invisible. In fact, physics is mostly nothing BUT the study of the invisible realm, called energy, since it cannot be seen.

As a person with degrees in both interior design and in engineering, both disciplines incorporate intelligence into their design. Neither one just throws things randomly together and hopes they will gel and work together because that's not how intelligent creation occurs. But that's the way science explains how we were created through random selection, which by the way is not repeatable. If you don't believe me, try it. Randomly throw things together like wood, metal, glue, and maybe some grass; add water too if you want. Then see, for example, if a working car or bicycle or whatever you choose, gets created. Don't hold your breath as this is not the way to create anything, whether by man or by nature. It's not going to happen, I guarantee.

At the beginning of any intelligent design or creation, designers tend to put a lot of thought into their work, and part of the process is specifying items that will strategically be placed in the design of the space that *will work together toward a specific **purpose***. As an example, an interior designer will never randomly put a tree in the middle of a kitchen or put an airplane in the middle of the front yard. And an engineer will never randomly just place a tree in the middle of the aisle of an airplane or inside the engine as part of the design. This is because in either case, the items *will not work together or gel by themselves the way science teaches that we evolved through **random selection***.

For intelligent design to happen, all the parts have to be specifically and strategically be (1) *selected*, and (2) *placed or planned so* that they (3) *work together*, which means each item has a purpose. These are the keys to creation and God's intelligent design. God's intelligent design and evolution together is called out in the Bible, in Genesis 1 and Genesis 2, which state what ***specific items*** God *wanted to create, their **specific purpose**, and how they are to **work together*** within the system so that they sustain life growth or evolution.

Genesis1, KJV:

11: And God said, Let the earth bring forth grass, the herb yielding seed, and the fruit tree yielding fruit after his kind, **whose seed is in itself, upon the earth**: and it was so. *(Note: This states how vegetation will have seeds to continue its evolution and that it needs to specifically work together with the ground to make this happen; the seeds* *cannot be randomly placed in the ocean or the sky for growth, after all, there's more space in both—if you try that, it will not grow and evolve; it will die.)*

14: And God said, Let there be lights in the firmament of the heaven to divide the day from the night; and let them be **for signs, and for seasons, and for days, and years**. *(Note: This states the purpose for dividing the day and nights so that we may have seasons and days that just happen to be a perfect combination to sustain our lives so that evolution can happen; if it were random, why not all be light or all be darkness which would have been easier to create than the dual day and night scheme—either way this randomness could not sustain the life of evolution as we know it.)*

20: And God said, Let **the waters bring forth abundantly the moving creature that hath life**, and fowl that may fly above the earth in the open firmament of heaven. *(Note: Here he created water and air molecules so that they are in the **perfect combination** to sustain the life of creatures in both water and land creatures—how awesome is that! If randomness were at hand, why wasn't the water made of mercury or liquid nitrogen or any of the other toxic gas and the same thing with the air? Why wasn't it made of some other material that was toxic? Why were they perfectly made so that they work synergistically with the creatures in them to sustain their life's evolution?)*

22: And God blessed them, saying, Be fruitful, and multiply, and fill the waters in the seas, and let fowl multiply in the earth. *(Note: This instructs us to keep growing and multiplying the earth, which is part of evolution—this is our purpose!)*

26: And God said, Let us make man in our image, after our likeness: and let them have dominion over the fish of the sea, and over the fowl of the air, and over the cattle, and overall the earth, and over every creeping thing that creepeth upon the earth. *(Note: Here it states that God specifically designed man in his image with the purpose of having dominion over all of the earth. If it were random, how come only man was given the ability to dominate the earth, why not the fish or the trees or other animals randomly given this same power? Population-wise, there are more of them that randomness could have selected than man. If you look around, who's dominating the earth but humans—not chickens or fish or trees or water or air.)*

Genesis 2, KJV:

4: These are the **generations** of the heavens and of the earth **when they were created**, in the day that the LORD God made the earth and the heavens. *(Note: Day here is explained as actually generations, which is part of the evolution; it's not the twenty-four hours that we define today as day. We have to remember that in ancient times, units of measure like millions or billions of years did not exist then, so generations were probably the highest unit of measure at that time. Scientists today like to use billions as a unit of measure for the age of the world, which is currently at 4.5 billion years and the universe at 14 billion years old.)*

9: And out of the ground made the LORD God to grow every tree that is pleasant to the sight, and good for food; the tree of life also in the midst of the garden, and the tree of knowledge of good and evil. *(Note: Here again it states that the garden was to grow and evolve to be beautiful and used for food for man. Again, there's this synergy from the beginning between man and Garden. The trees help feed man to sustain its life, and in Genesis 2, man is supposed to take care of the garden to help sustain its life evolution. If this were randomness at hand, there would be no reason for the connection between the two objects because all the trees could have randomly been poisonous and not be edible to man, and they could have randomly been producing poisonous gas instead of oxygen to help sustain man's life of evolution—but this isn't the case.)*

10: And a **river went out of Eden to water the garden**; and from thence it was parted, and became into four heads. *(Note: He created the river that went through the Garden of Eden with the specific purpose of watering the garden. Both garden and river were designed from the beginning to work together to sustain life, which means they had a perfect working synergy from the beginning. If this were random, the probability that the river and garden would have this natural synergy would be impossibly infinitesimal; after all, there are many other gases that the river could have been made from, like liquid nitrogen or hydrogen or mercury or any of the many other gasses and combinations of them, but it's specifically water, the exact material that is needed to sustain the life of the garden and everything in it.)*

15: And the LORD God took the man, and put him into the garden of Eden to dress it and to keep it. *(Note: He created man and specifically put him in the garden with the purpose of feasting from it but also to care for it.)*

The point to all this is that God or the universe could not have created water animals, land animals, plants, man, etc., by random selection as science has been teaching for years. It's impossible for all that to happen by chance and all happen to work out together at the end, as scientists believe. This idea is actually a contradiction of another one of their teachings in biology, that for something to exist, it must be repeatable—because *randomness is not repeatable.* There's too much synergy of everything working perfectly together for randomness to have happened in God's universe.

On the other hand, *Intelligent Design,* by definition, has purpose, organization, and a definite relationship between the objects to make it all work together. Whereas randomness is the opposite—it has no purpose, no organization., and no definite relationships between the objects. Any honest look anywhere in the universe will see the evidence of this.

Even the inside of our body is amazingly designed—how the systems within systems are created to work together for the purpose of the body to function properly. Here's an example of an eighth-grade science assignment where the students had to explain how the circulatory system works in synergy with other systems within the body. Notice how each system has a purpose and placement, and at the same time, they are connected. This is evidence of the intelligent design behind just even our bodies. If this is not intelligently designed, then why do science teachers spend so much class time teaching and trying to explain the complexity of our world, like how the various circulatory systems work together, how the cosmos work, how the universe works, etc.?

Circulatory System Working with Other Systems

(From: https://sites.google.com/a/apps.svsu.org/waterwheel-science/home/the-circulatory-system/ circulatory-system-working-with-oth-er-systems)

Each of the following systems are **connected** to the circulatory system.

> **Nervous system:** The nervous system is made up of the brain, spinal cord, and nerves. The brain sends messages to the heart, telling it to beat. The heartbeat pumps blood throughout the body so that nutrients and oxygen can be brought to cells and waste can be removed.
> **Digestive System**: The digestive system breaks down foods and takes out needed nutrients. These nutrients are put into the bloodstream for the cells to use as energy. Minerals and vitamins are also put into the bloodstream to strengthen bones and the immune system.
> **Muscular System:** The heart is a muscle. The expanding and contracting of this muscle is what pumps blood throughout the body.
> **Respiratory System:** The respiratory system is how oxygen is brought into the body. It enters through the lungs into the alveoli. From there it is sent through

blood vessels into the bloodstream for the body to use. At the same time, carbon dioxide is brought to the lungs through the blood to be exhaled.

Skeletal System: Marrow inside of bones produces red and white blood cells. These blood cells are parts of the bloodstream and are responsible for carrying oxygen and fighting off disease.

Endocrine System: The endocrine system is where hormones are produced. Hormones and other chemicals produced by these glands use the circulatory system to travel to needed parts of the body. Example: adrenaline, created by the adrenal gland, travels through the bloodstream to the heart, causing an increased heart rate.

Immune System: The immune system is made up of white blood cells and antibodies. These things travel inside the blood so that they can be transported to the site of infection/invasion to remove and/or hopefully destroy it. This is how you fight off sickness.

The probability of everything working out together randomly, as the theory of random selection as part of evolution suggests, is unimaginable if you understand statistics. If this were the case, it would be as if all the 8 billion people of the world population winning the lottery every single day for the rest of their lives. This is why I call the theory of evolution and the Big Bang theory a scientific miracle since a miracle is defined as something that is a "highly improbable or extraordinary event, development, or accomplishment."

With Christians, at least they are honest upfront and actually call their story of how God's universe started as an actual miracle, though they debate whether the "days" of creation were twenty-four hours or long geological time periods. *"Days"* is used in Genesis as ***multiple generations*** (Genesis 2:4) or **1 day=1000 years** as Peter describes it (2 Peter 3:8). We have to remember that in Bible years, the units of measure *billions* did not exist yet, that is why they used the term multiple generations as the largest unit they knew at the time. According to

Wiktionary, the word billion was coined by Jehan Adam in 1475. This is just an example of how **science and religion could work well** ***together***—if more people would take the time to look at creation and evolution in a different light than what we have been used to.

> *Beloved, be not ignorant of this one thing, That one day is with the Lord as a thousand years, and a thousand years as one day.*
> —2 Peter 3:8, KJV

> *These are the generations [could be thousands or millions of years] of the heavens and of the earth when they were created, in the day that the LORD GOD made the earth and the heavens.*
> —Genesis 2:4, KJV

I heard a Western doctor on the radio recommending the combination of both Western and Eastern medicines to promote a healthier, longer life. Today, more and more Westerners are accepting Eastern medicine. By themselves alone as separate disciplines, they are great; but together they are even more useful and awesome in improving the existence of humans.

There is a movement through New Thought to merge both disciplines, spirituality and sciences energy, together as one so that the union is more effective for the good of all. Understanding your spirit, developing it, and learning how to elevate your own energy level so that you are always performing at your highest level are the keys to attaining happiness and peace of mind.

> *Love not [only] the world [of objects], neither the things that are in the world. If any man love [only] the world [of objects], the love of the Father is not in him [he does not love God].*
> —1 John 2:15, KJV

For most of us, our knowledge of our own invisible spiritual energy or divinity level that is inside us, is very immature and confined by our own very small world, like a baby that doesn't know how to use their body parts. We need to wake up so we can grow up and start maturing spiritually. We need to learn to work together as one universal unit that is in love with God instead of working alone as separate small beings. We need to learn to stop the struggling, the fighting, the anger, the hatred, and the madness we are experiencing in our lives with our spouses, our families, the people we work with, other countries, and other religions. It's time we learn to love each other so that we can all live together in peace. But it all has to start with you—inside of you.

In my daughter's fourth-grade science book, *Discover Science, Grade Four* by Scott Foresman, talks about the food web as the flow of energy and materials through food chains that are connected. If one part of the food web changes, the rest of the web changes in some way. Then he goes on to talk about the natural changes in food webs and the ways in which people can change food webs, such as pollution in the water and air, and the removal of trees from communities that animals need for their homes. This is just another example of how the entire universe is connected as one, so we all need to start seeing ourselves as one unit so that we behave responsibly as one unit in God's universe. This is why it is so important to learn who we really are—so that we reach our highest spiritual energy levels.

At this highest energy level, we can then work together with God or nature as one, as a partner, in making this entire universe a better place to live for everyone. You see, He is alive because He is in you, in me, in the water, and in the trees. He is in everything as energy that is always moving. He is the creator of the physical world of objects, and He gives life to everything in the universe; to you and me, and to all. But as humans, because we were made in His image with our minds, we have chosen to try to destroy the world of objects, *his Garden of Eden*, by giving *it* a slow death. We are the cancer within. It's the humans who created the cars that are polluting the air. It's the humans who are polluting the waters. It's the humans who are killing the trees faster than they can replenish themselves. It's the humans who are killing other humans with our bombs, our anger, our hatred, our prejudices, and our policies. We all need to wake up and start taking care of *God's*

Garden of Eden [the object level], because if we continue to destroy *it,* we destroy ourselves because we are *it* and *it* is us, *connected as ONE.*

> *Behold, the kingdom of **God (his spiritual energy)***
> ***is within (inside) you.***
> –Luke 17:21, KJV

> *So then, let us not be like others, who are*
> *asleep, but let us **be awake** and sober.*
> –1 Thessalonians 5:6, KJV

Only humans have the antidote to get rid of *its* cancer, and that antidote is to love *it*—all of *it!* You see, when people hate something, they tend to want to destroy that something; but when they love something, they tend to treat that something differently by taking care of *it.* Take for example, if you have children, don't you love them so much that you want to nurture them and help them grow? In the same way, we need to learn to love *it* all so that we can help make *it* grow and evolve. As we individually evolve, *it* evolves.

We're not here to destroy and use up all our natural resources faster than nature can replenish them, giving nature a slow death—or a quick one with our bombs. Our purpose is to help it grow and flourish at the object level, which means helping each other evolve and be better because we are all part of the whole. We are part of *it,* and *it* is part of us, so if we don't grow and evolve ourselves, that part of us that is part of *it* cannot grow. We are all in this together as ONE unit, with God the Universe. Can you see that?

So it's okay to grow and learn about your spirit but help others do the same. You can grow a family or your own business, you can help others grow by being a teacher or a parent, or you can be an engineer who helps come up with ideas for environmentally friendly cars if that is what you want to create for yourself and for others. But whatever it is, help *it* grow and be better. Be the creator, not the destroyer. You were given talents for this purpose, so use *it* up and share your talents and gifts by giving and serving yourself to others so that you can help them grow, thereby helping *it* grow. Don't waste yourself by not sharing.

You are good enough; you are God enough. You do matter because you are part of the universal puzzle, and what you do or don't do affects everybody else in the big picture. If you are not growing, then you are like the scab that refuses to heal because we are all part of God's body as one. Therefore, if you are not growing, you are dying. God specifically created us to help manage and take care of His Garden of Eden, the physical world of objects, by improving it and making it better. This is His purpose for us.

> *The LORD God took the man and put him in the*
> *Garden of Eden to **work it and take care of it**.*
> –Genesis 2:15, NIV

PART II

(+) Mind

"Garbage in; Garbage Out"

4

Silencing Your Mind by Controlling It

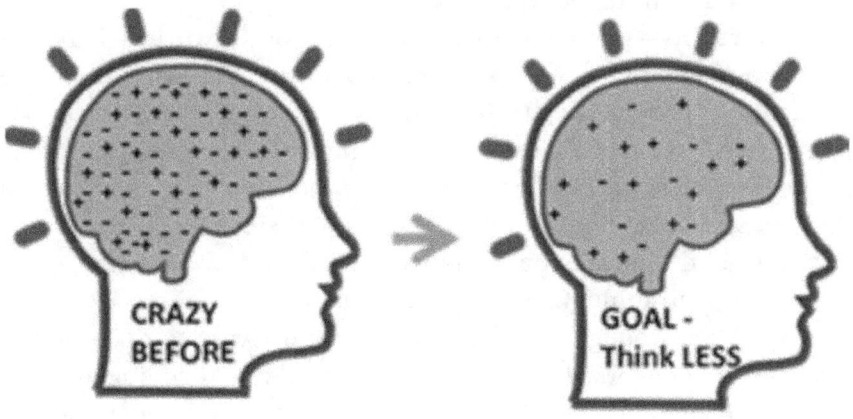

CRAZY BEFORE

GOAL - Think LESS

Rule your mind or it will rule you.
−Buddha/Horace

In recent years our knowledge of modern technology has increased considerably, and as a result we have witnessed remarkable material progress, but there has not been a corresponding increase in human happiness. There is no less suffering in the world today, and there are no fewer problems. Indeed, it might be said that there are now more problems and greater dangers than ever before. This shows that the

> *cause of happiness and the solution to our problems do not lie in knowledge of material things. Happiness and suffering are states of mind and so their main cause are not to be found outside the mind.* **If we want to be truly happy and free from suffering; we must learn to control the mind.**
> –Modern Buddhism

If you're not familiar with it, "garbage in, garbage out" is a term used in the computer world, meaning that when you put bad data in your computer, the results that come out of it will, obviously, also be bad. Your mind is like a computer, and "garbage in, garbage out," applies to it also. If you think your life is messed up, it's because you have put garbage into your mind to make it so. These are your negative thoughts and beliefs that do not serve you. Because your mind tells your body what to do, the only thing your body can produce is "garbage out" when you are always thinking negatively.

Your reality—your very own perspective of the world—is always a reflection of what thoughts you have put into your mind since you created it, and you are the only one in control of your own mind. In other words, your success rate in creating love, happiness, peace, and joy in your life is first determined by your thoughts and beliefs, which then determine your life's production level in these areas. The only way to change and improve your world is to (1) identify what garbage you have put in your mind, (2) get rid of the garbage, and (3) replace it with positive beliefs, thoughts, and behaviors that do work so that you can create a life that works for you. If you do not have underlying love and peace in all areas of your life, and your life is not easy for you, then it's probably because you have put garbage in your mind that your body is acting upon based on those negative beliefs.

Start questioning your beliefs, and if they are not working for you, change them by learning from experts in the particular area you want to improve. For example, when I needed to learn about love, forgiveness, peace of mind, and spiritual development, I turned to people who were experts in the field and read books by Eckhart Tolle, Neale Donald Walsch, Stuart Wilde, Elizabeth Clare Prophet, Dr. Wayne Dyer, just to name a few. When I wanted to learn and understand money in a way that enabled me to be more comfortable with it so that I could create more of it, I turned to experts like T. Harv Eker, Jack Canfield, Ernest Homes,

Stuart Wilde, Deepak Chopra (see appendix A). When I wanted to learn about real estate, I turned to experts in the field like Robert Allen, Ron LeGrand, Robert Kiyosaki, and others. So, when you want to change your thoughts and get in the flow so that creating your happiness goals is much easier and faster, I recommend learning from the experts in your field of choice. Most importantly, make sure you also learn to work with God's spiritual energy as your source for creating and materializing your happiness goals. Trust me, doing it all alone is harder than working with God. Let Him do the heavy lifting for you, once you figure out what you want to create in your life, to make you happy.

> ### *Your beliefs and thoughts determine what you can and cannot create for yourself.*

Your thoughts are spiritual energy that have negative and positive values, depending on which words you choose to describe your environment, your marriage, your family, your job, your financial status, your business, etc. Once chosen, these words eventually become your experiences or objects that you attract and create into your reality. That is why your world is always a reflection of your thoughts, the words and beliefs that you have placed into your mind, and that you use in your everyday conversations. That is why it is so important to be conscious of the words and thoughts you choose to describe your environment because thoughts are just energy forms that you experience negatively or positively, depending on the strength and power you put in your beliefs of the words you choose.

Dr. Masaru Emoto was a Japanese author, researcher, and entrepreneur who said that human consciousness has an effect on the molecular structure of water. According to him, words are ALIVE. His water experiments showed images of various crystals generated as a result of how positive and negative words affect frozen water molecules. Negative words created dark, ugly crystals, while positive words created beautiful white crystals. If thoughts can affect water molecules like that, how do you think our thoughts affect others since our bodies are made up of up to 60 percent water? This is why we all have to be careful how we talk to ourselves and each other, especially our kids and loved ones, since negative words can have adverse effects on people.

If we can teach our kids to stop bullying and parents to stop abusing their kids verbally or physically, maybe we can save lives. IF only we were allowed to teach kids in all schools how to treat each other with love and kindness, maybe we could change the next generation. But currently, such form of courses are illegal to teach in public schools since books like this are considered religious, because of separation of church and state laws we currently have. Schools are allowed to teach about HATE in history classes, for example about the KKK, Hitler, slavery, and wars, but definitely not about LOVE, FORGIVENESS, ACCEPTANCE, and KINDNESS. It's no wonder we are where we are, with suicide rates and school bullying on the rise and their repercussions like school shootings. Divorces are on the rise, and illegal/legal drugs are becoming school norms. This is because our educators refuse to teach our kids how to use their minds properly so that they are more effective human beings. They can and must learn to control their minds—if only they were taught how to. Isn't this supposed to be the main purpose of education, to educate our kids on how to use their minds most effectively?

Anyway, your ability to think and use your imagination to create is your greatest power. This is what makes you special. Your mind tells your body what to do, so you need to learn to be conscious of your beliefs, thoughts, and feelings since your thoughts, whether positive or negative, affect your behavior. So you need to learn to control your thoughts and minimize the number of thoughts you generate at a time so you can avoid going mentally crazy and stressed. That way we can all reduce the need to get drunk or take drugs every time we get depressed or stressed.

Remember, we are all together as one with the universe, or God. So, whatever you put out as negative or positive thoughts and behaviors are always what gets returned to you. You can easily see and evaluate how you are by assessing what you currently have in your life. If you are miserable or you have a broken marriage or you are unhappy at work, then look within, because the answer is inside of you. The only way you can change and create the world that you dream about is by taking responsibility for your own life's results because only you can change it from the inside out since you are the only one in control of your own mind.

<u>BE SILENT – Control Your Thoughts:</u>

80 % of Thoughts Are Negative...95 % are repetitive

ON MARCH 2, 2012 / BY FAITH HOPE & PSYCHOLOGY / IN JUDGE-MENTALISM

https://faithhopeandpsychology.wordpress.com/2012/03/02/80-of-thoughts-are-negative-95-are-repetitive/

 In 1985, medical research conducted at the University of Maryland School of Medicine showedhow internal and external dialogue significantly affects our blood pressure, hearts, and alter the biochemistry of individual tissues at the farthest extremities of our bodies

In 2005, the National Science Foundation published an article regarding research about human thoughts per day. The average person has about 12,000 to 60,000 thoughts per day. Of those, 80% are negative and 95% are exactly the same repetitive thoughts as the day before and about 80% are negative.

These studies reveal that the quality of our existence rests on the quality of our internal and external communication. It also reveals how our bodies respond to the way we think, feel and act. This is often called the"mind-body-spirit connection." When we feel guilt and shame or stress and anxiety our bodies cry out to tell us that something isn't right. For example, high blood pressure or a stomach ulcer might develop after a particularly stressful event.

Casting down imaginations, and every high thing that exalteth itself against the knowledge of God [stop negative thinking], and bringing into captivity every thought [control your mind] to the obedience of Christ [instead, focus on God's love].
–2 Corinthians 10:5, KJV

How negative are we? According to research by the National Foundation, we generate about 12,000 to 60,000 thoughts a day, of which 80 percent are negative and 95 percent are repetitive. So, the big question is, how do we stop this repetitive negative thinking, so we can have mental peace without drugs, which this section covers?

To help you have peace of mind, you need to learn to create space between your thoughts by reducing the number of words you generate in your mind. Most of your thoughts are nothing but mindless chatter anyway, and if you believe your own negative stories and lies, they can be detrimental and destructive to you and to others. Unless you are at school where you need to remember a lot of data or at work requiring a lot of thinking, you don't need to think so much.

My father, for example, was very abusive because of the thoughts and beliefs he generated in his mind that it was okay to beat his wife and children to a pulp. Another example is one of my daughter's friends who was sent to a mental institution because she had thoughts of killing her abusive parents. The father was probably abused himself so, then he abuses his daughter, and his daughter wants to return the favor. This kind of negative cycle is what we need to stop; otherwise, we will continue to pass it on to our children, generation after generation. This is what the Bible calls the generational curse. Everything that we do always starts with our thoughts and then becomes our reality. That is why it's important to learn to be conscious of our thoughts, and then learn to manage and control our thoughts. To manage our thoughts, we need to do two things:

1. We all need to reduce the number of thoughts we generate.
2. We need to make sure the thoughts we generate are good, positive thoughts.

When we learn to refocus our minds' eyes on the invisible realm and learn to silence our minds and the number of thoughts we generate, we align to the silence of God the Universe, where there are no objects to judge; only peace and unconditional love resides. This is how we can achieve freedom from hell and slavery from the object-level chaos by breaking our mental separation from the God within and learning how to work with it naturally.

If I were to take a rose bush and ask ten people what they think about it, they would all come up with varying thoughts. One might say, "I hate roses." Another might say, "I love roses." Another might say, "I hate the thorns." Another might say, "I love the smell of roses." And yet another might say, "I hate the smell of roses." So who's right and who's wrong? Nobody is. Your opinions don't matter because there are no right or wrong answers in the world of chaos of visible temporary objects that are always changing forms; there are 8 billion mental perspectives. You must learn to detach yourself emotionally from everything by trying to control your own thoughts, not other people; otherwise, you can't have mental peace. Especially if your mind is only focused on the temporary object level, where there is nothing but chaos. Only people disagreeing and fighting with each other all the time.

The people who have very large egos and have a need to be right all the time are people who are stuck at the object level. These are the most miserable people, and they often make others feel just as miserable because these people want to control everything in their universe. Whenever you want to stop an argument with one of these self-righteous people, just tell them, "Yeah, you're right." Even if you disagree. Then just leave the room, or go to the bathroom, or go play with the dog or kids, or watch TV. The point is, as part of the universe of God, the rose doesn't care what you think of it because ultimately the stories you create in your mind about it or other objects don't matter. And it will drive you crazy if you take your own stories too seriously. That is why so many people are on drugs and drink themselves into a stupor because they can't stop the chatter they create in their minds. People create their own hell, their own Twilight Zone scripts in their heads.

My husband, for example, drove himself crazy when our oldest daughter was a teenager wearing thongs. He seriously thought in his mind that if she wore thongs, it was going to cause her to lie, take drugs, have sex, and get pregnant. All this mental craziness over a piece of underwear that she wears covered up! The thong was just underwear; everything else was just stories, lies, and illusions he made up in his head about the underwear. The story he created in his mind was what drove him crazy! He then picked a fight with my daughter about wearing them, then he picked a fight with me because I disagreed with him. To me, the underwear was just that, a piece of undergarment that was made of electrons and protons just like everything else. It was nothing but pure energy, which is nothing! He used to get himself very upset over little things by creating wild stories in his head about nothing. And don't even get him started on cell phones. I am so glad he's learned to silence his mind somewhat. Previously, we were all fighting all the time because of this kind of craziness, and I was guilty of it too. Remember how I said I had this private mental conversation about how I thought all men were jerks based on something that only my father did? Now that I've learned to silence my mind, I'm not afraid of men anymore and I'm at peace.

Ever since my husband and I learned to stop our mental craziness, fighting used to be the norm in our family. Now it's the exception. I finally have the family I've always dreamed of. We are happy, loving, peaceful, and supportive of each other. It's pleasant to come home now. The point is that if we can do it, you can do it too. You can get yourself out of your own mental hellhole because you created it. You are in control of your own mental perspective of your universe.

The secret to having mental peace is learning to stop creating the mental chatter, the stories, the craziness, the assumptions, the lies, and the narration of everything you see with your eyes on the outside. Stop judging everything because everything is made of energy that is ultimately made of nothing. Don't make an issue of every little thing. All your judgments and opinions, your mental chatter, whether spoken or in silence, are wasted energy. They are futile! They mean nothing because they don't matter. There are no right or wrong answers or good or bad ones; an answer only works or doesn't work in achieving the task and goals you are working on.

So the next time somebody cuts you off in traffic, let it go! You don't know why they cut you off. Maybe there was a good reason, like the wife is having a baby and needs to go to the hospital. Maybe they burn their hand and need to go to the hospital, or maybe they are in a hurry because they are late for work or to school for their finals. Because you don't know why they are in a hurry, forgive them and let it go. Don't go after them angry that they cut you off or give them the middle finger and start a road rage. Rather, forgive them and say a silent prayer for God to keep them safe during their journey.

It's the constant automatic judging of things around you that causes you to go mentally crazy. You can only achieve mental peace when you start seeing everything from the standpoint of objects existing at the invisible spiritual energy level as one, rather than as separate objects. Learn to place your mental focus in **God's invisible spiritual energy realm in love**, rather than on people's craziness and drama. Otherwise, you yourself will also go crazy or get physically sick.

Learn to be silent. You need to create lots of space between your thoughts by reducing the number of thoughts you generate. Remember, God is within the space, the silence. Like matter in a solid state, nothing gets through because of the lack of space between the particles. That's why if you talk too much, you do not allow anything else to get through. So the less you think, the more peaceful you will be and the better you will feel because it is only in the silence that you can actually hear God answer your prayers and questions. When you are too busy with your own chatter, you cannot hear Him answer.

Only in the silence can you mentally be one with God the Universe, because He is only in the space, in the present moment, in stillness and quietness. So create lots of space between your thoughts to allow God's thought energy to go through you. Your power to create and to use the universe's energy to its fullest, boundless, limitless potential is by focusing all your energy where it is—in the present by being quiet. The goal is to match nature or God. Be mentally where it is—in the present moment in time. And put your mental focus on Him, not on people or things or problems. By being silent, creative, flexible, and loving, you can reach your highest self.

> *There is one that keepeth **silence,** and is found wise:*
> *and another by much babbling becometh hateful.*
> Sirach (Apocrypha) 20:5, KJV

There are several ways to silence your mind, which are listed below. What you want to do is to combine them all and experiment to see which are working and which are not working. Again, all these are interrelated; they are not separate. And it's a combination of all that makes them more powerful and useful as a way of helping you silence your mind. Learn and master them all and make them live in your heart and soul at your deepest being. There is no other way of having inner peace (other than taking synthetic drugs); otherwise, your stress and mental craziness will continue to rule your life. These concepts are all covered in detail in various sections of the book. So master these concepts:

- *Learn that we are not just temporary separate objects, but together as one in God's energy that, according to physics, everything is made of.*
- *Learn where your source comes from.*
- *Learn to stop being so sensitive and judging everything you see in the material world of objects because this is not what unconditional love is or where God's love is.*
- *Learn to live in the present moment so you can reduce your mental thoughts.*
- *Learn to forgive yourself and everybody else because we all mess up in the material world of objects, and no one is better than anybody else.*
- *Learn to give unconditional love to all, especially to yourself and those you have most difficulty with, like your enemies.*
- *Learn to send silent blessings to everybody, especially to those you have difficulty with, like your enemies.*
- *Learn to be grateful for all the blessings you do have.*
- *Learn to speak to God on a daily basis by praying and meditating while doing your day-to-day activities.*
- *Learn to be in sync with God's positive energy flow of love.*
- *Learn to make God your life partner in everything that you do and create by putting Him first rather than the crazy world of objects.*

The other important reason you want to learn to be silent is that if you ever hope to create your own Garden of Eden, it's difficult to do when your mind is preoccupied with negative judgments of hate, anger, fear, jealousy, blame, complaining, and putting down of yourself and others. Silencing your mind eliminates or redirects these self-destructive thoughts and instead creates space in your mind to allow you to focus on the things that are most important to you so you can be more creative.

In other words, negative thoughts and useless chatter will always get in the way and distract you. In fact, they destroy your ability to create your very own beautiful, peaceful world. That's why most people cannot accomplish their dreams because their mental focus is directed toward death or fears, which is negative and destructive, rather than helping God create new life into this world, the positive and creative. As a result, they cannot grow and instead die early instead of living.

It's similar to a plant that is placed in darkness; it cannot grow but dies quickly because it lacks light. God's Light, as I said in the beginning, is knowledge. It's knowing the truth about who you really are as part of God's spiritual energy, and knowing how to use it and work with it, that will help you from struggling. You are a divine perfect being in God because you are not separate but together as one with God at the invisible spiritual energy level, created in His image.

You know some of these struggling people, maybe it's you. These are the people who are suicidal, depressed, dependent on drugs or on alcohol, unhappy, or angry all the time. These people lack the ability to grow their lives in happiness, peace, and love because of their lack of knowledge and limiting thoughts of how to effectively work and use God's universe together as ONE unit. These people are imploding from within.

You can save yourself from destroying yourself if you can master the concepts above. When you learn to silence your mind, not only will your mind be lighter due to less babbling, but you will also feel it in your body as less stress. So, learn to divert your attention to doing something you love or being around people and things you love, like your dog or cat, praying or meditating, going to church or synagogue, reading the Bible or your favorite book, gardening, watching something on TV that makes you laugh, or changing your environment to reduce your mental stress.

For example, when my youngest daughter was in the fifth grade, she would get massive headaches on a regular basis from school when her mean bully teacher yelled at the students all the time. My daughter would be creating these negative thoughts in her head that she did not know how to get rid of, so her headaches would get worse and worse. Because I hated giving my kids drugs, even aspirin, I would purposely try to divert her attention by turning on her favorite TV show, SpongeBob, which always worked to get rid of her headaches. The other thing I used to do to try to divert her attention from her mean teacher while driving home was to try to talk about something positive, for example, a party that was coming up, or to hold her hand and silently pray for God to give her peace of mind and for Him to give me guidance to help her. These all worked temporarily, but the headaches kept coming back the next day after her class with the same bully teacher. Eventually, when we transferred her to a new school, she was able to stop her negative thinking and thinking about death because, at that age, she didn't think there was a way out. Then her headaches automatically went away, her vomiting in the mornings stopped as well, and she stopped talking about death—all just by removing her from that bad environment.

> *For many are deceived by their own vain opinion;*
> *and an evil suspicion hath overthrown their judgment.*
> –Sirach (Apocrypha) 3:2, KJV

Extracting What's in Your Mind And Your Beliefs That Are Not Working For You

One way to extract what you are thinking is by writing a journal of the thoughts you are harboring. Be very honest. Nobody has to read your journal except you. This exercise is extremely powerful, especially in dealing with the painful thoughts you keep replaying in your mind about family, friends, people at work, your work, your school, and everything that you are concerned about. Write down your thoughts, and then go back with a marker and highlight all the negative words and thoughts in your journal.

The words you are looking for are control, anger, hate, can't, sadness, depression, fear, etc., and phrases like "He/she won't listen or help," "He/She doesn't do anything," "I can't control him/her," and "I might fail." Negative habits you are looking for are overeating, eating junk food, drinking, smoking, using illegal drugs, etc. Also, using a red marker or pen, make a note on the left side of the journal of the date or your age when certain painful incidents first happened. Again, using a different colored pen than you used for the date, write down on the left side of the journal how often these thoughts keep repeating in your mind. Is it about five times per day, daily, weekly, monthly, once a year, or another frequency? Don't worry if you don't know the exact dates or ages; estimates are good enough. This exercise does several things for you.

First of all, it is a good way of data dumping your thoughts. This is also a great way of releasing some of the stress that you keep stuck in your head. This journal is basically the story you are telling yourself about yourself. Second, the highlights will show you how negative you are being, which most people don't even realize they are doing. Third, the dates and times on the left side of the journal tell you how automatic, or subconscious, you are being. Fourth, this journal tells you all the different areas in which you can improve yourself. Because it's only a story, this is an opportunity for you to change the story that you tell yourself about yourself, especially your past.

The past is gone, so it can't hurt you anymore. The story that you have decided to keep and repeat to yourself and to others is what keeps hurting you when you repeat it in your mind. These stories are the things that make you feel trapped and crazy. You can't have freedom until you learn to let them go. Remember, only you are responsible for your own thoughts and creations—nobody else, since you are the only one in control of your own mind. Therefore, you can always change your perspective in how you view your world by changing your thoughts and creating better ones. This is where your creative power begins.

Most of us keep repeating the past pains, the past abuse, the bad words somebody said, and whatever bad experiences we may have had. This exercise will help you view these things differently so that you can move on with your life. The story that you tell yourself, the one in your journal, is the source of your stress and behaviors that do not help you grow. If you can't let your story go, you should at least change it. Because it's only a story, it's okay for you to change the story and make it positive so at least it's not hurting you anymore. If you really want to stop hurting and start healing within, learn to master forgiveness and to love *all*! Peace can only happen from the inside out—through the love and forgiveness of *all*. This is the secret to having mental peace.

Remember, nobody is right or wrong in the world of objects. Everybody always does the best that they know based on their age, culture, experiences, history, education, and religious background. There are only perspectives, and every single person alive today has their own individual perspective of the universe they interact with. No two people share the same view of the world. That is why there are so many divorces, sibling rivalries, and wars. Even by reading the same book, you may get many interpretations or views. Take, for example, the Bible; it's only one book, yet there are so many Christian sects. There are Catholics, Baptists, Nazarenes, Methodists, Foursquares, Unitarians, Jehovah's Witnesses, Church of Christ, Mormons, etc., and these are just the ones I've gone to. All of them have a different interpretation of the Bible. If Christian theologians can't even agree on one interpretation of the same book, how can average people be expected to believe in one interpretation?

The bottom line is that there is no right or wrong way of interpreting or writing a story. A more effective question is whether it is working or not working for you. Are you getting the results you want? Are you at peace or suffering with the stories you tell yourself? Are the stories you keep in your mind helping you to grow in love and giving you mental peace or not? If it's not working, simply adjust your beliefs until your view of the world works for you. Don't waste your mind and time in petty arguments about who's right or wrong, or by blaming people for what's not working in your life and relationships. This is thinking too small, too negatively, and stuck at the material level. Instead, you should think big, thinking God in the invisible energy level, so you can redesign your life from that vast empty space as your source and focus on creating your perspective of the world from the God-view of love, so you can co-create your own Garden of Eden through love.

You can't change what actually happened in the past, but you can change how you view the past by retelling your personal story in a positive way instead of a negative way. I recommend reading this book to the end, and I invite you to rewrite your story about what you tell yourself about who you are after you read this book. Change your story, and make all your stories positive instead of negative.

Remember, you are the author of your own story. You can tell it any way you want; after all, they are just words. Don't get yourself stuck in a negative story that is not working for you. This exercise will help you shrink the thoughts and the stressors that are in your mind. This is helpful in letting go of your past.

The rest of the book will help you change your underlying beliefs. To make this exercise as successful as possible, you need to be extremely honest about yourself. Many negative people come to my office, and most of the time, they don't even know that they are being negative. They are in denial. If you ask yourself if you are happy most of the time at home, with all your family and friends, at work, and everywhere you go, and the answer is no, then this exercise can help you.

Another way you can make your journal useful is by recording yourself while you are reading it. Then keep listening and replaying your story over and over until you get sick and tired of listening to your own sad story. It's like being your own therapist. Pay special attention to all the negativity. Count the number of times you are being negative. Bringing your thoughts into the open, to your awareness, helps you to realize how you are thinking because often most of us don't realize how negative we are being. When you get sick and tired of listening to your own story, you will be ready to rewrite your story about yourself in a different light. Again, wait until you read this book entirely to rewrite your journal so that you can write a more effective story that can help you create a better you by redesigning who you are from the inside.

Here's how we reduce our world: As children, we are all born with clean minds that are like blank sheets of paper. However, as we get older, we fill it up with good and bad memories, but they are mostly bad because of our environment (parents, TV, religion, school, etc.). Often, we form beliefs and rules that we live by from what we hear and experience. However, because we often don't question statements like "Money is a sin," "Our way is the only way," "Sex is a sin," "Blondes are dumb," etc., we don't even realize that these thoughts are constricting and limiting our lives. These rules that we subconsciously accept limit our abilities to experience the universe in its vastness. The negative thoughts and fears we adopt and collect through the years are what reduce our view of the world from a clean blank sheet of the universe to just the confines of our neighborhood.

For years, I kept repeating in my mind the negative story about my abusive father. I dwelled on how much I hated him and how much I thought he was a jerk, and then in my mental script, I increased it to include all men. I told myself that all men were alike and that they were all jerks like my father. As a result of my negative thoughts, I lived in fear and grew up hating all 4 billion men around the world, even though they did not do anything to me, I blamed them anyway. Then I grew to hate all the Filipinos in the world since the kids in my neighborhood were not allowed to play with us after their parents found out my parents got divorced when I was nine, so we were basically ostracized by my own people. In my mind, I was so angry with these people and thought, "If you're going to hate us, I'm going to hate you all too!" In my crazy mind, I wanted so much not to be Filipino like these people and hated myself so much for being so. The only remaining group I liked in the universe were women. Then I told myself that I was a Republican and took on their beliefs, so I became angry with half the women. Then because I thought I was being a good Christian by believing that Jesus was the only way to salvation and that we were right and all other religions were wrong, I was taught to hate the other religions. Then when 9/11 happened, I became fearful of traveling outside the United States. I was reading murder mystery books, so I had fears of being murdered and of my kids being murdered. Of course, with news of gangs, kidnappings, and murders, the media didn't help; they only made me even more scared and freaked out.

As a result, I refused to do business outside of Orange County because I was too scared otherwise. My perspective of the world shrank from loving the entire universe as a child to only loving Republican

Christian women in Orange County as an adult because I was too scared of everybody and everything else. That pretty much summed up my little world. I was afraid of or angry with or didn't like anybody outside that circle because of the various reasons. I became so afraid and paranoid of everything and everybody that I became afraid of leaving my own house. I created a mental hellhole so deep that I knew if I didn't get myself out of it soon, I would lose it. I felt so trapped. I had problems breathing at night, and I was literally suffocating myself from the inside out with these negative thoughts that I had made up in my head. I got to the point where I was just sick and tired of my life. I was tired of being angry and depressed all the time. I didn't want to be afraid anymore, and I was tired of struggling and fighting with everyone.

I knew I needed to reverse the process somehow. So to stop putting negative thoughts in my mind, I did what Dr. Wayne Dyer said to do—turn everything off, since there is so much negativity out there, he said. So I stopped watching TV, especially the news. I stopped reading murder mystery books. I stopped fighting with and talking to my family until I figured things out. I stopped going to church. I stopped what I was doing because these things were all making me mentally crazy. Nothing seemed to be working. When I first heard Dr. Dyer on TV, I started flooding my mind with nothing but positive thoughts with books and DVDs listed in Appendix A. I listened to DVDs while driving, I read positive thinking books while at the gym, every night before going to bed, and on every break I could get. I was taking all sorts of expensive seminars like Ontological Design and Lifespring. I had to learn to stop the mental chatter, the lies, the illusions, and all the negative thinking I was creating in my mind because they were making me crazy, hateful, fearful, and physically sick.

To do a mental reversal, which was more like a mental cleansing without drugs, I had to go back into my personal history. Once I changed my story about my father, which I had been carrying for almost thirty years, from negative to positive, my life changed!

First, I had to forgive my father; I thought that if it weren't for him, neither I nor my beautiful children would exist today, so I had to thank him for that. By simply changing my story, my beliefs, and my attitudes about my father from negative to positive, I was able to change how I saw my husband and all the men that I had to work with. This has created many job and business opportunities for me. For my husband and I, it helped to create a more loving relationship for us.

Do your own mental cleansing or reversal so that you learn to love all again. Change your own personal story so that it is more useful to you. The last chapter will focus on how to re-create yourself so that the stories you tell yourself about yourself and about your world will be more positive. This is why all permanent change has to begin inside of you, in your mental belief system.

In a seminar I attended by John Grey, Ph.D., author of *Men Are from Mars, Women Are from Venus,* he stated that based on scientific research, men's and women's brains are wired differently. There are more connections between the left and right side of the brain for women; whereas, men tend to be one-sided and are either stronger on the left or right side of the brain only. But most men, he said, are actually just left-brained. He gave the example of a map. He said that women can see and focus on the entire map all at once, but men can only see and focus on a small portion of the same map at a time. Because of this, he said women tend to work more than men because of their brain function. This is another reason why men and women view the world differently and why so many couples fight and divorce. *(See Scientific American online article, "How Men's Brains Are Wired Differently than Women's,"* https://www.scientificamerican.com/article/ how-mens-brains-are-wired-differently-thanwomen/)

Those of us who were born in the '50s and '60s are familiar with old TV shows like *Ozzie and Harriet, Father Knows Best,* and *Leave It to Beaver* because the characters on these shows were our role models. This was a different time in our history. This was a time when most women stayed home to take care of the housework and kids. But times have changed, and we all have to change with the times. The reality today is that most women work—full-time most of the time—along with their husbands. Most of my friends today are enrolled in some kind of family counseling to keep their marriages intact. As a society, our divorce rate is up to about 50 percent. The impression that I get from listening to my friends' conversations and from my own experience is that most of the men who grew up in this era are still suffering from what I call the "*Ozzie and Harriet syndrome.*" These men are mentally stuck in this era with the belief that women should do all or most of the housework at home. This belief system is an example of a belief system that no longer works for the society that we currently live in because most women today work a regular forty-hour-a-week job just like men.

Once I was trying to solicit my husband's help with the housework, when he said, "*It was better (for him) before, when women didn't work,*" because to him, housework is for women. He grew up in the '60s believing that is the way it ought to be because of his role models at the time, like *Ozzie and Harriet-style* show and his mom, who didn't work. This is a big problem for many couples.

If determining who does the housework is a problem in your family, hire a maid; and if you can't afford one, simply split all the tasks equally. If you truly love each other and accept each other as equals, then this will be an easy task to do as a couple. If both husband and wife are each already putting in forty hours of work per week, then the men should not expect the women to take care of the bulk of the work at home too. Dividing and sharing the housework and childcare responsibilities is a more loving and responsible way of taking care of this common problem. Split the task, but be flexible at the same time. For example, because both our daughters went to different schools, whenever my husband had to work really late at the apartments and couldn't pick up my daughter, I automatically took over his task. Remember, solve the problem for the greater good of the family as a whole (for all), not just for what's going to benefit one person or a few people in the relationship. The solution is always best when everybody comes out being happy and at peace.

This is an example of how we accept our society's beliefs without being conscious and aware of whether they work for us or not. This particular belief system may have worked in the 60s, but it no longer works in today's society. If your beliefs no longer work for you, change them, improve them, and choose new ones that do work. Fortunately, there's been a shift in the male role in our society, and men are now sharing more of the housework and childcare than they used to. I'm not saying one is better than the other or that one is right and the other is wrong. What I am saying is that you should just be aware of the changes in society and that you should make a conscious choice, not a subconscious choice, to make your moment-by-moment decisions. Don't get stuck accepting subliminal messages your environment is throwing at you.

Always ask yourself, "How am I portraying myself to others?" Read your journal to get a clue about your predominant thinking, because chances are that you are showing up exactly like the story you created about those whom you are afraid of, angry with, hateful toward, jealous of, etc. Until you forgive and learn to love and send silent blessings to all those on your hate list, you will continue to struggle in your life story about yourself. And you will suffocate from the minutiae that you created in your mind. If this is what you choose for yourself, then don't blame anybody else. Your own thoughts are your own responsibility and nobody else's. Take back your power by taking full responsibility and control of your own thoughts and destiny. Don't give your power away by blaming others or complaining because this will only weaken you.

CHAPTER

5

Reduce the Time Frame in Your Mind by Living in the Moment

Let go and learn from the past, set goals for the future, but live only in the present moment.

Time is relative and flexible, and according to Einstein, "The dividing line between past, present, and future is an illusion."

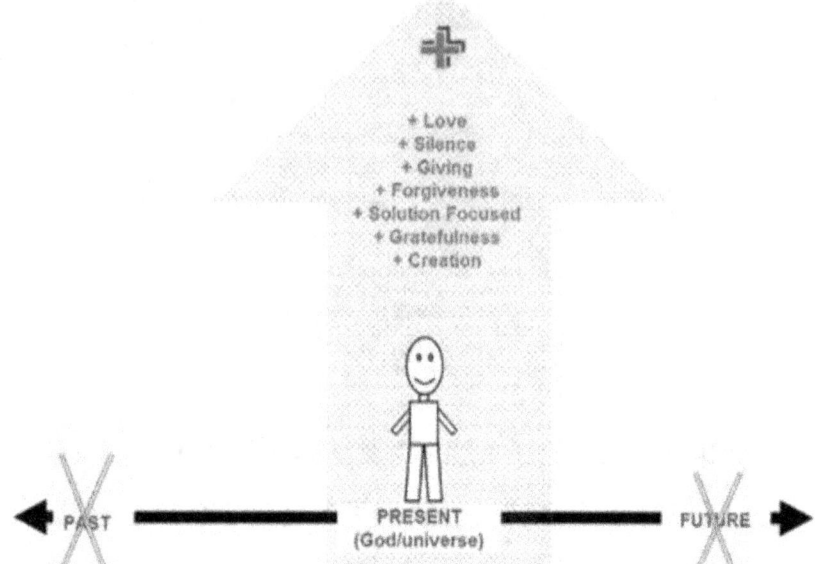

+ Love
+ Silence
+ Giving
+ Forgiveness
+ Solution Focused
+ Gratefulness
+ Creation

PAST — PRESENT (God/universe) — FUTURE

* Forgive, love, and send blessings to all those who have hurt you in the past so that you can let go of past pains.

* Clear your mind & body of negativity.
* Keep your minds thoughts in vertical alignment with your body.
* God only exists in the present moment, so creation can only happen here.
* Write daily to-do lists and follow through. This keeps you on track and moving toward your goals.

* Write your future goals down; don't keep them in your head, as they cause mental stress.
* Studies have shown that 97% of all written goals are met

- Destruction
- Unforgiving
- Unloving
- Problem Focused
- Mindless Chatter
- Ungratefulness
- Stress
- Fear

YOUR PRESENT MOMENT:

For most of us, we carry our entire lifetime (past, present, and future) in our minds, which causes a lot of mental stress. To heal our minds from this form of stress and mental sickness, we all need to learn to reduce the time frame we keep in our minds by learning to live only in the moment, so we can mentally be present at all times. To do this, we need to have a different understanding of time so that we limit it to just the present moment. Remember, **time is just a series of moments strung together.** In terms of real-time, there is no past or future. This is another one of our mental illusions that we need to correct. As Einstein says, *"Time is an illusion."*

Your BUBBLE – limiting time in your field of vision or where your physical body is by living in the moment

In the book *The Power of the Now* by Eckhart Tolle, he talks about the importance of living in the present moment, which he calls the NOW. So, I have developed the *bubble* as a symbol of what I define as *the space that is within your field of vision or where your body is that represents your present moment.* If you can't see it or touch it, it's not part of your present moment. This is a trick I use to keep my mind in the present moment, in the Now. Remember, you can only maneuver within this moment.

You do not have control over your past (because it has passed) or your future (because it will never arrive). Here's a helpful mindset: The universal God only exists in the present moment, so you need to learn to work within the present moment (your bubble) to be highly effective in life. This is where the source of all creation is at, in this moment. This is another way of keeping in alignment with God by keeping our mind focused where it is, in the present moment. That is why spiritual books refer to God as Presence and say, that "God created all things." It is because all that is created in the universe as part of God is all created and done in the present moment and not at any other time, such as the past or future. The concept of time that there is a past and future time is just an illusion in our minds; it was created by humans. We only have this moment to live—there is no other time. So if you keep your mind worried about the past or the future, you have just missed the moment. Do you see and understand that?

Think of your bubble as your present space. This space is really the only space you have control over at any moment in time. The reason that most people have so much pain, sadness, anger, etc., is that they are mentally too focused on spending most of their time replaying a painful past or worrying too much about not getting what they want in the future instead of being in the present. If you look at the timeline above, you will see that your power is in learning to live in the present moment. Your present moment is all that you can maneuver around, and this present moment is restricted only to what you can see within your field of vision and where your physical body is. This is what I call your bubble. The past is gone and the future isn't here yet, so don't waste your precious time with them. God is only present in this instant moment. So, this is where you need to keep your mind focused—in this present moment.

One day while I was driving home, I asked my then ten-year-old daughter how her day was after I had just picked her up from school. She proceeded to tell me about her day, and a few minutes into her story, she woke me up out of my trance when she yelled, "Mom, you're not even listening!" I was so busy thinking about what to serve for dinner—which at the time was my future—that I could not even pay attention to her and really be with her at that moment. So **wake up** from your trance so that you can live in the present, or you will miss out on precious moments with your loved ones. Learn to be present and be in the moment at all times.

Just because you are physically next to a person does not mean you are mentally with them. *Your body, mind, and spiritual energy are now out of sync when they are not all in the same time frame in your mind.* When you are at work but thinking or worried about your children at home or at school, then you are not in the moment. This causes you to perform at a negative energy level, which means that you are giving less than 100 percent of yourself to what you need to be doing at that moment. If you are at home, but your thoughts are what you forgot to do in the past or what you have yet to do in the future at work, then you don't know how to live in the moment. Again, you are performing at a negative level and giving less than 100 percent of yourself to your family or work. You need to learn to keep your mind and your thoughts in the same time frame, and you need to keep them in sync with where your body is so that you don't miss what is going on around you at that moment. Not knowing how to keep your mind aligned with your body causes unnecessary mental stress and worry. You can learn to control where you put your mental focus in the present moment within your bubble.

I noticed that for me—now that I have stopped worrying about the future and stopped thinking about things that I might have forgotten to do at work—I am driving safer and more slowly, and I am noticing more of what's happening around me while I drive. I am not getting tickets or getting into accidents anymore or missing my exits on the freeway. Previously, I was getting tickets and getting into accidents a lot because I was so negative and always worried about this and that. My mind was always preoccupied and wandering, and I was easily distracted with past or future thoughts that really did not have anything to do with what I was doing at that moment, not really paying attention to what was going on around me. I was such a mental mess and so stressed all the time, just out of control!

As a mother of two, I was worried about the kids 24/7, whether I was physically with them or not. I was worried about their health, their safety, whether they were warm enough or not, whether they were getting their homework done, and about getting them to and from all their activities. I found this to be very stressful and ineffective. Once I learned to trust that God will take care of my children even when I am not physically with them, and once I learned to keep my mind limited to only that which I can see at the moment so that my mind is always in sync with my body, I was able to stop the stress, the worry, and the automatic constant babble that was continuously streaming out of my mind. Because I have learned to keep my mind with my body, I am able to give 100 percent of myself when I am at home, at work, or wherever I am at that moment. I am able to do more because my mind is focused only on the people and the work I find myself in that moment. My mind is not wandering as much, which keeps me from wasting time and energy on things I cannot change.

Thoughts of the past and future that are kept in your mind slow you down and lower your energy level. They distract you from doing what's most important, and they constrict your life flow, which can cause physical illness. Learning to live in the moment helps to elevate your energy level and make you feel better so that you are able to do more with less effort and you are able to reduce your cycle time in meeting your happiness goals, whatever you are working on.

YOUR PAST – Learn And Build From It, But Let It Go

This means learning to let go of the past by accepting that whatever happened in the past as past by forgiving and loving yourself and anybody else that's ever hurt you in the past. This is the way you heal yourself. In the next section, I will be talking more about the importance of forgiving and loving. This is important if you want peace in your life. Seriously examine your beliefs and the stories you tell yourself about the past, and change them from negative to positive, if they are not working for you so your mind will let them go. Write a journal or get feedback from friends as I discussed earlier to help you with your self-assessments and to identify areas for improvement.

For some people, this is going to be a difficult exercise because most of us are in denial, and it's often much easier to keep doing what we've been doing, even if our methods don't work and we're miserable, than it is to have to think about such things. I wasted thirty years being angry toward and blaming all men about my life for something that only my father had done when I was a child. I missed many opportunities for love and happiness as a result. I kept replaying the past pains by not forgiving.

Don't waste your time like I did. Learn to forgive those who have hurt you in the past so you can love again and have mental peace in the present. Learn to *let go of your painful past!* Your history is useful when you can look at it from the perspective of what you can learn from it and use it as a building block to improve your persona in the same way that most engineers use past science, technology, and engineering knowledge to help build better or faster technologies. Don't keep the past in your head; it's a waste of your precious time and mental space. This only lowers your energy level and keeps you stuck in a state of pain, which will manifest in your body as a form of illness. This was the main cause of my brain tumor that I spoke about earlier. So master letting go of your past through love and forgiveness of your past negative experiences.

YOUR FUTURE – CREATING an abundant life by knowing what YOU want and how to have it all by writing your goals down on a list

The reason that some people get so stressed about their future is because they often don't have a clear written direction of what they want and how to get there. They don't have a sense of purpose. They focus too much on what they don't want or have instead of what they do want, so what they don't want keeps showing up, and they can't figure out why they are so miserable. They want a lot of things, but because they fail to write down what they want in terms of goals, set schedules to meet the goals, or break the goals into smaller pieces as daily-to-do lists, they can never follow through. However, while writing goals down is important; it should not be the daily focus. It should only be used as a compass to give you guidance and direction as to where you want to go to avoid unnecessary stress. It's like looking for a needle in a haystack: If you don't focus on the needle, you will never find it; instead, the straw that you don't want will keep showing up, and you will only get frustrated. So, if you want something, you need to tell the universe exactly what you want, so that what you want is what gets attracted to you. Writing your goals down on a list helps to remove negative thoughts and worries about the future from your mind.

Remember, goals are in the future. You can only control your present moment. For example, if your goal is to drive from Los Angeles to New York, you know that you are going to New York because your goal directs you there, but while driving in the direction of your goal, you should only focus on the road in which you find yourself at each moment; otherwise, you will get in an accident. Goal setting is explained in more detail in the goal-setting section.

6

Clear Your Mind of Negativity by Being Positive

Insanity is doing the same thing over and over again and expecting different results.
–Albert Einstein (Nobel Prize in Physics)

The goal here is to help you get over your negative thoughts of fear, and there are many ways to do this; facing your fears and learning to be positive are a couple of ways. Remember, while some of your fears are legit—such as being in the same room with a tiger—most fears are mental illusions and lies you made up. Other negative thoughts to learn to get rid of are feelings of guilt, anger, loneliness, jealousy, not being good enough, feeling that nobody loves me or cares about me, etc. When you allow your negative thoughts to get stuck in your head, they can cause you to hurt others physically or verbally, or hurt yourself via suicide, or they can manifest as a heart attack, tumors, backaches, headaches, cancer, and much more. Getting rid of your mental illusions by getting over yourself is what this section is about.

YOUR MIND (Examining and making changes in your beliefs, behaviors, attitudes, and effective creation)

Again, all lasting behavioral changes start with your mind and your beliefs. Your mind tells your body what to do and where to focus, whether you should think about the object level or the invisible spiritual energy level in a balanced way. So if you are doing something but you are not getting the results that you want, then you should examine your beliefs to see if they need improvement or adjusting, so you can start changing your behavior accordingly. Your minds' thoughts can affect your body because your brain is connected to your body, which is connected to the spiritual energy that physicists say everything is made of inside. We all need to learn how our body parts work best when they are in sync, going in the same positive direction, and working together as one whole unit to achieve our happiness goals faster.

The reason there are no courses you can take on this topic so we can improve our human efficiency rate is because our expert scientists and educators haven't discovered the connection between our body parts yet and how they work better together as one unit. Most religions, not all, are actually more advanced in this topic of our connectivity, especially with our connection to our invisible spiritual energy level that, according to physics, everything is made of.

Remember, thoughts are energy. Thought energy has both direction and vibrational speed. Positive, high-energy thoughts go up one direction, like water vapor molecules that are vibrating really fast; and negative, low-energy thoughts go down the opposite direction, like water molecules of an ice cube that are vibrating really slowly. God's unconditional love is positive high energy. Thoughts of love, forgiveness (*when you release your negative thoughts*), and creation elevate your energy level so that your molecules vibrate and move faster, which causes you to be more active.

When my daughter was a teenager, she used to let her negative thinking overwhelm her and had severe panic attacks because her mind was so focused on the object level, constantly judging it, and she did not know how to control her thoughts. As a result, she was often depressed and slept a lot. Then when she started seeing various psychiatrists, they prescribed antidepressant drugs for her, but that only made her panic attacks worse, and she got addicted to the drugs and became suicidal. I have a friend who, because her depression was so severe, unless she was on meds, she'd just sleep all day, and she's been on antidepressants for over fifteen years! Our society has become so depressed, that many adults (*30 million Americans*) today are on some kind of prescription or illegal drugs. *(See articles at the end of the SUMMARY section titled: "US Antidepressant Use Jumps 65 percent in 15 Years," "Recent Study Confirms That Antidepressants Increase Suicide Risk," "EXPOSED: Our dangerous dependency on antidepressant," "Making Money from Addiction: 30 Million Americans On Antidepressants. Twenty Facts on America's Big Pharma Nightmare," "The Half-Trillion-Dollar Depression," "Money For Nothing.")*

By being made in God's image, you were given a mind, which allows you the freedom and free will to choose to follow Him by controlling your mind's mental focus toward Him in the invisible realm of energy by being positive like Him, immersed in unconditional love, peace, creation, and our oneness. Conversely, you can choose to go the opposite direction and be negative all the time, immersed in hate, anger, destruction, separation, and have chaos in your life by putting your mental focus primarily on the temporary object level of chaos and drama. Only you can control where you place your mental focus. People whose mental focus is only in the world as separate objects are often lonely people who are always looking to fit in or looking for love or attention or happiness from other objects, which are all temporary, such as people, drugs, liquor, sex, etc. It's your choice, and it's your responsibility where you place your mental focus—nobody else's. You can blame others or God, but ultimately, you are where you are because of the choices you have made based on your subconscious and conscious thoughts, which most likely are not working for you. Otherwise, you would have peace, love, happiness, and good health in your life already.

For example, it wasn't too long ago that women in the USA were not allowed to vote (1920) or work certain jobs or get an education. The situation was the same with people of color. We all need to look at our individual beliefs as well as the things society is feeding us as truth, and then we need to ask ourselves whether this is working for us as a whole or not. If it's not working, be open to changing your beliefs so it does work. Do not just accept beliefs and allow yourself to be automatically swept away with anything that society feeds you, such as your religion, your politics, etc. Look at what TV advertisers are telling you; you need drugs, you need to live in a mansion, you need to weigh ninety pounds, you need plastic surgery, etc. Because we don't have all those things, our entire society is depressed. It's all crap! Don't buy the stories and ads they are trying to sell you. Those things won't make you happy or give you mental peace. If anything, a bigger house and a more expensive car are just going to give you more mental stress since now you have a huge mortgage and car loan to pay for every month. Unless you are able to pay cash, they're not going to give you mental peace or happiness. This is one reason so many celebrities, once rich and famous, commit suicide. *(See: "100+ List of Celebrities Who Killed Themselves," ranker.com).*

Here's another example. In the entertainment industry, we always hear about couples getting married, getting divorced, and getting married and divorced again. This is evidence that just because a person is rich doesn't mean they are going to be happy. These people are our role models, not just for ourselves but also for our children, so it's no wonder that 50 percent of all marriages end in divorce. It is our responsibility to question whether our society is working or not working and whether they are promoting love and unity with all or separation and destruction. So please, **be conscious of who you are following.**

God is Love and He Gives Us Free Will

*And we have known and believed the love that God hath to us. **God is love [invisible level]**, and he that dwelleth in love dwelleth in God and God in him.*
1 John 4:16, KJV

*A new commandment I give you, that you love one another: just as I have loved you, you also are to love one another **[in the object level]**.*
–John 13:34, ESV

John 4:16 and John 13:34 are my two favorite verses in the Bible because they are so simple to remember—it's all about LOVE! So, if you have a difficult time remembering Bible verses like I do, don't worry, the only one you have to remember is to learn to **LOVE EVERYBODY UNCONDITIONALLY, NO MATTER WHAT,** the way God loves us all. That's it, so simple! John 4:16 just says that **God is love**; therefore, the only commandment we have to remember on how to treat others on the object level, is to bring out God's unconditional love from the inside, out to others on the outside world of objects (John 13:34), by learning to love everybody the way God loves us unconditionally.

Knowing that there is only one commandment for me to remember, gave me a sense of peace because I didn't have to remember the Ten Commandments anymore since I had a hard time just remembering three. I just use the Ten Commandments (*e.g., not to lie, not to kill, not to commit adultery, etc.*) as rules and guidelines to what it means to act and behave lovingly to everyone at the object level on the outside. The Ten Commandments are not rules for us to abide in so that God can love us accordingly, as some churches teach. No, the Ten Commandments and all the other Bible verses about love, are just verses to teach us *how to act and treat people lovingly on the outside at the visible object level, and how that might look like on the outside* if we do not know how to be loving to others. For example, 1 Corinthians 13:4–5 (NIV) explains love this way: *"Love is patient, love is kind. It does not envy, it does not boast, it is not proud. It does not dishonor others, it is not self-seeking, it is not easily angered, it keeps no record of wrongs."* At the same time, we are supposed to rely on God's love from the inside invisible level for our own source of love. John 4:16 (NIV) says, *"And so we know and rely on the love God has for us."* Not on human love, which has restrictions and limits. For example, most people think, "I will only love you if you act the way I act, believe in what I believe, and do as I say."

We must learn to focus our minds on God's unconditional love for us, because most people do not know how to love each other unconditionally and eternally the way God loves us, since we're not taught in school. Not knowing and understanding this form of love is why so many people are mentally sick and are suffering and why so many commit suicide. Their mental focus is getting love from the outside world full of limits, like from other people, drugs, liquor, sex, which are all temporary, instead of accessing God's eternal love that exists inside all things already.

You have to be careful though, as there are a lot of religions, including some Christian churches, that actually teach the *God of hate*—that God's love is limited to only it's followers and that God hates everybody else, and that he hates gays, and on and on with the hate. John 4:16, says "God is love." It doesn't say, "God is love, except for the Jews, the Muslims, the Buddhist, the infidels, the non- believers, the gays, the aliens, etc." We don't need a God that hates because I think we can all do *hate* pretty well on our own; we don't need Bible instructions for that. We have to remember that in the invisible spiritual energy of God, because everything there is invisible, there is nothing to judge, there are no separate religions, no people, no countries, and no objects at all. So make sure to **look for a religion that teaches about the "God of Unconditional Love,"** when choosing a religion to follow.

What we all need, which would be a miracle, is if we all learn God's unconditional love that exists inside all things (*at the **invisible** spiritual energy level*), as well as learn to love everybody else unconditionally on the outside (*in the **visible** object level*) at 100 percent. *We have to remember that God's energy resides inside all our enemies too*, even when our enemies may not be aware of that or behave the way we want them to behave. This is why we need to *forgive them and love them anyway*, since we are not taught in school how to use our minds to improve and control our thinking. This is the hardest part about love to learn for most people, but it's one we all must learn to master if we want to have long-lasting eternal love, mental peace, and happiness in our own lives. **This will also help heal our body, mind, and energy back together as ONE whole unit in our MINDS, through unconditional love for all.** There is no other way! No amount of antidepressant drugs can make a person feel mentally whole and loved, without understanding our connection to God's universe and how it works. We have to imagine, by refocusing our mind's eye, on God through (*inside, where the invisible energy of God resides*) all things and people, including our enemies, as Ephesians 4:6 (NIV) says,

> *"**ONE God** and Father of ALL, who is **over ALL and through [inside] ALL and in [inside] ALL.**"*

The statement "no one comes to the Father but through me," just means **inside** him beyond the atomic level in the invisible spiritual energy level, but again, this is true for everybody. To know God, you have to imagine God's invisible spiritual energy inside **ALL objects,** through their physical bodies, or what Einstein calls the illusion. If everything is made out of invisible spiritual energy, that means God also *exists inside ALL things*, including you and me, not just Jesus, the way it's taught in most Christian religions. There are many Bible verses that support this interpretation, like Ephesians 4:6 above and Luke 17:21 (NIV) which states that:

> *"**The kingdom of God is within [inside] you.**"*

This means we are all together as ONE invisible energy force field in God, since everything is made from his invisible spiritual energy that according to physics, was never created and cannot be destroyed; therefore, we are ALL eternal in God the universe. This is why there are over sixty Bible verses that refer to us ALL as God's *children,* since we are all made from the same spiritual energy as God, just like any family with children who are made of the same DNA. Jesus knew He was just another brother in God's family when He said, and I'm paraphrasing John 14:12-14: *You can do what I can do but even better (due to human evolution over time), if you believe and learn my teachings about how to use your body parts properly.* This is also why, as God's children, we are referred to in the Bible as **mini-gods**, with a small letter "g" in Psalm 82:6 and John 10:34,

> *"**You are gods [mini-gods]; you are all children of the Most High.**"*

We all need to understand this at 100 percent or as humans, we will remain in darkness and cannot evolve to the next level generation of who we really are as mini-*gods (here to create our own perspective of our own universe)* and not knowing how to use our body parts more effectively like Jesus. God loves us so much that He gave us minds to choose to follow Him in His positive direction so that we can choose either to have love, peace, joy, and abundance *(focused on the invisible spiritual energy level where unconditional love resides)* or to go in the negative direction and live in fear, pain, and chaos *(focused mainly on the object level where love is rare, full of limits and conditions).* Because He loves us unconditionally, He gave us our own individual minds so that we have the freedom to choose our own perspective and our own ability to create our own reality. This is His gift to us, but we have to learn to use it properly if we want love, happiness, and peace in our lives, instead of chaos.

Unconditional love means He loves us no matter what; even if we choose to not follow Him, He loves us anyway. Unconditional love means He loves us just because He wants to, without having any expectations from us or requiring anything in return. God loves us all unconditionally no matter what we believe or do not believe, what we do or do not do, or whether we are good or bad. God is love, period! If this is a difficult concept for you to understand, think of how loving parents love their babies. Even though all the baby can do is eat, burp, and poop, they still love their baby no matter what. You've got to remember that **we are all God's children** and that He is inside us all as energy/spirit, which is why He loves us unconditionally. This kind of love is the highest form of energy level you can have, and we can choose it if we want, when we *learn to be mentally one with God and have a two-way loving relationship with Him.*

Because we are part of the whole universal energy, and we are made of the same energy as God, we create chaos for ourselves when we choose to be at odds with Him by moving in the opposite direction of God's directional energy. It's like being in the middle of the ocean. You can choose to panic and drown, or you can work with it and relax, and let the ocean help you float with ease. God works the same way. You can choose to learn to either work with Him, be immersed in His unconditional love, or work against Him. The choice is yours to make. It's always been your choice. However, most of us just don't know that because we mostly operate on an automatic, subconscious level, mostly focused on the material world of objects. It's time to wake up and start thinking for yourself and take back control of your mind and your life, by being aware of your thinking—and then controlling it so it's going in a loving direction.

You might ask, then, why would it matter to follow Him then? The answer is whether you want mental peace, love, and abundance in your life or not; it's your choice. It's your own peace of mind that is at stake here, not God's or anybody else's because you get to choose how you want to live your own life. Your mental stability, your physical health, and your entire life are your own responsibilities. Again, God loves you so much that He gave you the freedom to choose how high or how low you want your energy to go. Heaven (*high energy level focused on the invisible level*) or hell (*low energy primarily focused on the chaotic visible object level*), are all created in your mind. You get to choose to create a life of heaven or hell, depending on which direction you have chosen to place your mental focus—either positive: high LOVE (*ALL inclusive*) energy; or negative: low HATE (*highly exclusive*) energy level, mainly focused on the visible object level chaos.

If you choose to follow and put your mental focus on moving in the same positive direction as God's invisible spiritual energy level, immersed in his unconditional love for ALL, then you will create a loving, happy, peaceful life for yourself. This is creating heaven on earth, no matter where you are in your life or your economic status or what you've done or didn't do. On the other hand, if you choose to be negative, you will create a living hell for yourself by choosing to be unhappy, stressed, and sickly, and you will always be struggling, focused only on the object level where everything seems to be in broken pieces. Believe me, going against the cosmos is a living hell. I went through this with my negative thoughts about my relationship with my husband, my father, my brother, and people at work. If you choose to practice negativity, separation, and destruction, you will continue to suffer until you consciously choose to change the direction of your energy flow. It's your choice. Actually, most people are thinking subconsciously. They just need to wake up and choose for themselves which way to go: peace or chaos, positive or negative, believing in the invisible God energy or believing only in the temporary visible world of material objects, where there's only chaos, wars, divorces, and fighting.

Because we are so used to using only our five senses, it is very difficult for most people to understand that invisible energy level has a particular flow—because it's not visible. It's easy to see the effects of the energy flow of the ocean's current or the wind current, but it's not so easy when it comes to the energy flow of relationships or money, which are also energy. Here's a simple way to tell if you are with the flow or not. If the creation of relationships or money is easy for you, then you are going with His energy flow. If you are having a difficult time with people, work, relationships, or whatever, then you are going in the opposite direction as God's love flow, which is causing constriction in your life flow either in spirit, mind, or body, or a combination of the three. Find out where the constriction is, and change its negative direction, so that life becomes easy and effortless for you.

IT'S ALL ABOUT LOVE – Three Distinct Relationships
Why Is Agape Love So Confusing?

I love to watch various religious shows on a regular basis to learn and to get inspired. I don't often stick to one, however, because I'm kind of selective and only believe thoughts that make sense to me. Anyway, I noticed there's this conflict between preachers who teach that God loves us ALL unconditionally through God's grace or love alone, and not by needing to do anything in the physical world of objects; therefore, we can ignore the Ten Commandments altogether. The other teaching is that God's love is earned and it's only through our own good works, like how well we follow the Ten Commandments, that God loves us in return. While I believe God loves us unconditionally, I do not believe we should ignore the Ten Commandments altogether. After all, "Though shall not kill or lie" are good rules to follow. Then I realized the mass confusion has to do with the source of who loves whom and how we should apply the various Bible verses. So, (1) How God loves us? (2) How are we to love God? (3) How are we to love others? These are distinct relationships, and the Bible has versus that apply appropriately. So I hope the diagram below helps clear this up.

1. How God Loves Us? – Unconditionally:

Because God is pure love, and He created us as part of His own spiritual energy inside us; therefore, the only thing there is inside of us is His love for us, which is forever eternal, according to the Bible. Another way to explain this is the way physics defines energy that it cannot be created or destroyed, which means He's always loved us and that His love for us has no conditions or rules on the invisible, energy level. Remember, God's love is spiritual energy that is inside all things. His love is not at the object level that has separatism, conditions, and limits, like human love has for one another, which can easily be broken. The source of God's love comes from the inside, not from the outside visible object level.

> For **God so loved the world** (visible objects).
> –John 3:16, KJV

> *I have loved you with an everlasting love;*
> *therefore, I have continued my faithfulness to you.*
> –Jeremiah 31:3, ESV

> *And so we know and rely on the love God has for us.*
> **God is Love.**
> **Whoever lives in love lives in God, and God in them**.
> –1 John 4:16, KJV

2. **How We Are To Love God?** – With All Our Heart and Soul

We are supposed to love God first, with all our heart and soul, unconditionally, then ourselves and family, then others, as we love ourselves.

> *Thou shalt **love the Lord thy God with all thy heart,***
> ***and with all thy soul,** and with all thy strength, and with*
> *all thy mind; **and thy neighbour** [other people] as thyself.*
> –Luke 10:27, KJV

3. **How We Are To Love People?** – As Ourselves

We are supposed to bring out God's love from the inside out, by loving ourselves and others unconditionally, as God loves us unconditionally, meaning with no conditions, no matter what! If you can think of other people as your brother and sister under God, it makes it easier, because God only sees us all as one family under God. There are many Bible verses that you can use as guidelines on how we are to behave and act lovingly toward each other on the object level if you don't know how. If you come from an abusive family like me, and schools refuse to teach this stuff, you probably only know how to fight, but you probably don't know how to treat people with love and kindness on the object level. For example, the Ten Commandments or these verses below are helpful guides on how to act lovingly toward others so you don't hurt yourself or anybody else:

*I say to you who hear, **Love your enemies,***
do good to those who hate you.
−Luke 6:27, ESV

***Above all, keep loving one another** earnestly,*
*since **love covers a multitude of sins.***
−1 Peter 4:8, ESV

Love is patient and kind; love does not envy or boast; it is
not arrogant or rude. It does not insist on its own way; it is
not irritable or resentful; it does not rejoice at wrongdoing,
but rejoices with the truth. Love bears all things, believes all
things, hopes all things, endures all things.
−1 Corinthians13:4–7, ESV

See what great love the Father has lavished on us,
*that we should be called **children of God**! And that is*
what we are! The reason the world does not know us is that
it did not know him.
−John 3:1, NIV

To develop pure and unconditional love between husband
and wife, parent and child, friend and friend, self and all,
is the lesson we have come on earth to learn.
-Sri Sri Paramahansa Yogananda, Journey to Self-realization

15 Great Principles Shared by All Religions

1. The Golden Rule / Law of Reciprocity – The cornerstone of religious understanding. "Do unto others what you would have them do unto you." – *Christianity*

2. Honor Thy Father and Mother – Knowing them is the key to knowing ourselves. The day will come when we shall wish we had known them better.

3. Speak the Truth – "Sincerity is the way of heaven, and to think how to be sincere is the way of a man." – *Confucius*

4. It's More Blessed to Give than to Receive – Generosity, charity and kindness will open an individual to an unbounded reservoir of riches.

5. Heaven is Within – "Even as the scent dwells within the flower, so God within thine own heart forever abides." – *Sikhism*

6. Love Thy Neighbor / Conquer With Love / All You Need is Love – Acts of faith, prayer and deep meditation provide us with the strength that allows love for our fellow man to become an abiding part of our lives. Love is a unifying force.

7. Blessed Are the Peacemakers – When people live in the awareness that there is a close kinship between all individuals and nations, peace is the natural result.

8. You Reap What You Sow – This is the great mystery of human life. Aware or unaware, all are ruled by this inevitable law of nature.

9. Man Does Not Live by Bread Alone – The blessings of life are deeper than what can be appreciated by the senses.

10. Do No Harm – If someone tries to hurt another, it means that she is perceiving that person as something separate and foreign from herself.

11. Forgiveness – The most beautiful thing a man can do is to forgive wrong. – *Judaism*

12. Judge Not, Lest Ye Be Judged – This principle is an expression of the underlying truth that mankind is one great family, and that we all spring from a common source.

13. Be Slow to Anger – Anger clouds the mind in the very moments that clarity and objectivity are needed most. "He who holds back rising anger like a rolling chariot, him I call a real driver; others only hold the reins." – *Buddha*

14. There is But One God / God is Love – Nature, Being, The Absolute. Whatever name man chooses, there is but one God. All people and all things are of one essence.

15. Follow the Spirit of the Scriptures, Not the Words – "Study the words, no doubt, but look behind them to the thought they indicate; And having found it, throw the words away, as chaff when you have sifted out the grain." – *Hinduism*

All credit to Jeffrey Moses. For a full list, please visit http://www.onenessonline.com/

Keeping Your Field of Vision (Bubble) Clean & Clear

Clear your mind by being neutral or positive at all times in all areas of your life, not just at work or at home or while golfing or doing whatever you are into. Your mind cannot separate your feelings and thoughts into separate compartments; you only have one mind and one body. The key is to be positive in all areas of your life. You need to neutralize or make positive any negative thoughts of the past and create passion in any future projects you might want and are trying to create; otherwise, they will be difficult to materialize.

> But he that **hateth his brother is in darkness**, and
> walketh in darkness, and knoweth not whither he goeth,
> because that **darkness hath blinded his eyes**.
> −1 John 2:11, KJV

Taking Care Of Your Bubble:

Your bubble, as I said, is always just limited to your field of vision—what you can see. This is your present moment. Don't bog down your mind with past and future thoughts of worries because they cloud your bubble, and therefore, they cloud your ability to make the best choices and decisions at that moment. Also, negative thoughts slow you down and distract you from creating and doing anything positive at work or with your family or where ever you are at that moment. Living with negative thoughts is literally like driving through a fog. It's difficult to see where one is going because it's too foggy and dark, so accidents happen. How often have you collided and fought with people because of your uncontrolled anger, fear, or hatred, and how often have they collided with you because of their uncontrolled negative thoughts?

To illustrate what your bubble is, let's say you move from your kitchen to your bedroom. If you burned your hand in the kitchen, you need to let it go and accept what happened and forgive whoever was involved. Once you are in the bedroom, that becomes your new present moment, and the kitchen then becomes your past because you are no longer in the kitchen. The kitchen is no longer in your field of vision, so whatever pains happened moments earlier in the kitchen are now in the past. So train yourself to let go of your past pains through forgiveness and love so that you can have mental peace. It's really dangerous to allow yourself to get mentally stuck in negative past thoughts because some people can go into a downward spiral that can be extremely difficult to get out of unless they get professional help.

You need to learn to stop carrying your entire lifetime in your mind; it's very draining and ineffective, and it will make you mentally and physically sick. This doesn't work for anybody! Also, blaming won't do you any good because it only keeps you stuck in the past. What's done is done; learn to let it go. Forgiveness is more useful because it allows you to let go of your past thoughts so you can go on with your life. Holding on to past pains only hurts you repeatedly mentally and physically and will drag you to the ground. So learn to forgive your past. The key to living moment by moment and keeping your bubble clean is forgiveness.

Remember, YOUR bubble is your responsibility and no one else's. Only you are responsible for keeping it clean and clear. You can also choose to keep it dirty and cloudy (remaining in darkness) by thinking negative thoughts. It's up to you. Observe your thoughts and your actions. Keep them positive. People always wear their thoughts, and it shows up in their bodies as bad or good behaviors. For example, I work with a lady who is in a constantly bad mood, and as a result, nobody wants to be around her. She is so automatic in her behavior that she's not even aware that she is exhibiting it. Every day, I purposely choose to avoid her by taking a different route when I see her. If I have to be in the same meeting with her, I purposely choose to ignore her bad comments because I choose to be in a peaceful and happy mood at every moment of my life. Within my bubble, I always choose to love the people and the things that I do. Therefore, I am almost always at peace now. Because now I know that *only **I AM responsible** for my own thoughts and actions. And every day I purposely keep them in control by being positive, focused only on the moment in time, because that is what I choose to be: a loving, peaceful, forgiving person.*

Remember, if you are not happy or do not have peace in all areas of your life, it's because you chose and created that world for yourself whether you did so subconsciously or consciously. You are responsible for all of it! Don't blame others for it—doing that is ineffective, since you are the only one in control of your own mind.

If you have to deal with people who are constantly in a bad mood, avoid them. Remember, only you are in control of your own moods. So start taking control of your life by learning to control your mind. If you can't avoid people who are always in a bad mood, learn to ignore their bad moods because their moods are their own responsibility, not yours. Try to be kind and loving anyway, even though it's hard. Trust me, I know. Mostly, I avoid negative people.

What also helps is changing how you view people. For example, instead of thinking that my co-worker is doing this to me and getting angry with her, I simply choose to forgive her because I know she does not know that she's even doing this as she is on automatic pilot and does not even know and realize she is hurting others by her negative attitude. I think she learned this bad behavior at some point in her past, and because she hasn't learned to forgive and let go of her pains, she wears the pain and anger everywhere she goes and takes it out on everybody else without even realizing she's doing it. **(Actually, most people are like this since we are not taught in school how to control our minds since our scientists and educators have not discovered it yet. So, it's not people's fault; they don't know how.)** Because I know better now, I am able to forgive her and love her no matter what. This is what unconditional love is. I will not let her bad moods directly affect my moods, or for that matter the mood of anybody who comes into my bubble. If I do, once I realize I'm letting somebody else's bad mood affect me, I stop it very quickly, and the bad mood doesn't stay that long in me because I know that only I am responsible for my own thoughts and actions. This is how I remain at peace. This is how I am able to control my mind, by being aware of the thoughts I allow going in and out of my mind.

Positive people do not allow themselves to get stuck too long in a negative energy level because they know better. Choose it! It's a mindset. Which do you choose? By choosing how to act and accepting responsibility for all your own thoughts and actions, you can take control of your life. Blaming others puts the responsibility on others; however, only you can make yourself happy and peaceful—no one else can—that's why keeping your bubble clean and clear is your responsibility. **It is your mind, your brain, your own perspective of your own reality, all under your control.**

Subconscious Thinking

Subconscious thinking is an automatic reaction to situations out of habit and negative beliefs. The key word here is *automatic*. Most people perform at a subconscious level, like zombies. Most of the time they react to whatever comes their way without even realizing how automatic they are being because there is so much negativity out there on TV, radio, schools, politics, and all over our society and the world. We allow ourselves, without being conscious of our thinking, to be swept away in the negativity that surrounds us. We often don't stop to think that perhaps these negative thoughts are the reason that we, ourselves, are so negative or the reason things are not working for us. Also, we often don't consider that there may be a better way. To stop the madness, you need to start taking control of your own life by becoming aware, by being conscious of the conversations you are letting into your mind. From now on, just observe yourself and your thoughts.

When my daughter was a baby, while getting into the freeway, I was stopped by the highway patrol. When the officer stopped me to write a ticket, I asked him what I did wrong. He said, "You were driving in the carpool lane and you don't have a passenger." You see, I had forgotten that I did not have my daughter in the car seat that day. Because I'm usually driving with her, I was used to driving in the carpool lane. A month later, when I had to go to traffic school, the officer said that most accidents happen within a ten-mile radius of where people live because they are on automatic pilot. Because they often drive the same streets over and over again to go to work or school or whatever, they often don't pay attention to what's going on while driving. That's why so many accidents happen to people who are near their homes. You see, most people are unaware and are ignorant of what they are doing most of the time because they are on automatic pilot, but we are always quick to judge, and even that is automatic. You need to wake up and be aware of what you are doing and thinking if you ever hope to stop the mental craziness and accidents you are creating in your life. And, as I have said, you are doing it to yourself—nobody else is. **You are the only one in control of your own mind. Do not give away your power of control** to others by blaming and believing the wrong people. **Take back your power!**

> *Having the understanding darkened, **being alienated from the life of God** [not knowing God] through the **ignorance** that is in them, **because of the blindness of their heart**.*
> –Ephesians 4:18, KJV

Sometimes, making changes at the subconscious level can be done by simply changing your understanding or perception about an issue. An example of this is the time I changed my perception of God from one of an almighty superior being from whom I was separated, who was to be feared, and who lived in heaven, up above the clouds, watching my every move and waiting for me to screw up so He could punish me and beat the crap out of me and throw lightning bolts at me. I shifted to believing in a God who is loving, supportive, guiding, and is made of a creative energy force of which I am a part of because he lived inside me as invisible spiritual energy, therefore allowing me to create in the same way He creates. When I understood this, it was instantaneous for me at the subconscious and molecular level.

Another way of changing your subconscious is through affirmations. Affirmations are simply repetitive positive thoughts that you follow until the change is made and becomes permanent at the molecular level. I have found that the shorter the affirmations, the easier they are to repeat and the faster they seem to work for me in getting the message through at a deeper level. For example, when I was trying to accept that everything is part of God, since He is in everything as invisible spiritual energy, the affirmation I kept repeating as I touched every object (the walls, the telephone, the steering wheel, my children, my husband) was, "I love you, God." It seemed that I was repeating this at least a million times a day until it became a part of me at the subconscious and molecular level. I needed to learn that God's spiritual energy was in everything and everywhere. Just a caveat, do not do this loudly; people will think you are crazy. Doing it silently works just as well.

Getting personal coaching from experts who know how to help you extract bad data or negative thoughts and stories you are mentally stuck with can also help you change your perspective of your past. Also, acting or pretending until the positive change becomes a natural habit is another way of changing. There are many different methods of change; you just need to find one that works for your personality. But whatever you choose, do not give up before you get the results you want. The biggest problem people have is that they often give up on themselves too soon.

Be careful if you choose legal or illegal drugs or liquor as an option, as a way to stop your thinking. These are just temporary fixes because after the drugs wear off, you will still need to keep taking the drugs because the thoughts will still be there, and over time your thoughts accumulate. This is why you will need to keep taking the drugs to make the thoughts temporarily stop. And the side effects of these drugs can be detrimental to your health and life because they are addictive and can cause suicidal thoughts. If they work for you, that's great; but if not, all I'm saying is, why not learn to control and manage your thinking naturally, the way God intended for us to function more efficiently instead?

Unless you face your problems head-on, you cannot heal. I know because my daughter became addicted to antidepressants that the so-called expert doctors prescribed to her for four years, and instead of getting better, she became worse. Not only were the drugs addictive, but she also became suicidal because of them. The same thing happened with my brother-in-law who had throat cancer. After his chemo, he was prescribed antidepressants, and he too became addicted and suicidal for years because of the drugs. He became so angry with both his oncologist and psychiatrist because he felt he did not even need the drugs. I have a friend who's been taking antidepressants for fifteen years! She's finally reduced her need for the meds from reading and doing the exercises from this book. I believe if you're still on antidepressant drugs after two or four years or more, that means the meds are just treating the symptoms, not the real source of the problem, which is uncontrolled thought energy stuck in the mind. In this case, you just need to learn to get the thoughts out of your mind to get them unstuck naturally using various methods suggested in this book since we are not taught the process in school.

See articles at the end of the summary section titled, "US Antidepressant Use Jumps 65 Percent in 15 Years," "Recent Study Confirms That Antidepressants Increase Suicide Risk," "Exposed: Our Dangerous Dependency on Antidepressants"; and online: "Making Money from Addiction: 30 Million Americans On Antidepressants. Twenty Facts on America's Big Pharma Nightmare," End of the American Dream (2014); "The Half-Trillion-Dollar Depression," *The New York Times Magazine*; and "Money for Nothing," *U.S. News*.

Conscious Thinking

Conscious thinking is what happens when you stop and really think about your options in handling a particular situation and then choosing what you think is the best option at the time by *being aware* of your thinking and your environment by being present, within your bubble or field of vision and not be easily distracted with nonsense. And if you believe in spiritual consciousness, your options are unlimited because God is the universe of limitless abundance. The key word here is *your choosing*.

For example, I am now more conscious or aware of my surroundings when I am driving, being mentally present, and not allowing myself to be easily distracted with fast or slow drivers and people who cut me off or with my kids or thinking about work when I shouldn't be. I am driving more carefully and slowly than I used to and paying more attention to my environment at each moment. As a result, I am a safer driver and not getting tickets like I used to.

Negative Thinking

Negative thoughts produce negative results;
while positive thoughts produce positive results.

Negative thoughts and feelings that you need to overcome are fear, hatred, anger, stress, depression, worry, blame, complaining, and resignation: "I can't do this or that." "It's too hard." "I'm not smart enough or good enough." "I don't deserve this." "I'm better than they are." "They're stupid." "I'm stupid." "They're ugly." "I'm ugly." "I'm too fat." "They're too fat." "Women can't do this." "I can't lose weight." "I can't stop smoking." "I can't stop drinking." Every negative thought that comes out of your mind, whether it's targeted at someone else or yourself, is very destructive to others and to yourself. These thoughts separate you from others, and they are extremely limiting and sometimes dangerous. For example, I did not speak to my brother for six years because I was so *angry* with him for something he had said about me to my other siblings. My friend committed suicide at twenty-eight years old because he was mentally stuck in the negative thought that he was a *mistake*.

All negative thoughts from your mind are reflections of how you really feel about yourself inside, even when you target your words at others. For example, if you call people *fat or skinny*, it's because you really don't like your own weight, and so you like calling others names because it temporarily makes you feel better to call someone else fat or skinny. Out of habit, like a drug addict, you need to have a fix, so you keep calling people *fat or skinny* to feel good about yourself. Because of this, calling people names and judging them becomes a vicious cycle. I saw this with my older daughter when she was in high school. She was always judging the models and movie stars on TV. She was constantly judging whether they were pretty or ugly, or fat or skinny; but in reality, this was just a reflection of thoughts about herself because, like most teenagers, she put so much focus on how she looked that she was always saying things like, "I hate my looks." "I hate my legs." Because she was what she believed, she was miserable as a result.

Negative thoughts cloud your judgment and your bubble, and this can make you sick, which I spoke about earlier. That's why negative people tend to be less accomplished than positive people. I remember in college how I failed the SAT entrance exam the first time I took it. I'm one of those people who have panic attacks before and during a timed test. My brain just goes berserk, and I would keep thinking negatively that I would not pass the test or that this was too hard. When I found out the college provided another SAT testing just for people whose English was not their first language, and that was not timed, I signed up immediately. I used the race card (okay, I'm not ashamed). I told them I was not born here and that Tagalog was my first language, and they let me retake the test, even though English was the only language I knew. The fact that it wasn't being timed gave me such peace of mind and allowed me to think only of the test material, so I was able to complete the test faster than if it were timed. Apparently, I scored so high in my SAT test the second time, that when I was trying to sign up for an English class, they told me I didn't need to because my test score was so high. If I had not found another way of taking the SAT test, there is no way I would have ever been an engineer, even though I was capable of taking the classes.

Another time I was supposed to take the state exam to be a realtor, but my panic attack was so bad that I just gave up and never took it even though I had already paid for it and had taken all the classes. I could not do it. I let my negative fear and stress consume me. So basically, I failed myself because I couldn't control my mental stress.

Now, with my husband weird things happen to his body when he gets mentally stressed out. For example, about a few weeks before he was supposed to take his brokerage exam, one of his eyes got so swollen it was popping out. His doctor gave him antibiotics because he thought maybe it was a bee sting. When that did not work, the doctors wanted to surgically remove his eyes because they were worried he was going to go blind anyway if it continued to get bigger. Luckily my husband ran out of the hospital fast. Two weeks later, after he passed his state exam, his eyes simply went back to normal. When my brother's eye popped out like my husband's, he told his doctor he thought it was poison ivy since he had just come back from camping. But his eye doctor told him no, that's not poison ivy, that's from stress! And I know this to be true because my brother was being threatened with a potential lawsuit at the time by his apartment tenant, but once it was settled, his eyes popped back in. This is how our mental stress can make us so sick if we are not careful, or it keeps us from doing what we want sometimes.

This is because thoughts are invisible spiritual energy forces that originate from our physical brains that are connected to our physical bodies. That is why what you think affects your physical body, because energy, according to physics, just changes forms. This is because all three—your body, mind, and invisible spiritual energy (*that everything in the universe is made of, according to physics*) are all connected as ONE whole unit. This is the key to understanding why and how you create your own negative hell or positive heaven in the universe. You get to choose how you get to live your life since you are the only one in control of your own mind and what thoughts come out of it, since you are the creator of your own universal reality.

Negative thoughts produce low energy levels in your body. They make you inactive rather than active, and therefore they make you less productive. Because negative thoughts are going against the grain and in the opposite direction as God's positive energy, they also slow down your energy's vibrational speed. Again, it's like swimming against the current; it's difficult. It's much easier when you swim with the current. Remember, energy has both direction and speed. Negative, low-energy thoughts slow you down. Negative thoughts limit what you can do and have. The negative or positive beliefs and thoughts you have subconsciously and consciously combined in your mind directly affect the things you will create in your life. In other words, your world as it appears to you is a reflection of your thoughts, both negative and positive. So, if your life isn't as abundant in love, peace, and joy as you would like it to be, using journaling exercises, examine your beliefs to see what limiting thoughts you have put inside your mind, then delete them.

> **For God is not the author of confusion, but of peace**
> *[in reference to the invisible energy level where there are*
> *no objects to judge].*
> —1 Corinthians 14:33, KJV

Positive Thinking

The most important positive thoughts that need to be maintained within your bubble are forgiveness (of your past), love (your moments), and creation (of your future). Even though these are not the only positive thoughts out there, they are the most important, and they must be practiced and mastered in your every moment, regardless of the situations you happen to be in. Positive thinking opens up your life to opportunities to learn and practice love and forgiveness and to create a life of abundance. As you practice love and forgiveness, they will become your new automatic behaviors, and peace will be the result.

Maintaining a positive attitude clears your bubble and your vision so that you are able to solve your problems at a faster rate. With a positive attitude, you are able to see answers that you couldn't see before because being positive magnifies your intuition and improves your ability to read God's messages or signs that show up when you talk to Him and ask Him questions, and pray for His help.

If you want to be successful in all areas of your life and live abundantly, you need to learn how to change your current energy level to a higher energy level. This is what spiritual writings call your higher self. Always reach for the highest energy level you can be. You can do it! It is easy once you learn to change your beliefs from ones that do not work to ones that work, such as from negative to positive and from hate or fear to love.

If you remember, we are all made out of invisible energy or spirit. There are laws in science and religion already in place that, when used concurrently, help us to understand and develop a better way of living, a way to help you reach your higher self—a better way to be. I will use water to illustrate what happens to its energy level when it is energized. When you remove heat from water, H_2O, it freezes and solidifies. Its shape is then bounded and limited to the container in which it resides. Remember, all atoms and molecules are always moving, according to science, and the only difference between the various states is the vibrational speed at which the atoms and molecules are operating. In ice, for example, the water molecules are compacted and moving so slowly that they appear solid. Because solid ice is very dense, there is very little space between the atoms for anything else to go through. In this state, they cannot interact much with their environment. Ice is hard to work with, it breaks easily, and its behavior is extremely predictable. However, if you add a little bit of heat to the same water molecules, you begin to energize them. The molecules begin to vibrate faster, and they become liquid. In a liquid state, the water molecules become easier to move, and there's more space between the atoms because it's not as dense as ice, but the liquid is still confined by the volume of its container, even though you can shape it to anything you want within the container.

Now, if you keep energizing the same water molecules by adding heat until it reaches its boiling point, what happens to the water? The water molecules evaporate; they become so energized and active that they begin moving and vibrating so quickly that you can't even see them anymore because there are more spaces between the atoms. In an open container, they have become boundless, invisible, and unlimited. They've joined the cosmos as one!

You too can join the cosmos, which is God! When you are able to reach and perform at your highest energy level of unconditional love, you can activate yourself so much that you can create miracles in your life. At this higher energy level, you will be able to create much more in a shorter amount of time than you could previously, simply by learning to love all and by learning how to work with God. You will realize that you are in this state when people ask you, "How do you do all that?"

In life—again because we are all made of energy, like water—we can change our energy level depending on how much love we have for ourselves and for others when we partner with God to co-create our life so that it is boundless, unlimited, and abundant. Love energizes us! Conversely, a lack of love lowers our energy levels. The more love you have inside of you and for others, the more you become like God.

Love unites us all together into one energy, one God, boundless and unlimited. Love allows us to perform at our highest level of energy. That's why positive people are able to create more than negative people; they have more energy, more love, and more passion for themselves and for the things they do. They don't waste their time with negative thoughts and pettiness because they are too busy focusing on creating their projects. So if you want to get out of depression, learn to love all. Get in alignment with God's energy flow of unconditional love.

In physics, *energy* is defined as the ability to do work; therefore, when you increase your energy level, you are able to do more. In other words, the more energy you have, the more you can work to create your projects and happiness goals; the less energy you have, the less energy you have to work and create for yourself and for others.

You can see then that having an abundant life has nothing to do with intelligence. It has to do with your energy level and the amount of positive energy of love you are able to produce within yourself so you can mentally focus on materializing your pet projects. If you can master these things so that they become your new automatic habits, your chances of success in meeting your goals will also be increased. The reason for this is that love unites people, and you need to be able to work with other people in order to be successful. After all, we are all God's children as equals. God does not love any one person or group any more than any other. Under God, we are all brothers and sisters, so we need to all treat each other as such. Those who have children and love them unconditionally understand this. As a parent of two, I don't love one child more than the other; I love them both equally no matter what they do or say. I love them no matter what, and that's how God loves us too.

We are all given gifts and talents that we can use to help each other succeed in meeting our goals. This is where your genius resides—within the gifts that were endowed upon you. Your purpose in life is to leave this place a better place than it was when you got here by creating a life of abundance for yourself and by helping others do the same. Like God, you can create your own Garden of Eden by using the gifts and talents God gave you to serve others. This is your function, and we all have different functions in life; however, we need to work together as one unit to make it all work together and to help it grow and evolve. It's like a bike, each part has a function, and all the parts have to be working together; otherwise, it will not work. This is the process of giving and taking. In life, you need to give yourself to others by helping them attain their own Garden of Eden, and at the same time, you will receive their help in creating your own Garden of Eden. It has to be a partnership because you cannot do it all alone. It's this partnership— with all, with everything, with God—that you have to develop if you want success in all areas of your life. For example, can you imagine how successful my business would be if I hated all men, everybody living outside of Orange County, and the other half of my political party? If I want a successful business, I cannot be limiting the people I do business with because everything is a partnership. And unless I learn to love everybody unconditionally, my business will not grow and succeed. That is why loving all people is so important.

Positive Attitudes To Live By

Forgiveness (the healing switch)

In order to help clear the cloud off your bubble, you need to be able to forgive yourself and others. As stated earlier, all changes need to begin with you, and they need to begin in your mind. Change the thoughts and beliefs stuck in your mind, so you can change the behaviors that are not working for you so you can create a new world that does work, simply by changing your perspectives.

For example, if you want to help others, **never try to use force** to change them, as this only causes them to want to hate you and fight you. You can only try to **teach** them so that you give them the freedom to choose whether to want to change on their own or not. This is a more loving way to go. However, if you have a problem with them, then **you** need to change because the problem is with **you,** with your perspectives and ideas about people. Also, I've learned that because not everybody learns the same way, you may not be the right teacher for them. For example, I'm a visual person, so I learn better through diagrams and pictures. Books with just words are difficult for me, as my brain has to translate the words into two or three-dimensional objects before I can understand. My husband and oldest daughter are both auditory, so they learn best when they listen to a person talk. Our old gardener was tactile, so she learned best through touch. Then there are those who are dyslexic, like my sister and nephew. On top of this, God gave everyone different gifts. That's why each person will need to find their own way that works for them and find the right teacher for themselves whenever they are trying to learn something. Because everybody is different. The point of all this is that we need to learn to let go of people and forgive them and not take everything so personally and seriously when they disagree with our views. This is love if you can learn this concept.

The way I learned to forgive was by changing my own perspective on forgiveness by coming up with a new understanding of it that worked for me. Once I realized that most people were operating by using their subconscious minds, that they didn't even realize they were on automatic pilot, and that most people did not know how the universe operated as a whole (since we are not taught in school how to use our body parts effectively), I was able to forgive everybody whom I thought ever hurt me. The picture that came to mind was of the moment when Jesus was being nailed to the cross and He said, *"Father, forgive them for they do not know what they do."* This is one of his most profound teachings for me. Because He's right, we don't know what the heck we're doing, since most of us live in the world of MADNESS, not knowing who we truly are, as mini-gods, all here to create our own perspective and reality of the universe. So being angry, hateful, and making ourselves sick is all unnecessary when we learn to control our minds and live in God's universe of win/win, LOVE, and ABUNDANCE; not the world of MADNESS based on limits and conditions and the win/lose way of uncontrolled automating thinking.

I figured that if Jesus could forgive these unthinking, automatic, subconsciously driven people who were about to kill him, then I could certainly forgive my husband, my abusive father, and my brother for hurting me as well. After all, I was once like them, living in darkness, not knowing how my body parts worked together best in God's unconditional love for all as ONE unit. So forgive people, and accept them for not knowing any better. Remember, we are not taught in school how to manage our thinking because our scientists and educators have not yet discovered that our thoughts are even real or how thoughts work naturally in God's universe. Therefore, there is no way they can teach us how to manage and control our thinking naturally so that we can all become better thinkers and better humans overall.

> *Then said Jesus, Father, **forgive** them[since we're not taught the importance of love in school]; for they know not what they do.*
> –Luke 23:34, KJV

People are like children to God because He is our source and creator. If you understand the relationship between LOVING parents to their children (*not all parents are loving*), then forgiveness will be easier to understand. With **loving** parents, we pretty much forgive our own kids no matter what they do, don't we? Even when they say, "I didn't know that," we still forgive them when they mess up. Like children, most of us are immature regarding our spirituality. God is like a parent to us. Even when we do things we shouldn't do, He forgives us anyway because He loves us all unconditionally, no matter what. God will not punish you or kill you if you do things you shouldn't do, as some religions teach and make you believe, because you are His child and He loves you unconditionally. God does not want you to be afraid of him because He wants you to go to Him with your concerns. If He punished you, as some religions teach, then that would only create fear in you, which would cause you to be too scared to go to Him for help with your problems. Think about it; would you kill a child that you created? Of course not. Not if you are a **loving** parent, anyhow.

God is about creating, growing, evolving, and loving. If, on the other hand, He killed off what He created, that would be like killing part of Himself because you are part of Him as invisible spiritual energy, and He is you at the same time, ALL together as ONE UNIT. What would be the point of creating you in the first place if He didn't love you? Would you cut off your own leg because you didn't like it anymore? Of course not! Well, actually, with so many movie stars going under the knife in our current society, cutting off body parts is becoming the norm. So many kids on social media are committing suicide because they want to look like these movie stars but they can't afford all the surgery that stars have to make themselves beautiful. But they aren't even real people anymore; they're more like plastic barbies. Don't buy this crap that they are selling you! Better to learn to love yourself instead. That's how you will find peace—no other way but through unconditional love for God, for ourselves, and for everybody else.

In one of Dr. Dyer's books, he says that the people you dislike the most are your soul mates because they push you to your limits. For example, when this lady at work was giving me a hard time about work, I grew to hate her really quickly. I hated to go to work because of her, and this caused me to be in a bad mood every day. Because of her, I learned forgiveness. I asked God to teach me forgiveness, which He did by bringing me a book by Dr. Dyer called, *Your Erroneous Zones*. Once I learned to forgive her, I forgave my brother, whom I was angry with and had not been in contact with for over six years. By forgiving him, I went from anger and hate to love. This was only possible because I chose to forgive him and to love him.

To reiterate, negative energy separates and destroys people and relationships, whereas, the positive energy of love unites people. And forgiveness allows you to switch from a negative to a positive energy flow. The first step to love is always forgiveness. You have to learn to forgive yourself and everybody that ever hurt you in order to learn to love and ultimately to attain mental peace. It is impossible to go forward without forgiving the past. Forgiveness is the key to going from negative thoughts to positive thoughts of love.

Forgiveness is like a switch in your mind that allows you to go from negative darkness to positive light. Without turning on that forgiveness switch, you cannot heal your pains, and you cannot learn to love yourself and others. Only through forgiveness can healing begin. Maintaining a negative attitude only hurts you and others in the long run. Sometimes, depending on how strong your anger and hate are and how often you repeat your negative stories to yourself, it will manifest in your body in the form of an illness. It keeps you stuck from being successful in the different areas of your life. It keeps you from experiencing the love and peace—which is God—that you deserve and crave. That is why positive people tend to be healthier than negative people. When positive people get sick, they don't stay sick for very long. This is because thoughts are energy, and energy changes forms, according to physics' definition of invisible energy.

When I was twenty-four years old, I was diagnosed with a brain tumor in my pituitary gland, the size of a pea, that my doctor said was growing. My first reaction was sheer panic "I'm going to die! I'm going to die! I'm going to die!" Then my doctor told me my blood pressure was high. And I yelled at him, "Yeah, what do you think? You just told me I have a brain tumor!" That was when I began to realize that maybe my thoughts affected my body because five minutes before the doctor told me I had a tumor, his nurse measured my blood pressure and said it was normal. The only thing that changed during the five minutes was the doctor saying the words, "You have a tumor."

Wow, how powerful were his few words, only four words, as I believed him. As a result, my blood pressure shot up. Then not only did I have a tumor; but I also had high blood pressure. Then I thought, "How did I get here, so messed up, with a body falling apart, dying, at only twenty-four years old?" I was only 105 lbs, so my weight was not the reason for my high blood pressure. I asked God, "Why me?" I had just graduated from college and started my engineering job six months earlier, so why now? For a moment, I was angry at God and blamed Him. Most of the conversation with the doctor was a blur because I was having a hard time concentrating. I was too busy having a private mental fight with God. Why me? What did I do to deserve this?

Anyway, my endocrinologist at that time said I needed to take these expensive pills twice a day for the rest of my life to control the growth of the tumor. I hate taking pills; I don't care if they are prescribed. Because of the type of person that I am—an engineer always trying to figure things out—I am always telling myself when things are not working for me, "There must be a better way." One day I heard a voice in my mind that said, **"All ailments, the source is thought."** *This is what I call God's voice, answering my question.* Then I thought, "If indeed the tumor was caused by **thought**, that must mean the pills my doctor was prescribing were only taking care of the symptom and not really getting rid of the source of the problem, which was **thought.** So then I thought, what would happen if I reverse-engineered this and figured out what that thought was, that was creating the tumor? And what would happen if I deleted the thought or shifted it? Would the tumor go away? This was the premise that I worked from, as my goal was to heal myself without drugs. I prayed a lot and asked God to help me find the answer.

I was so determined to find my own answers to fix what was in my mind with the hope that my tumor would go away. I sought the help of a psychiatrist since they are thought doctors, but after a year, I fired her since she could not help me much. Also, I took lots of mental courses such as Ontological Design, Lifespring, and the Forum, and read lots of books about the mind. But what helped me the most was hiring a life coach. She had me do journaling to help me discover what negative thoughts were stuck in my head. By changing my perspective on my abusive father, my life coach helped me to relax and not be so stressed at work. I learned that my headaches and tumor were caused by my own negative thoughts, fears, and stress about working with men, which I had created in my mind.

In my mind, I thought that all the men I worked with would beat me the way my father did when I was young. Immersing myself in the field of engineering and having to work with a lot of men caused me to get stressed, have headaches, panic attacks, and develop a tumor. I was literally killing myself from the inside with my negative thoughts. I really believed and thought that they would all abuse me, like my father. But this was the lie, the illusion, the reality I created in my mind. None of it was true, yet I lived and behaved as if it was true! Going to counseling, reading books on positive thinking, and going to classes all helped me to view my world differently. I began to see things in a positive light. Once I forgave my dad and got rid of all the hate and anger that was stuck in my head and learned unconditional love for all and made God my life partner in everything I created in my life; my tumor went away, my headaches went away, my allergies went away, and my skin problems went away. This is how God's peace and unconditional love heals the body, when you learn to let His love take over your negative thoughts of fear, hate, and anger. Also, learn to control your mind to focus from the visible objects of madness and chaos that are always changing, to the INVISIBLE spiritual energy level where there are no objects to judge... where only love and peace reside.

Here's a caveat: If you are currently on medications, continue them as your doctors recommend. However, at the same time, start getting positive. Learn to love everything and everybody, remove your past and future from your mind, meditate every day to get closer to God, learn to have internal peace, forgive everybody, and know God at 100 percent. By doing these things, you will increase your own positive energy level naturally, and only then should you consider asking your doctor if you can safely reduce your medications once you start feeling better.

At the time I had all this illness, I did not really know God at 100 percent, maybe only 50 percent. And I only prayed when I had an emergency, like in this case. I honestly did not have much faith in the God process because of my lack of understanding of who He really was and how to work with Him from an engineering and science perspective. So I always looked for answers in the medical field (my other 50 percent) whenever I was sick. But because I hated taking drugs I always prayed at the same time, asking God for a miracle healing (God's 50 percent), so healing this way for me took almost three years, instead of being instantaneous. I had no experts who could explain to me the natural process of how our body, mind, and energy or spirit worked together from an engineering process view. And I knew no scientific point of view that made sense to me and could reduce the chaos in my brain. I had to figure it out myself to try to save my own life. So for me, it was a matter of life or death. I did not know how to get rid of the bad thoughts and their results since they don't teach us in school. And of the 25 percent-to-50 percent belief in God that I did have, the only small glimmer of hope for understanding how God's light worked inside me, science and education in school was trying to kill by teaching all their students that God did not exist. This is what the Bible says about the splitting of the mind and the creation of chaos and madness in our brains:

No man can serve two masters:
for either he will hate the one, and love the other;
or else he will hold to the one, and despise the other.

Ye cannot serve God and mammon.
–Matthew 6:24, KJV

I believe this separation between religion and science/education regarding the existence of God—and just not knowing how to manage and control our thinking naturally—is why so many people are mentally sick from stress; young people committing suicide is on the rise; and thirty million Americans on antidepressants! Surely, more drugs is not the answer. *(See articles at the end of the Summary section titled: "US Antidepressant Use Jumps 65 Percent in 15 Years," "Recent Study Confirms That Antidepressants Increase Suicide Risk," "Exposed: Our dangerous dependency on antidepressants"; and online: "Making Money from Addiction: 30 Million Americans On Antidepressants. Twenty Facts on America's Big Pharma Nightmare," End of the American Dream (2014); "The Half-Trillion-Dollar Depression," The New York Times Magazine; and "Money for Nothing," U.S. News.)*

Your mind is so powerful that whatever you believe in is always true for you—but only for you! If, for example, you believe you can do something, then you can. However, if you believe you can't, then you're right—you can't because you are what you believe. You are the creator of your own reality, your own perspective of your own mental universe. Because there are literally almost eight billion mental realities out there; everybody gets to create his or her own perspective of how the world works for him or her. This is why it's almost futile to have arguments or fights with people.

I saved my marriage when I gained an understanding of this concept. Now whenever my husband and I have a difference of opinion as to whether something is good or bad, I just accept that he has a different point of view. I don't argue with him, or at least I keep it brief and tell him, "Okay, whatever you say, honey." If it's something that needs to be done, and I feel strongly about it, then I either compromise or do it myself. I find that by handling problems this way, I eliminate a lot of our arguments, and it saves me a lot of time and headaches. To me, this is a more loving way to handle our differences than forcing my opinions and beliefs on him. All our relationships could be improved if we could just learn to stop being so righteous. Most of us are stuck in ego, that there is only ONE mental universe, as currently being taught in our education, and that our perspective is the only right one! IF you want to stay in the world of MADNESS, then keep believing this lie. So, I ask you, "How's that working for you?"

Thoughts of "I'm right and everybody else is wrong," and "I'm better than (*or not as good as*) they are" is just your ego talking. Learn to silence your ego by learning that we are all made of the same thing, which is invisible energy. We are all equal, and we are all connected as one with each other in the invisible realm. Our obsession with the thought that we are **only** here as separate objects is what causes the inflation of our egos—our need to be more important or better than the next guy because this is the only way we feel we matter. Stop feeding your ego (*the object level*) with garbage. Know that you do matter because you are part of God's universe together as one unit. We are all here as one to help each other grow and evolve to the next higher spiritual level of unconditional love for all.

So learn to refocus your thoughts on helping and healing God's universe as ONE whole unit, but with almost eight BILLION **mental** perspectives. Stated differently, don't just feed you; help feed the rest of the world with this new knowledge if you understand this 100 percent since our scientists and educators don't know this. The sustainment of life is not just about you, it's about God, and you were purposely created to help do just that. So ask, "God, how can I serve you?" and "How can I help make this world a better place to live in for everybody?"

Always focus on the love for all, rather than being right all the time, because in the long run, your relationships with others will always be more important than just proving you are right. I think more marriages would be saved if people understood this. Instead of focusing on being right or wrong, it's more useful to ask yourself, "Is this working or not? Am I getting the results I want or not?" If you are not getting the results you want, adjust your beliefs or your tactics until you get the results you want without needing to hurt anybody along the way. Remember: Nobody has to lose to get what you want. Life doesn't have to be a win/lose, right/wrong, or either/or situation. **Nobody should have to be sacrificed along the way to get what YOU want.** Working together through cooperation and helping each other out so that everybody accomplishes what they want is more loving and effective. This concept could be applied to all your relationships at home, with other family members, with friends, at work, or with anybody for that matter. Aiming for a win/win situation is a more loving way of showing up in this world; that way nobody loses. The universe is big enough so that everybody can win because it is all based on our own individual MENTAL PERSPECTIVE anyways, which is unlimited and abundant—and true for almost eight billion mental realities.

When I was eighteen, I had an argument with my mother about which college I should attend. I told her I wanted to go to a Christian college in San Diego, and she insisted I go to the local community college. I tried to explain to her the various college levels, but with her having come from a different country, it was beyond her comprehension. When I realized this, I ended the conversation with, "Okay, Mom, whatever you say." So I saved the relationship by not arguing, because my love for her was more important to me than being right. Two weeks later, I left home for San Diego without arguing. I did what I wanted. In the end, she was so proud of me that I didn't listen to her because I ended up getting my engineering degree as a result, which was what I wanted.

Ask yourself, "Is there somebody I am not at peace with?" If so, you need to first forgive yourself for your negative thoughts and then forgive them. This way, you open the door to loving that person. Then you can expand your forgiveness to the next person, and then the next, and then to all people you may be prejudiced against because of their color, religion, sex, political beliefs, or nationality.

Basically, you should learn to forgive and love everyone and everything so that you can have mental peace. God's spiritual energy of unconditional love is everywhere and is in everything. So learn to love God and be like God by loving and forgiving all people even though they don't know this, so your experience with life will be easier. It's like swimming with the flow of the ocean instead of swimming against the flow. Think about it; which one would be easier?

Unconditional Love

> *And we have known and believed the love that God*
> *hath to us. **God is love**; and he that dwelleth in love*
> *dwelleth in God, and God in him.*
> –1 John 4:16, KJV

Unconditional love is accepting others and treating them as equals without conditions or expecting anything back. Love is easy when you practice forgiveness. You know when you understand unconditional love when you love everybody without expecting anything in return and without consideration of their color, sex, religion, or politics.

Remember, **all changes have to start inside of ourselves first, inside our minds by changing our mental perspective, not outside**. If you don't have love in your life, it's because you haven't learned to love yourself. Most of us spend our lives looking for love in all the wrong places. At churches, they do an exercise where they turn to people around them and say, "Peace be with you." I think a better exercise would be for each person to hug him- or herself and say, "I love me." In fact, every time you look in the mirror, you should point to yourself and say, "I love you." Learn to start loving yourself no matter what you've done or didn't do in the past and no matter what people have said about you. Learn to love yourself abundantly with absolutely no conditions so that you can give love to others unconditionally, because as Dr. Dryer says, **"You cannot give away what you don't have."**

As a Christian, I never understood the meaning of unconditional love, which God is. After all, I didn't see too many Christians practicing unconditional love. We all need to learn this concept to be one and to be like God. I once went to a service in a Baptist church and listened to the preacher talk negatively about the president. You could tell from his tone of voice that he was angry and mad; he was virtually telling the congregation not to vote for him. I was so shocked that I never went back to that church again. I am one of those people who question authorities who don't practice what they preach. This includes church leaders and politicians. He was supposed to be a preacher. I was expecting him to preach about love, togetherness, and forgiveness; but instead, he was preaching about hate, anger, and separation. What was wrong with this picture? Anyway, it's people like this who turn me off from organized religion. After all, aren't we all searching for the same things in life—love, peace, and happiness? If the churches can't teach us about love, peace, togetherness, and happiness, isn't there something not working with what they are teaching? Otherwise, what would be their purpose, Sunday brunches?

Fortunately for me, I found a center that believes what I believe—that God is unconditional love—and they actually practice what they preach. Wow, what a difference from what I'm used to. They don't care about your sex, your race, or your religious beliefs. They are not prejudiced at all. They accept all people and all religions. In fact, the leader is a female, and she often references a variety of spiritual teachers and books such as the Bible, the Torah, etc., and books like those listed back in Appendix A. They have seminars on yoga, meditation, energy flow, love, forgiveness, the healing power of the Holy Spirit, love in action, the path to Christ consciousness, etc. In fact, I learned what unconditional love is, not at church, but rather after forgiving my husband and learning to love him from the books on spirituality. I learned to stop expecting my husband to think and act like me, especially when my expectations were unspoken; after all, he is not a mind reader. I learned to let go and let God guide me. In my mind, I learned to release my husband from the responsibility of being my source as a provider for our family. I learned to stop focusing on what he was or wasn't doing, because it was driving me crazy. Instead, I focused my attention to improving my relationship with God and taking full responsibility for creating my own happiness goals. I learned to accept my husband, and I allowed him to be himself even though he was in a different phase of his life than I was spiritually, and I was okay with that. Once I learned to accept myself, it was easy to accept him and others just because they thought differently (8 billion realities) than the way I thought and perceived how the world worked.

Unconditional love, I learned, is loving people without expecting anything back and with no conditions. So, I stopped expecting anything from my husband and started trusting him. I became surprised and happy when he started doing more and giving more, because I wasn't expecting it. Once I learned to love him, I noticed that we started doing things together again without force or guilt. We started to enjoy spending time together as a family and as a couple. We even went to seminars together and we were making plans together. Previously, I made all my plans without him, and he would make his separate plans, but we never made plans together. Now, we do everything together. By really loving my husband, we became as one! As I said before, I was seriously thinking of divorcing him or separating from him. All my thoughts of him were negative. But once I changed my thoughts from anger, hate, and jealousy (which only separated us) to forgiveness and love, I was able to be one with him. In other words, through love we were able to think together as one. Love is the answer. Love is the way through which we can all become one with God, because God is love. Love unifies people, it brings them together. Do you get that? It's so simple.

To repeat, positive thoughts of love bring us together as one with people and with God, while negative thoughts destroy us and separate us from each other and from God. This can't get any simpler. The most important decision you can make for yourself is the choice of direction to operate from. Do you choose positive or negative? Do you choose the direction of love and peace mentally focused in God's eternal love, or do you want to continue in the same direction with fear and chaos, mentally stuck on the object level? It's up to you, because you are in control of your own mind's perspective, and you get to choose how to live your own life the way you want to—happy or miserable, with or without GOD, heaven *(invisible energy)* or hell *(visible objects)* focus.

If we could all learn to love ourselves and everybody else unconditionally, we could have mental peace within ourselves and with everybody. It's only through the love of *all*, the way God loves us *all*, that we can put Humpty Dumpty's broken pieces together again. This is the only way we can have mental peace with all, as one unit, with God. Remember, focus on the goal, which is to be like God, not the path to God. Focusing on the path only causes prejudice, wars, and fights. Solve problems for what is best for all, not just your part of it. If your solutions are only going to benefit you or a small group of people, I guarantee you will create a breakdown somewhere.

This is extremely easy to apply to the bubble concept. If we learned to control our own thoughts in this world, each one of us could make a difference by choosing forgiveness and love over hatred and fear for everything that entered our bubble. We can actually put this into practice at every moment of our lives very easily.

So the key is to love yourself and everybody so that working with people becomes very easy and stress-free. Also, learn to love your work or studies; however, if you hate it, change your job or subject to something that you do love so that you can have peace and happiness. Make life easy on yourself by doing the things that you love to do, or learn to love your chosen field. For me, because I learned to love the people I work with, my job became easier, and because I learned to love my husband, I no longer have marital problems the way I used to. I'm more forgiving and understanding, and I don't take every little thing personally the way I used to. Life is too short to waste your time doing something you struggle with and hate. Too many people drag themselves to whatever they do, looking tired and unhappy with their work and lives. What a waste!

Learn to love life, all the people around you, and all the things that you do. Focus on love, so life will become easier for you. Without mastering forgiveness and unconditional love of all, it is impossible to create an abundant life full of love, joy, happiness, and money because they go hand in hand. And this love has to be implemented in all areas of your life, not just parts of it, or you will create a breakdown somewhere else, as mentioned earlier.

Here are a couple of stories about love and the creation of abundance and how they go hand in hand. When my husband and I were just starting as real estate investors, I wanted to try the strategy I was taught to turn ugly houses into pretty houses and then resell them to generate income. So when we bought our first fixer-upper ugly house, you could tell from the outside of this property that there was a lot of hate and anger in the house, and compared to the other houses in the neighborhood it stuck out like a sore thumb. The owners, a divorced couple, had destroyed both inside and outside of this property. You could tell the love in this house was all gone. One of the windows was boarded up; the entire yard was practically dead; the fence was incomplete; the paint inside and outside was old and peeling; the carpet was all torn and dirty; the walls had holes; and the inside smelled of urine and feces. Needless to say, this house was on the market for over a year. Nobody wanted to buy it, and I was too new of an investor to turn it down. Since there was nothing structurally wrong with the building, I just knew inside of me that we could make it better and beautiful again, which we did. The neighbors were ecstatic when we bought it, and when we were through with the project, you could tell from the outside and the inside how much love and work we put into making it beautiful again. As a result, we did make a lot of money when we finally sold it.

When we started to fix the yard of this house, I found some plant bulbs in the ground that, because of their lack of water from the previous owners, were barely surviving. I didn't know what they were, so to save the bulbs, I gave them to my mother, who happens to have the gift of making plants grow and thrive. I don't have a green thumb, but since I love plants and flowers, I wanted to make sure they were taken care of properly. My mother was just perfect for the job because within three months, her yard was full of these big, bright, beautiful red flowers growing all around her fence, and to this day, they still thrive and grow in abundance in her yard. And when you drive around my mother's neighborhood, you can always know which house is hers because it's the one with the most beautiful garden. She partners and works with nature, or God, to create her own Garden of Eden. In fact, people come and take pictures and stare at her creation, and you can see the love and the care she has put into her yard. You too can create abundance when you put love and passion into the things you do.

Do not limit your love to only family members or friends or those who believe only what you believe, but expand your love so that it overflows to include everybody, no matter what color, race, sex, or religion they are. When your thoughts and attitudes come from a boundless or unlimited source, that's what will be returned to you. However, when you give only in terms of limits and boundaries, then only the amount you have given out to the universe will be returned to you. Hindus and Buddhism describe this phenomenon as your karma or what the Bible says, what you sow is what you reap.

So, what and how much you give of yourself to others is pretty much the same as what you will receive from them. If, for example, you are experiencing a lack of love, don't blame others; just look at yourself in the mirror. Most likely it's because you don't have enough love for yourself to give to others; therefore, you are giving and receiving a lack of love. Remember, you are together as one with God the Universe; therefore, you are it and it is you. Your experience with the universe (God) will always just be what you feel and think about yourself. Change the way you feel and think (about yourself and the universe) if you want to change what you want to experience with it.

> *There is no fear in* **love**, *but* **perfect love casteth out fear: because fear hath torment**. *He that feareth is not made perfect in* **love**.
> 1 John 4:18, KJV

Perfect love, which is God, has no fear because it resides in the invisible energy level where there are no objects to judge as fearful because there's nothing there; therefore, as the verse states, God is free from torment. He will not judge you since there is nothing there to judge at the invisible level; he will not punish you or hurt you, even though some religions teach that. Do not believe them! God the Universe only sees Himself as perfect love inside you at the invisible energy level. That is why He can only love you as Himself unconditionally in you and as you.

Blessings

Bless those that persecute you.
–Romans 12:14, KJV

Learn to give blessings to everybody, especially your enemies, people you hate, and people you are angry with or are fearful of. The reason this is so important is that whatever thoughts you send out to the universe are always what gets returned back to you. Again, this is because you are part of the whole universe as eternal non-destructive invisible spiritual energy. You are it and it is you! So giving silent blessings to others is like giving yourself blessings. As the saying goes, "What goes around comes around." If you want to create an abundant life for yourself, then wish it for everybody else first. I especially give blessings to all the people whom I perceive to have a difficult time with to help me redirect my energy from negative fear to positive energy of love. This concept took a long time for me to learn, and I didn't understand its significance until I had to hire a lawyer.

For the longest time, my husband and I refused to get our will or do estate planning because of our negative fears and beliefs about lawyers. As a result, we had no written plans as to who would take care of our children in case we died. We know it's a good idea to set up a will and do estate planning; on the other hand, I have read lawyers' jokes about how they are all sharks and how all the dead ones live in hell. You know the jokes I'm talking about that float around in cyberspace? I was stressed and struggling for years about this dilemma because these two trains of thought were colliding inside of me going in the opposite direction. To combat my negative thoughts, I started giving and sending out silent blessings and love to our lawyers. This was the only way I could get through the process peacefully and effortlessly; as a result, I am more at peace now that we finally created our estate plan.

These jokes, by the way, even though they seem harmless, are actually harmful to you when you believe these negative thoughts. They can subconsciously stop you from creating what you need or want, just like the will we needed to create for our family. Unless you become aware of them, they will stop you in your tracks.

Remember, mental peace that is naturally long-lasting is only attained when you focus your mind in God's invisible energy level, where there is nothing to judge as good or evil, no one is rich or poor, no one's sick, no one's fat or skinny, no one's smart or dumb, there are no religions, no countries, no races of black or white people, no pain or abuse, no problems—but only perfect love, joy, and peace that is eternal, which is what all objects are made of inside. However, because most people focus on trying to get love, joy, and peace on the outside from other objects that they can only see with their eyes, such as people, money, cars, houses, and things as their source for happiness; their experience with love, joy, and peace are also as temporary as the objects they focus on. For example, my kids just have to buy the latest and greatest new cell phones every time a new upgraded version is advertised on TV, even though the old one still works, but they insist on getting the latest new thing to be happy. This is what advertisers always want us to believe, that we must buy the latest phones, the latest cars, and gadgets, the biggest house, etc., to make us happy. This is pure madness!

This is why not very many people are happy. Their minds' focus is misguided on temporary physical objects that they feel they constantly have to buy, upgrade, or replace to be happy. Therefore, we are creating mentally unstable crazy people, happy one day, unhappy the next because they can't buy the latest toy. This is one of the reasons why so many unhappy people are popping happy pills and are now addicted to legal and illegal drugs—all searching for mental peace and happiness that last, but sadly they are all looking in the wrong places on the temporary outside world of objects—instead of God's spiritual energy level on the inside that cannot be bought because it's FREE. And this form of love, peace, and joy can never be broken or destroyed, according to physics. God's love for us can never be broken because it is eternal, and we are all physically part of Him, and He is in us as spiritual energy that cannot be destroyed according to physics. But what's broken is that most of us do not reciprocate our love back to Him. It's this mental separation that we each created in ourselves by NOT believing and loving the invisible God energy that everything is made of, and not knowing how to work with Him, that is causing our mental suffering and sickness.

What's scary to me is how our society seems to easily accept and be okay with all the druggies we are creating—thirty million Americans on antidepressants that do not work and growing, according to these articles! Basically, our society is supporting and creating the next generation of children addicted to drugs, and doctors are basically high-end DRUG PUSHERS! According to the article: "US Antidepressant Use Jumps 65 Percent in 15 Years," it states that one-fourth of those surveyed have been on antidepressants for at least ten years or more! Does anybody see, what I see as a major problem, that our society is clearly headed in the wrong direction? *(See articles at the end of the Summary section titled, "US Antidepressant Use Jumps 65 Percent in 15 Years," "Recent Study Confirms That Antidepressants Increase Suicide Risk," "Exposed: Our dangerous Dependency on Antidepressants"; and online: "Making Money from Addiction: 30 Million Americans On Antidepressants. Twenty Facts on America's Big Pharma Nightmare," End of the American Dream (2014); "The Half-Trillion-Dollar Depression," The New York Times Magazine; and "Money for Nothing," U.S. News.)*

Because the media does not want to lose their billions of advertising money, they often purposely mislead people when it comes to shootings caused by people with mental issues who are on anti-depressants, so that the focus is on their weapon of choice, not the fact that the person was probably addicted to drugs prescribed by "expert" doctors who are messing up the person's head. For those who commit suicide, whether they want to take others with them or not, often their weapons of choice vary, as some use guns, and others use knives or cars. So now we have this "get rid of all the guns" movement as if it's the gun's fault that magically decided to attach itself to the person's hand, and it's the gun's fault that magically decided to push the trigger on its own, and it's the gun's fault that magically decided to target people! Next, they're probably going to have a "let's get rid of all the knives" movement, "let's get rid of all the axes" movement, "let's get rid of all the cars" movement, "let's get rid of all the ropes" movement since sometimes they are the weapons of choice used to kill people too. Do you see how ridiculous this is? They don't look at the source of the problem that there is a high probability that the antidepressant drugs that are being prescribed by doctors are probably the culprit to our society's mental crisis. According to the article *"EXPOSED: Our dangerous dependency on antidepressants. A study giving 'happy pills' a clean bill of health is seriously flawed."*

Being Grateful

Every day, I thank God for everything that He has given me, especially for my family and all the people He has brought into my life. This is an example of practicing gratefulness. This allows me to start my day at a neutral level, or ground zero. If you can't find anything to be grateful for, it's because you are focused on what you don't have, and thus you have no peace. Take inventory of all the good things that you have working in your life and be thankful for all of them. Learn to accept yourself and the world you have created for yourself. Learn to stop complaining about what you don't have. Instead, start your every morning in a positive direction by thanking God or the universe for all that you do have. Maybe it's your family, your kids, your health, your job, or just having a home.

Creation

> *And you, **be ye fruitful, and multiply; bring forth abundantly in the earth, and multiply** therein.*
> –Genesis 9:7, KJV

The Bible states that in the beginning, God created the Garden of Eden. The Bible also states that God wants us all to have abundant lives. Because we were made in His image—unique with a mind—we too can create our own Garden of Eden. For example, rocks and monkeys cannot create, but humans can. All creation starts with your mind and your imagination. So, use your mind to the highest level by creating the life you want out of love. It's a gift God has given you so you can learn to be like him. You deserve it. All you have to do is ask yourself, "If I could have anything I want or do anything I want, what would it be?" Once you answer this question, write the answers down on a list of what you want to achieve, then break those goals down into bite-size daily to-do lists and follow through so that you can work toward your goals one day at a time. Goals are discussed in detail in the section titled "Working Toward Your Purpose/Goals."

If you can grow anything in your Garden of Eden, don't you want to grow it abundantly? After all, who would want to grow weeds in his or her garden? However, most people I observe are good at producing partial gardens. Like most people, I was good at creating a career; however, I was terrible at creating a peaceful family life. My husband and I fought constantly, and my kids then reproduced our behavior because we were their role models. Here's another example: Even though Johnny Carson was extremely successful as an entertainer, all the news media could talk about when he died was that he died unhappy, had many failed marriages in his past, and that his kids would not even talk to him. Look at all the failed marriages in the entertainment industry that are constantly in the news; the people in these marriages are our role models.

Most of us only water one side of our garden and grow weeds on the other side. Right now, you are building your garden of life whether you think so or not. Creating your own Garden of Eden or perspective of the universe means creating a beautiful world out of love, which makes you happy without destroying others along the way. You can create a happy, peaceful you. You can create a happy, loving family. You can create your dream job. You can pursue the education you want. You can create your dream home, or you can do whatever you want. I know many people who are unhappy with their relationships and many people who are unhappy at work. Most people are wasting so much of their precious time being miserable by creating misery in their life, which is a shame, instead of creating more love, peace of mind, joy, and happiness. Our time in this life-form is too short to be miserable. So take control and responsibility for creating your own happiness goals since it's **your mind** that creates your own reality. Nobody else can make you happy but you—because it's your brain. You are the only one in control of it, you are the only one that knows what you want to make you happy since people are not mind readers.

My husband once told me, "Why do you have to be miserable all the time? For once, why can't you just be happy?" This was one of those wake-up moments for me when he woke me up from a negative automatic behavior that I did not even realize I was doing. It was a behavior of misery and constant fight-ready mode I learned from my parents. But once I took inventory of what I really had by counting my blessings—a wonderful loving husband who never hit me, two beautiful and wonderful daughters, nobody was sick, we had great dogs, wonderful jobs, and a nice house. Then I realized, there was nothing for me to be miserable about! That was when I told myself, that I was going to create a different family than what my parents had created, from a house of misery to a house of love and peace. To break the negative cycle, I was so determined to learn and lead my family into this new endeavor by creating love scenes instead of fight scenes. I elevated my mental level to positive love and peace instead of operating from automatic, negative, constant anger and misery. Because I changed, my family changed too, for the better. As I became a better role model for my family, we all became happier as a result. This is my miracle love story, and you can do the same, by creating your own love story. To paraphrase John 14:12, Jesus said, you can do what I can do, but better, when you learn the God process.

When you choose to follow God in love and be positive, anything is possible for you. You can actually be happy if you want to, right now! You just have to choose to believe in God, believe in yourself, and follow or copy God by going with His energy flow of unconditional love and forgiveness for all. He can help you meet your happiness goals quickly and peacefully instead of being stressed and worried all the time by believing you have to do your life all alone, which negative stressed people tend to do. You just have to believe in a loving God and hire Him as your life partner to help you co-create your own Garden of Eden, so you can meet your happiness goals faster. God becomes very important when it comes to mastering creation. The reason for this is that all of us have our own minds, our own versions of the world and how it works for us, and our own individual desires and goals. Oftentimes, our spouses may not understand our visions because they have their own brain and are busy creating their own little world to deal with. All the negativity in the world of objects can be overwhelming and frustrating. This is when it really helps to know and to believe that there is something grander than you that can help.

When you focus your mind on the bigger picture, on the invisible God, instead of the things you are trying to create, or instead of focusing on yourself as a separate object from the whole universe, then all the negativity disappears, and peace is restored in your mind. It's much easier to give up on yourself when you only have yourself to count on and do things for. That's why it's important that when you set your goals, you do it with loved ones in mind. When you don't believe in or have faith in the invisible God or the universe, you will have a difficult time believing that either you or others can help you accomplish your goals because they are part of the universe as you are. Having faith in God is simply believing that everything and everybody is here connected in the invisible spiritual energy realm as one universal unit—but with separate bodies and brains with different functions in the visible object level. By being able to focus on the God of ALL as your source and creative canvas to help manifest your projects, rather than the negative parts of the universe (*your problems or people you hate or are angry with*), it is much easier to work and continue a project no matter how big or small.

We are all creative people. It is inherent in us to create. When we ignore that part of us, we get frustrated and lost because of our lack of direction and purpose. To feel a sense of purpose, you need to decide what it is you want to do or create for yourself by serving others. You need to ask yourself, if you could be and do anything, what would that be? Here are some ideas: Look at the gifts God has given you and use them to serve others. My sister, for example, was given the gift of artistry. She serves others by using her gift to do what she loves, which is being an interior decorator. In return, she gets paid for her time when she serves others through her gifts.

Creating is a give-and-take process. You need to give first in order to receive. We give by serving others what they need, and in return, we get what we want to help meet our own personal goals. This is why we all need to love and support each other. We all need to help elevate and teach others so that we can help each other create our own Garden of Eden. You can't do it alone because it's too hard, but with God, it's easy, if you let Him help you create your happiness goals. Maybe your goal is to be happy, have peace, have a better job, have more money, get better grades, or buy a new house. Whatever it is, you will need to give first, and your efforts will be rewarded. For example, by giving forty hours per week of my time at work, I receive money in return, which is one of my goals. Creating is serving others first by doing what you love; whatever it is, this is your purpose.

Choose These as Your Core Values and Positive Attitudes to Live by

- Be loving to all (*all people, races, religions, political beliefs, and countries*).
- Be forgiving to all (*all people, races, religions, political beliefs, and countries, since we are not taught in school*).
- Be creative (*create your own Garden of Eden and love scenes*).
- Be of service to others (*work and help others with your gifts*).
- Be accepting of all (*all people, races, religions, political beliefs, and countries*).
- Be giving (*pray and give blessings to all, especially your enemies; it's free*).
- Be accepting of all (*all people no matter what they believe, races, religions, political beliefs, and countries, especially your enemies since you don't need to hang out with them unless you want to*).

Being a Conscious Positive Thinker

Your power is in consciously choosing to be positive or neutral during every moment of your time within your bubble, or field of vision. Being conscious is having a focused awareness of what you are thinking and doing so that you are not so automatic. It's being immersed in negative thinking that causes constriction and problems in your life flow. So consciously choose to be forgiving and loving at all times so that you can have mental peace and mental stability until these becomes your new automatic thinking or norm.

Focusing on God's unconditional love and forgiveness for all are two of the highest vibrational words you can mentally meditate on. It requires mental control on your part at the beginning because it can be difficult if you are not used to it, but I promise, it does get easier and easier over time. These two words alone can get you mentally high without drugs and their effects. Without learning to live in unconditional love and forgiveness, both in the inside invisible spiritual energy level and outside the world of objects, it is impossible to achieve mental peace. These are two of the most powerful words you can mentally immerse yourself in to heal the body whole.

Transitioning from subconscious negative thinking to conscious positive thinking takes practice and time. You can't do it overnight because it's a learning process, an evolution on your part. It becomes easy once it is practiced and practiced; over time it becomes a habit, your new norm.

Read books on forgiveness and love and keep asking God to help you answer your questions about love and forgiveness until you understand them at 100 percent. If you ask, He will answer. Get into the routine of talking to God on a regular basis. Think of Him as an invisible partner whom you can talk to anytime and anywhere, not just on Sundays.

Stop The Mental Madness Cycle

You need to realize how powerful your words are and how detrimental they can be to you and how your words do affect others. Here are a few examples of how the giver of a thought and the receiver of the thoughts are affected. Shortly after I graduated from college, I was briefly dating an engineer who had major issues with love because he hated his dad and heard when he was young that his father did not want him as a child, and his father told him he was a mistake. He let these few words stuck in his mind as his life focus.

He let his negative thoughts of anger and fear of not being loved and rejection overtake his whole being, and instead of learning to let it go and forgive his dad so he could free himself from these negative thoughts, he chose instead to end it all by killing himself. And later he did. You see he was never taught how to remove these forms of negative thinking from his mind. He was never taught that his biological father was just a sperm donor or about God who created him. He never learned that his real father, God, loved him unconditionally and had created him for a purpose. I think we could save a lot of kids and adults from becoming suicidal if there were some form of formal education on this topic to manage our thoughts. Companies do it all the time with computer data that they remove from their hard drives on a regular basis by deleting bad data or old data they no longer need. We can learn to do the same with useless thoughts we create in our own minds; we can learn to purge them and at the same time learn problem-solving skills in schools because I believe this is a failure in our educational system to teach our kids these basic survival skills. I believe we can easily save and mentally heal a lot of kids and adults from potential suicide and drug and alcohol abuse if schools were allowed to teach about self-control through mind management and God's love and healing. So why aren't schools teaching our kids how to use their minds to think more effectively? Isn't this supposed to be their job function as educators to teach us how to process our mental data properly, so we can all become more efficient human beings? Can you imagine for everyone a life without drugs or alcohol or suicide? I believe it's possible when we all learn how to use God's power of unconditional love that is inside all things already.

Here's another example. When my youngest daughter was in fifth grade, I pulled her out of her school because she became so fearful of one of her teachers who apparently yelled a lot at all the children. My daughter internalized the teacher's anger and words of fear of never being able to pass high school and college if the kids didn't do well in all their assignments and tests. These words she believed from this teacher caused her so much mental stress that they manifested in her body, and she would start vomiting if she didn't complete an assignment or if she felt she was not ready for a test. Because the students were given so much homework every night, these negative thoughts kept recycling in her mind; and as she got more and more overwhelmed, she started writing notes about how she hated school and wanted to end it all. One night she had a mental breakdown. She was crying and vomiting incessantly, overwhelmed by everything, she had problems breathing, and she wanted to die. The next day I pulled her out of that school. Imagine, ten years old, and they pick up all those negative thoughts from adults!

This is an example of a teacher having good intentions of wanting to teach but using the wrong methods of yelling and threatening the children so that they would do their homework. She was willing to sacrifice some of the children to get her lesson through to them. It is these kinds of thoughts and practices that we pass on to our children, without thinking of their consequences or even realizing what potential damage we are doing to them.

We cannot afford to make these kinds of sacrifices anymore, especially with our children. We are their role models, and unless we ourselves as adults all take responsibility for our own thoughts and become aware of how we talk to others and ourselves, being consciously careful of the words we use, we will continue to pass on our mental madness to our children, generation after generation. This is what the Bible calls the "generational curse." We all need to work together (scientists, educators, doctors, politicians, religion) to stop this nonsense, the madness!

Even with our advancements in technology, why is it that the best that scientists, educators, doctors, and politicians (who seem to think they are so intelligent) can do as a solution to our society's mental crisis is to compete with drug dealers? Is this really the best that we can do for our children, the next generation, to teach them to be addicted to antidepressant drugs and to be suicidal? For money? Is this the best solution our so-called "experts" could come up with? Really?

There is another solution. A better solution is to learn and to teach our children mind management or data management, to use computer lingo. Now is the time to progress in this area without drug use because it doesn't work. According to Global Research, there are 30 Million Americans on Antidepressants, as of the writing of the article in 2014, and growing. If only we could set aside the billions and billions of dollars currently being made by Big Pharma, doctors, and government generated by these legal drugs. Aren't our children and our loved ones going through mental stress worth saving?

See articles at the end of the Summary section titled: "US Antidepressant Use Jumps 65 Percent in 15 Years," "Recent Study Confirms That Antidepressants Increase Suicide Risk," "Exposed: Our Dangerous Dependency on Antidepressants"; and online: "Making Money from Addiction: 30 Million Americans On Antidepressants. Twenty Facts on America's Big Pharma Nightmare," End of the American Dream (2014); "The Half-Trillion-Dollar Depression," The New York Times Magazine; and "Money for Nothing," U.S. News.

Healing Yourself And Others

> *The tendency of modern physics is to resolve the whole material universe into waves, and nothing but waves. These waves are of two kinds: **bottled-up waves** [visible objects], **which we call matter, and unbottled waves** [invisible], **which we call radiation or light.** If annihilation of matter occurs [e.g., tumors and cancers], the process is merely that of **unbottling imprisoned wave-energy and setting it free to travel through space** [e.g., letting go of stress and negative thinking]. These concepts reduce the whole universe to a world of light, potential or existent, so that the whole story of its creation can be told with perfect accuracy and completeness in six words: "God said, Let there be light."*
>
> –Sir James Jeans
> (English physicist, astronomer, mathematician)

To begin with, we all need to learn the *natural process* of healing ourselves first the way God intended for our spirit/energy, mind, and body are to work together more effectively as one whole system, so we can then help others heal themselves, especially our loved ones. It is my hope and prayer that this book will help you understand God's spiritual healing at 100 percent and mental healing at 100 percent so that you can help others do the same. Just by changing your own energy to perform at its highest level of unconditional love for all, you automatically affect others around you, since we are all connected in the invisible realm as energy in various forms of waves. Remember that the invisible energy that everything in the universe is made of inside us, according to physics, cannot be destroyed; therefore, everything is connected as ONE whole unit.

When we remove the God Factor from our life's equation, we all limit our ability to heal ourselves to only what doctors at the object level can tell us and to the drugs they prescribe to us, which may or may not work. But when we learn to add God into our lives, and we learn mind management for ourselves, and we learn how to effectively align our body, mind, and energy to work together for our good and for the good of everyone around us in a positive alignment, then we are able to add this deeper dimension into our lives that weren't there before. This will open greater options to be able to heal ourselves faster naturally.

According to A Course In Miracles, by Helen Schucman (ex-atheist) and William Thetford, Professors of Medical Psychology at Columbia University's College of Physicians and Surgeons in New York:

> *Miracles rearrange perception and place **all levels in true perspective.** This is healing because **sickness comes from confusing the levels [visible vs. invisible]** (4:23). **Miracles restore the mind to its fullness** [by learning how our ONENESS with God works] (5:34).*

The levels they are referring to are the visible physical world of objects that you can see with your eyes versus what everything is made of inside at the invisible spiritual energy level, as previously discussed. Even during Jesus' time, only a few people were saved and healed by His teachings, because very few fully understood and believed in the existence of God's invisible spiritual energy level at 100 percent. It is my hope that this book will help to simplify the two levels or dimensions so that they are easily understood so that more people can naturally be healed spiritually, mentally, and physically through understanding of how their body parts work together best as one whole system. Healing this way is not really a miracle, it's just the way humans are naturally created by God as to how our mind processes our mental thought data and how our body, mind, and energy/spirit work best together as ONE unit, in sync, and in positive alignment. Because we're not taught this in school, it may seem miraculous or supernatural, but it's not. It's just our ignorance of this natural process that makes it appear so because we can all learn the process; it doesn't have to be reserved to just a few people.

The reason psychiatry doesn't work for most of us is because they do not believe and do not know how to use God's invisible spiritual energy level, that everything is made of inside (*including you*), as a power to naturally heal us. Therefore, they will never provide that as an option for you. If you read the articles in the back of the Summary section, you will see that psychiatry is not in the business of healing, they are in the business of making as much money as possible by being high-end drug dealers, prescribing highly addictive drugs so patients keep coming back for more. You have to remember that this is a multi-billion-dollar industry. Americans spent $280 Billion alone in 2013, and the big pharmaceutical companies make so much money that they are willing to pay lots of money to psychiatrists to prescribe them, politicians to legalize the drugs, and the media to advertise them.

Another reason psychiatry doesn't work sometimes and is just a temporary fix for our mental stresses is that they are not there to **teach** you how to properly use your mind to control your own thoughts naturally without drugs, to reduce the number of thoughts you are generating so you don't go mad. Because psychiatrists do not know themselves how to do this process naturally, they can never provide this as an option to heal you. They only prescribe drugs, or happy pills as kids call them, to synthetically stop your negative thinking so you don't go crazy.

This temporary fix is the easy way out, but it comes with a price. The problem with taking illegal or legal drugs to help reduce the number of thoughts our minds are generating is that they are only temporary fixes. So you have to keep taking the drugs, and often times these drugs are extremely addictive, and this is just one of the side effects, and some even cause suicide. When the drug wears off, the problem is still there, so you're going to need more drugs again, and the cycle goes on. This is how drug addiction comes about.

My daughter is a good example of this when she was being treated by various psychiatrists for both physical and mental trauma that happened at her school caused by her teacher. During the four years of her seeing various doctors, they couldn't heal her. They just kept prescribing various antidepressant drugs to try to get rid of her negative thoughts, but instead of getting better, she only got worse. She got addicted to the drugs, and the drugs made her even more suicidal; as a result, she had to be institutionalized multiple times. This was our Hell On Earth working with all the expert doctors who didn't really know how to help heal her naturally! In fact, they almost killed her with their drugs. It wasn't until I fired all the doctors and hired God to help me help her that she was able to mentally heal, not only from the prescription drug addiction but also from suicide.

In my case, when I was about twenty-four years old, being treated for depression by my psychiatrist after I found out I had a brain tumor, my panic attacks got worse and more frequent. She was trying to get me to take antidepressant drugs, but I refused. I was searching for someone to teach me how to have mental peace naturally, without drugs. Six months later, she prescribed tranquilizers for me after my then twenty-eight-year-old boyfriend committed suicide. This was the only time I took her meds because I couldn't stop my thinking of, I shouldn't have said this or that, and the guilty feeling that it was my fault he died because I was the last person he spoke to.

After the tranquilizers wore off, I ended up in Venice Beach, California, not knowing how long I had been driving or why I had gone there. The drugs synthetically made me literally stop thinking, and I couldn't remember anything, absolutely nothing! When the drugs wore off, and I woke up from the trance, I realized how dangerous the drugs were, and I never took one again. I finally had to fire her after one year because she obviously did not know how to help me find mental peace naturally without drugs, which was my goal.

So basically, psychiatry did not work for me or for my daughter. I realized later that there is a big difference between **teaching** somebody how to have mental peace naturally by learning how to use our brains' computer properly by learning to control it versus psychiatry, which **medicates** patients for their mental suffering so they can stop the automatic thinking. Jesus for example, as the Bible states, was the Messiah who came to **teach** us *how to properly use our minds*, not to medicate, so that His followers could learn to mentally control and manage their own thoughts naturally without drugs the way God designed our body parts to function naturally. This is so that we can heal ourselves from mental stress naturally. That was his purpose, to teach us how to use our body parts more efficiently since we're not taught in school. That's all religion is all about, trying to teach us how to use our body parts more efficiently as ONE whole unit the way it's meant to work together naturally.

When I was taking a class called Ontological Design, a course on improving our thinking, one of the ladies who attended the course with me, with whom I commuted from LA to San Francisco, shared how her ex-husband died of cancer. After the doctors opened him up, the cancer had already spread all over his body, and the doctor had made a comment to her that "he was a very *angry* man." Imagine if this doctor had treated the source of the cancer, the *anger* **stuck** in this man's head. Imagine if that could have saved his life instead of just treating the symptoms of cancer in his body. She told me how he found her in bed with somebody else and how he could not forgive her.

I believe that when doctors treat only the symptoms of illnesses in our body, from mental stress, these are just temporary fixes that may or may not work. Often, these illnesses come back with a vengeance, especially if the mental stress of anger, hate, jealousy, vengeance, worry, etc., is still stuck in the person's head. Until they learn to release the negative thought energy and change it to positive thoughts of unconditional love, acceptance, and forgiveness, they will continue to suffer because, as physicists say, energy changes into forms. So do not hold on to negative thoughts. Instead, **focus on learning mental control by thinking less and thinking positively and learning to refocus the mind's eye to God's invisible spiritual energy level (where there's**

nothing to judge) that everything is made of inside all things, where unconditional love and peace reside. This is the only natural way to achieve mental freedom, away from the temporary world of object-level chaos and madness (8 billion mental perspective realities), which is healing to both the mind and body simultaneously since they are all connected together as ONE unit. This is how you master being whole again, by becoming ONE with God the Universe, with 100 percent belief and faith mentally in the God process. But anything less than 100 percent may or may not work.

Another good example of what happens to negative thinking is a manager at Boeing that I worked with as an engineer. This person always seemed stressed out having to deal with upper management and his team. He yelled at people all the time. He didn't know how to manage all the mental stress of work, so when he had his first heart attack and a triple bypass, he thought that changing departments would help eliminate some of his stress. Two years later he had another heart attack, this time with a quadruple bypass.

Why another heart attack when he was supposed to have already been healed by the doctor the first time? Because he never changed his way of processing his negative thoughts; he still kept getting easily offended and stressed out by the people around him. Even though he physically changed jobs, he could not get away from himself. His doctors were trying to heal only the symptoms of his body, not the source of his problem, which was mental stress. But once he quit work to get away from the negative environment, by taking an early retirement to stop his mental work stress, he was fine.

The only really permanent healing solution to mental and physical illness caused by mental stress naturally is through learning to manage and process our thoughts differently than we're used to. Surely, God's peace and love are worth a try and are a better option for ourselves and our loved ones than suicide, cancer, tumors, heart attacks, or stroke.

When my sister had ovarian cancer, what she did to naturally heal herself without drugs or chemo was to address her mental stress directly, one by one (*the source of her sickness*) by praying and forgiving her ex-husband for all the years of physical and mental abuse, and for his messing around with other women to get rid of her hate and anger that consumed her that was stuck inside her head for years. And through prayer, God answered her fear of being homeless and her stress about how to make money, because her husband was trying to kick her out of the house. As God answered all her prayers from her mental stress, she was healed naturally once she achieved mental peace.

Most recently my older daughter called me up, and said: "Mom, you can't believe what happened today! I wasn't feeling good, so I went to urgent care before work. The doctor took my blood pressure and said, "Your blood pressure is so high, I don't know how you're alive!" He told her to go to the hospital emergency room immediately because he did not have the facility to take care of her.

She had just started a new job, and there was a gal higher than her who would give her assignments and then go to their higher management and complain about how my daughter messed up again on her assignment. Because my daughter could hear them talking about her from the other side of the wall, she stressed herself out, thinking they were going to fire her. Days before she went to the doctor, she called me crying on the phone every day. "Mom, they're going to fire me! They're going to fire me!" She nearly had a nervous breakdown. I tried to calm her down by telling her, "Honey, please try not to think too much or you're going to hurt yourself." But to no avail. And she refuses to read this book on how to think less. She kept insisting that I did not understand her situation and refused to listen to me.

However, instead of going to the emergency room that day, as her doctor instructed her to do, she instead went to work and decided to speak with her senior manager, whom she had never met before, as this was a new job for her. She told her, "I know you're going to fire me, so I'm already looking for another job, and I will be leaving as soon as I find one." Her senior manager literally **saved her life with these few positive words** of encouragement, *"Why would you think we would fire you when we just hired you? We need you, that's why we hired you."*

Wow, how powerfully healing were her senior manager's kind words. Only twenty-one words saved her life! This happened just a few days after another employee had committed suicide by jumping off the roof of their office building. This was all during the Covid-19 drama with so many people mentally stressed. So please **be extremely careful with your words because negative thoughts can kill, and positive thoughts can save a life.** Thoughts are powerful! How you talk to yourself and to others can kill or save a life—and it may be your own. This is why being loving, forgiving, and caring for yourself and to others heals!

> ***A heart at peace gives life to the body***,
> *but envy rots the bones.*
> –Proverbs 14:30, KJV

> *Make a supreme effort to get to God. I am speaking practical truth to you, practical sense; and giving you a philosophy that will take away all of your consciousness of hurt. Be afraid of nothing....Meditate deeply and faithfully, and one day you will wake up in ecstasy with God and see how foolish it is that people think they are suffering.* ***You and I and they are all pure [invisible energy] Spirit.***
> - Sri Sri Paramahansa Yogananda, *Living Fearlessly*

My cousin had breast cancer after the economy dropped, and as a realtor, she was unable to sell properties. She became extremely stressed from the possibility of losing her house and cars, and of being homeless. Even though she was a Christian and prayed a lot, she could not be healed from her cancer because she did not know how to silence her mind. She did not trust God at 100 percent that He could help her with her mental stress and money problems, so after her chemo, she insisted on going back to work right away, only relying on herself, because she thought she was the source of her money problems. Two weeks later, she passed away at only thirty-nine years old. You see, she let her mental stress consume her. Unlike my sister, she could not be healed God's way because she did not believe, trust, and understand God's natural process at 100 percent. She let the negative mental stress of money consume her.

Also, I learned that praying negatively does not work to heal you or your relationships. For example, when my husband and I used to fight all the time, it seemed to me that I was doing all the right things. After all, I was going to church and praying for God to get rid of my husband, and nothing would happen. Then I'd get so frustrated with God and almost not believe in Him, since I would go home, and there would be my husband after praying so hard. After all, John 16:24, Matthew 21:22, and Luke 11:9 all pretty much say the same thing, "Ask and you shall receive." And here I was, praying, asking, and even begging God, and yet He did not answer my prayers. Why? Because my prayers were not about love, and my motive was very negative, about hate and anger that filled inside my heart and mind, that I did not know how to get rid of, which most of us do not know, since we're not taught in school.

But obviously, God had other plans for me and my husband because He works with us to bring the goodness out of us and the best out of us. It wasn't until I learned about God's unconditional love and forgiveness for all—and I learned that God was my source for everything, not my husband—that I myself started to act lovingly towards others on the outside, including my husband. Only then did I find unimaginable love and peace inside me. You see, once I learned to reconnect and believe in God's spiritual energy level at 100 percent (not at 50 percent), and I learned to get rid of all my negative thoughts of hate, unforgiveness, and anger that were consuming my mind and heart at 100 percent, did my body heal itself at 100 percent from a brain tumor and simultaneously saved my marriage. So learn to love God unconditionally, learn to love yourself unconditionally, and learn to love others unconditionally so you can heal yourself and your relationships. Achieving mental peace naturally heals when we learn to master the God process.

> *You desire but do not have, so you kill. You covet but you cannot get what you want, so you quarrel and fight. You do not have because you do not ask God. **When you ask, you do not receive, because you ask with <u>wrong motives</u>,** that you may spend what you get on your pleasures.*
> –James 4:2–3, KJV

The reason why *believing in God, prayers, forgiveness, and surrendering or releasing our problems to God works when it's done right*, when we are at 100 percent positive alignment in body, mind, energy/spirit, is as physicist Sir James Jean explains,

> *If annihilation of matter [e.g., tumors and cancers]*
> *occurs, the process is merely that of **unbottling***
> ***imprisoned wave-energy [thoughts] and setting it***
> ***free to travel through space.***

This is why letting go of our negative thinking by surrendering it to God the Universe, and not keeping our negative thoughts stuck and bottled inside our minds works to heal us! Remember, what physicists teach us is that energy(*including thought energy*) just **changes into different forms**. This is the law of conservation of energy on how invisible spiritual energy works to materialize into objects. Napoleon Hill, says it this way in his book *Think and Grow Rich*,

> ***Thoughts [positive or negative] become things . . .***
> *powerful things, **when mixed with definiteness of***
> ***purpose, persistence, and a burning desire** for their*
> *translation into riches or other material objects."*

Medical Daily, April 23, 2016, ran an article by Jaleesa Baulkman, "Suicide in America: Rate Reaches All-Time High, Especially Among Teen Girls." Also, the highest suicide rate among professionals is medical doctors; they are number one. See *Medical Daily*, "Top 11 Professions with Highest Suicide Rates." You would think that with all the medical and science education that these doctors have, that they would be at the bottom of the suicide list. A lot of people believe science has an upper hand over religion, removing religion from schools even. My boyfriend who killed himself at the age of twenty-eight was into science. He was an engineer, and his father who said he was a "mistake" was a professor in physics. If science alone is so great and better without the God Factor in our educational system, why are suicides on the rise and drug use on the rise? Why are thirty million Americans on antidepressants, all prescribed by doctors to control the mind's thoughts? If current science theories are such a better answer than the God Theory when it comes to mental health and living a long healthy life for people, why has science failed all these MILLIONS AND MILLIONS of people?

All suicides start with **thought energy** (*that scientist has not yet discovered*) that is why some will even leave suicide notes explaining what was in their minds, what they were *thinking* and *their mental pains and anguish.* All suicides are caused **by negative thought energy,** their source thought being, *"I'm going to kill myself because . . ."* There is nothing positive about this, not the *negative thought* itself, or the negative results, or the final behavior and action that they take to end their own lives. According to Medical Daily, Jaleesa Baulkman, in her June 29, 2016, article, "Take Me to Church: Attending Religious Services Linked to Lower Suicide Rates Among Women," God does matter in people's lives and God saves lives when we believe in him and put our mental focus on him, and asking God to help us solve our everyday problems.

That is why most religions teach about hope and the creation of a better future for ourselves and the importance of learning to control our thinking, and when we do think, to think positive thoughts of love, peace, and forgiving those who hurt us, and not to focus on negative thoughts. So that even when we think our parents hate us or they beat us up and throw us in the streets, we can still find hope and peace in God's love. I strongly believe the answer to our society's mental stress and all sickness associated with this illness isn't religion or science alone or separately; the answer is in both. I agree with Albert Einstein when he said: *"Science without religion is lame; religion without science is blind."* We need both, it's not one or the other.

The reason why I say this is that some people will get God easily right away at 100 percent, which is great. However, not everybody can do that, because it all depends on how mentally negative the person's mind is against God and their life overall, what trauma they've gone through, and the kind of negative education they've been exposed to against God. It's like learning calculus, some people will understand it and get it right away, some won't. It depends on the person's level of understanding.

Scientists and educators, for example, will find it difficult to teach about the invisible God since most of them do not believe that an invisible God/Universe exists—what it is and how it works naturally. This is because like most people, they only believe in what you can see and touch as their only reality, and teachers often tell students that God doesn't exist since it is invisible, which creates confusion and creates further mental separation from the real God of the Universe.

> ***You must unlearn what you have learned.***
> –Master Yoda (Star Wars)

For me, when I was young, since I was only a 50 percent God believer and 50 percent science believer, and I had my childhood trauma of abuse, I was a very sickly kid, both mentally and physically, and all doctors just wanted to give me drugs. So to mentally heal myself took years to undo all my education from science's teachings that God did not exist and to get rid of all the hate and anger that was stuck inside my mind from all the physical abuse and rape that happened to me. But **once I learned to quiet my mind, learned to think less, and replaced my negative thinking from hate and anger with positive thoughts of forgiveness and God's love and peace**; my brain tumor went away, my allergies went away, my depression went away, my panic attacks went away, my stress went away, all without drugs. **It was through understanding what God is and believing in God at 100 percent (not at 50 percent), having a strong relationship with God through prayer and meditation, learning how to use His spiritual energy on a daily basis, and controlling my mind's thoughts, is what healed my physical body.** This is why all doctors should include GOD as part of their healing program with all their patients so that they can help heal their patients faster.

The most effective way to heal one's own body is a combination of healing all three areas of yourself:

*1. **SPIRITUAL** healing only happens when you **believe 100 percent** in the **existence of God's invisible universal spiritual energy level** and that **your body is made of it**. A less than 100 percent believer will not allow you to see yourself as a whole being, and therefore, healing for you in this manner will be impossible. This is* *because, again, all three are interrelated: your spiritual energy, body, and mind are all connected as one unit with God's universe. This is where your inner power of healing resides, so we all need to learn to put our mental focus here, in the invisible realm that everything is made of, since no one is sick at this level. This is who we really all are already, energy that cannot be destroyed, according to physics.*

2.   MENTAL *healing is when you learn to reduce the number of thoughts you generate every day, learn to* **clear your mind from negativity, and be 100 percent in control of your own thoughts** *so that you are not easily mentally distracted with nonsense going on around you when you are only focused in the temporary object level of chaos that's always changing. A less than 100 percent mental clearing of useless thoughts will always impede your spiritual/energy, mental, and physical healing because all three are connected as part of who you are, together as ONE in God's invisible eternal energy force field. Also,* **NOT knowing** *how to work with your invisible spiritual energy force field, the universe's invisible canvas or screen, keeps you from successfully creating your happiness goals faster. Most importantly, achieving mental peace heals the body, when done naturally without drugs, when you are consciously in control of your own mental thoughts, and are focused on God's invisible spiritual energy level, where there are no objects to judge. So do not put too much focus and credence on the object level of madness and chaos, where there are 8 billion mental realities exist. Everybody fighting with each other for righteousness, stuck in the object-level ego because everybody thinks their perspective is the only right perspective of the universe. This is because we're NOT taught in school that there is a difference between the ONE* **physical** *Universe versus the 8-BILLION* **mental** *Universe we all get to create for ourselves and we're NOT taught in school how to control our minds naturally is society's biggest problem today.*

3.   PHYSICAL *healing only happened for me once I learned spiritual and mental healing first. My inability to manage and control my thoughts (since we're not taught in school how to control our mental thoughts) created all my mental stress, which then created my allergy, psoriasis, depression, brain tumor, and marriage problems. I used to* *get sick all the time, but once I learned to get rid of all the negative thoughts that were not working for me, and I learned about the God Factor, my body was able to heal itself faster naturally without drugs, and I was able to heal my marriage as well without the cost of hiring an expensive therapist. You can do the same to heal yourself and your relationships because you are the only one in control of your own mind that creates your reality, including all your sickness from mental stress. So take responsibility and start controlling your own mental universe by creating your own perspective out of love. That is why the Bible says:*

You are gods *[small 'g' for mini-gods as God's children];*
you are all sons of the Most High *[big "G" for God].*
–Psalm 82:6, KJV

Even though I thought I was a Christian, I discovered that I was more of a science believer, always wavering, and I found my mind split between the two disciplines. This mental anguish in finding mental peace in this area caused me such great mental and physical illness as it was very difficult for me to mentally consolidate and make sense out of the two seemingly different concepts. My mental confusion was because I grew up taking science classes with teachers and peers who kept insisting that God did not exist and that God believers were fools.

Then there were all the various Christian sects I listened to in search for mental peace, but unfortunately, they too added to the mass confusion in my head as some taught only from the Old Testament that focused on only good works I needed to perform. These churches taught that God would love me only if I followed the 10 Commandments, and they taught that we are separate from God physically and that God hated gays, and all other religions because God only loved Christians, so as a follower, I should also hate all these people was the subliminal message. This is the same message that other religious terrorist groups teach their followers who are mentally stuck at the object level.

Then there were some preachers who taught only from the New Testament, focusing only on God's unconditional love; and then there were those who kept switching between the New and Old Testament. So what I teach here is how I mentally consolidated all this mess that allowed me to have mental peace in this area that worked for me so that mental healing was possible for me. It wasn't until I learned God's unconditional love for all things that I found long-lasting happiness in my life, so that no matter what temporary changes or chaos was happening in the world of objects for me, it did not matter to me anymore because my mental focus was mostly on God's love, peace, and joy, in the invisible level that is inside all things already that gave me mental stability. After all, there is no chaos in the invisible realm to judge.

Therefore, **mastering the difference between VISIBLE vs. INVISIBLE levels heals. When you are able to heal yourself spiritually and mentally at 100 percent, your body becomes automatically healthier,** and you end up saving yourself from potentially deadly illnesses, not to mention saving lots of money from having to go to the doctor.

When I was young, my mother, who was a nurse, would automatically run and bring me a spoonful of antihistamine every time she would hear me sneeze and sneeze with my eyes teary; and I would get massive headaches from the allergies during the spring and summers when flowers were blooming. We had jasmine flowers growing outside my window, so half the year, my body was totally miserable from my pollen allergies. And because we lived in LA, the air pollution was so bad sometimes my body would just go crazy. I also noticed my allergies got worse whenever my mental stress from school exams and fighting with one of my many siblings was added to the mix. So I continually took antihistamines while growing up because that seemed to be the only option we had at the time, but the drugs never really healed me. The drugs were only temporary fixes to my allergy that always seemed to keep coming back. Because of the many years of taking drugs, I hated taking them because they didn't seem to work for me to permanently heal my physical illness.

Then two years after I was married, in my early thirties, when my first daughter was born, my stress level skyrocketed because my husband and I were fighting all the time. It seemed that the stress of being a new mom and work stress were causing brain overload. So all the negative thinking I was creating in my head—since thoughts are just another form of energy force that I was keeping bottled inside me—had to go somewhere. So it manifested as psoriasis. Psoriasis is a form of itchy, dry, red skin disease that seemed to flare up whenever I was mentally stressed, which seemed to be all the time. The doctors would give me topical medicine, but again, it was only temporary relief of the pain and irritation. The drugs never permanently healed my skin problem because the doctors were only healing the symptoms, not the source of the problem, which in my case, was the mental stress I was creating in my head from negative thinking. And because I didn't know how to get rid of the negative thinking, my psoriasis kept flaring up for years!

This was because I was following only what medical science could provide for me, but they were only temporary fixes. You see, they only focused on treating my body's physical symptoms, not the source of the mental problems I was having, and that is why my physical ailments kept coming back. Healing for me came years later, once I was able to resolve my mental issues in regard to my body, mind, and energy/spirit connection and change my belief system to the following:

- I now **believe** that God's invisible spiritual energy force exists as physics proves it as 100 percent real. So, I'm no longer just a 50 percent believer.
- I now have a **loving relationship** with God, and I'm still *learning to improve how to effectively work with Him* in dealing with various areas of my life since things are always changing in the material world of objects. Since we are not taught in school, I had to figure this out on my own.
- I now have another **option** for my mind to *place my negative thought energy forces (or demons as some religions call them) that I was creating in my head by letting these negative thoughts flow through me (ex: forgiveness, meditation) toward God or the universe* to deal with instead of keeping the thoughts bottled up inside my head that was making my body physically sick or acting out my negative feelings of anger or unhappiness toward others, thereby hurting others along the way.

Now if your body is already sick, or you are in a car accident and you are hurt, or you are having a stroke or heart attack, make sure you go to emergency right away. You want to combine your doctors' methods for healing your physical body with your spiritual and mind healing as suggested in this book so your body can recover faster. This is how you can help yourself and the doctors who are trying to help your body heal.

However, in helping others, we have to remember that not everybody is going to believe that God's invisible spiritual energy exists or believe what we believe, especially our loved ones, so we have to respect their choices and love them anyway. Since they are in control of their own brain, as you are only in control of your own brain. My brother who has a master's degree in theology, for example, even though he is religious, his religious beliefs for the most part are still mentally stuck on the object level ego. So, he is only a 50 percent God believer since he doesn't know the process of how to work with it at 100 percent; that is why he suffers from mental stress and severe back pains. My mother is another example of somebody who is religious, but because she too puts her mental focus on the object level as her religion teaches, she suffers from a lot of physical pains as a result. However, because I love her very much, I take her to the doctor and buy her pain medications to help ease her pain whenever she asks me to. I never force my loved ones or anybody about my beliefs, this is how I show others I love them no matter what and have mental peace at the same time. I only like to ***teach*** my beliefs to those who are willing to learn and want to learn and are ready to learn. However, if they don't, they don't. And I'm okay with that too, since they are the once's in control of their own minds, not me and I love them anyways.

Helping Others Heal without Book (*slow way*) and with Book (*faster way*):

> *Heal the sick, cleanse the lepers, raise the [mentally] dead, cast out devils [negative thinking]: freely ye have received [as you learn], freely give [teach others].*
> –Matthew 10:8, KJV

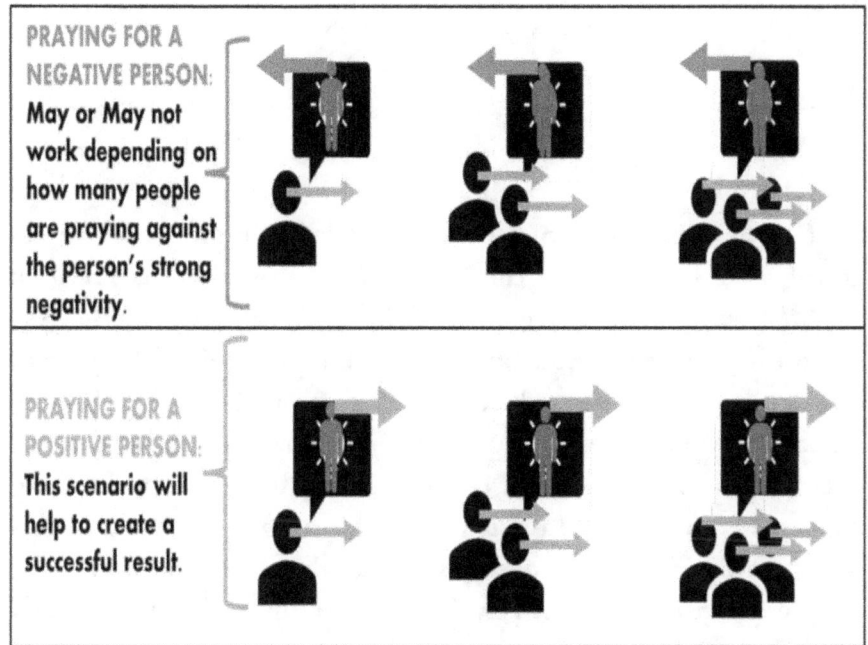

It's one thing to heal yourself spiritually and mentally since you are in control of your own mind. You can do it much easier and faster just by reading this book, reading other self-help books, or going to church. The more receptive you are to learning about God's love and peace, the faster you will receive your personal healing. However, it's another when trying to help heal another person, since they are in control of their own mind, not you.

Remember, all three, body, mind, and God's spiritual energy are all connected as ONE. This means you, and everybody else, are also all connected as one with God's universe in the invisible spiritual energy level.

This connection we all have with God's invisible spiritual energy level, allows us to help heal others through prayer, once we are healed ourselves first and understand the God process. The stronger our own mental connection with God (at +100 percent), the better we can help heal others.

This is why praying for others helps heal them **some** of the time; however, success in helping others heal spiritually, mentally and physically really depends on how high and thick the other person's mental wall is against God when trying to help them. No matter what, we always have to try anyway, even if the person has already given up on life. As long as there is a slight spark of life left in them, even if it's only 1 percent in the person's mind, I believe there is always hope that such a person being prayed on can turn around and be healed from an early death of suicide, cancer, or tumors.

It's the summation of all the invisible spiritual energy forces acting and surrounding the body *(since everything is made of invisible energy according to physics)*, **that results in whether the person gets healed or not. This is like a baseball being hit by a bat, to calculate the distance the ball falls is determined by adding up all the invisible forces acting on the ball at that time; like kinetic energy, gravity pull down, friction from the direction of wind energy, etc. that I spoke about at the beginning of the book. This is why praying for others works sometimes depending on how many people are praying positively for the person and how mentally negative or positive the person needing healing is.**

As an example, there were several things I did try to help heal my daughter since she refused to read my book, and my kids did not go to church since one of my daughters was traumatized there. I loved her so much that I wanted and needed to save her life no matter what because the doctors failed her miserably even after four years of their care. I had to help her using the long way.

1. Every morning and night I would pray and thank God for my daughter, for giving my daughter peace of mind, for surrounding her with His love, for His protection, and for His power to help her succeed in her projects **as if the projects were already done**.

2. I also instructed her to make sure to give me a call any time she started having panic attacks so that whenever her brain was thinking negatively too much, I would calm her down by teaching her to look at things from a different positive perspective or telling her not to take things too personally or too seriously.

3. I would tell her to pray for the job she might be interviewing for or to forgive somebody whom she felt was being mean to her.

4. I started coming up with creative ways to remind her that I loved her, like randomly texting her emoji kisses or sending her funny memes just to make her laugh almost daily.

She now only looks for videos by young people closer to her age for inspiration on YouTube that teach positive messages about loving and forgiving people and how to be successful with her projects. Now she rarely has panic attacks because she's learned to mentally control her own thoughts. She's so much happier now that she's not mentally stuck in her negative thinking, her mental hell of self-destruction—and no drugs involved! All I did was teach her how to build a strong relationship with God, lots of praying between the two of us, and I taught her how to look at situations more positively instead of negatively. It took about three years, but it was worth saving my daughter from suicide and addiction to antidepressant drugs prescribed by her psychiatrist. Of course, the process could have been so much faster if she had just read my book explaining about God, how to work with God, praying every day, positive thinking, learning to forgive and love all her negative-thinking friends, but hers was the long way of teaching.

All suicides lack the 100 percent mental connection with God, lack the knowledge of God's love that is inside them, and lack the knowledge of how to work with God's spiritual energy to help heal the cause of their mental suffering. Like most people, they only operate at the negative **mental** level (ex: thoughts of killing or harming themselves) and **body** level (*by killing the body itself*); *however, they have not learned to effectively work and use the invisible spiritual energy level that is inside them.* Other than the religious books, like the Bible or the Torah, we have to search and seek our own instructions on how to work our body, mind, and energy/spirit ourselves, since we do not come with instructions on how to use our body parts when we are born. Even man-made artificial intelligence robots come with instructions. Shouldn't we be seeking instructions from those who know best how to use our body parts *(body, mind, and spiritual energy)* more effectively so that we can be happy, have mental peace, and have love in our lives?

Here is an opportunity for all of us to teach our kids and others now, about God's unconditional eternal love that exists inside all things, and how to use our minds more effectively through mind management, and teaching problem-solving skills. This, to me, should be taught in all schools so we can help reduce suicide rates and reduce drug use in our children. But schools fail us and our children, and our government fails us because the money generated from legal pharmaceutical drugs is in the billions for both government and the pharma industry, which is their priority. Until we all change and learn how our body parts work best together as ONE unit; confusion, madness, and drug use will continue, and the madness will remain the norm.

Isn't it ironic, though, how we send our children to school to improve their thinking, yet our scientists and our teachers have yet to even realize that the "thoughts" we mentally generate are even real? Yep, that is our educational system! Think about that for a while. Then there are those who do not believe in God or the universe existing as invisible spiritual energy even exist. They come in different labels but they believe giving our children drugs to control their uncontrolled "thoughts" *(that mainstream scientists and educators do not believe exist)* and suicide is okay and is still a better option than teaching our kids about God's love that exists inside all things or about managing our thoughts naturally.

I believe that we, *as parents, aunts, uncles, grandmas, grandpas, and friends,* who are strong with God can all help save our loved ones from mental stress and self-destruction. I believe we can all help to reduce the suicide rate in our children in this country, the next generation, by teaching them about God's love and how to work with it. Together we can all help save lives by teaching them how to reach their higher energy level of unconditional love for all.

Honestly, the fastest way I have helped heal people spiritually and mentally is just by giving them a copy of this book because the book teaches the entire process of how our body, mind, and God's eternal spiritual energy work best together as one unit since they are connected so that they can learn it on their own. Depending on how much they already know about God or how much they hate God or people, and how hungry they are for answers, their own willingness to learn will determine if the book helps them at all because in the end, it's all between each person individually and God. Each of us has to be willing to break down our own mental barriers to let God's love into our hearts and minds, not the other way around. God is already inside us, knocking and knocking just waiting for all of us to open our mind's doors, to DISCOVER and see His FREE gifts of freedom from the visible object-level chaos. It is inside us and all around us, beyond the illusion of objects toward the invisible realm of God's spiritual energy level that everything is made of, where only peace, love, happiness, joy, and God's power reside. We just have to learn to open our mind's doors to release our power, which is God's love and power that is inside us already.

NOTE: If you need more help or want more examples of natural healing after reading this book, I recommend you watch Dr. Joe Dispenza's YouTube on "How I Healed Myself" from being paralyzed when he was hit by a truck while riding his bike. He healed himself naturally in spite of his doctors telling him, "You'll never be able to walk again". His bike accident happened in 1986; about the same time I was told I had a brain tumor that I was supposed to have for the rest of my life. So we both were doing our own individual research to heal ourselves naturally about the same time. I was looking at it from the engineering point of view since that is my background and he was looking at his sickness from his chiropractic background point of view, but we were both able to come up with a similar conclusion of healing ourselves naturally; through Body, Mind, and Spiritual Energy connection together as ONE unit.

Now he teaches others how to heal themselves naturally through his books, YouTube videos, and seminars. I found his work just most recently and I am so glad others are teaching this natural process of healing the Body, Mind, and Spiritual Energy

as ONE unit, that I've found to work to heal myself also, even though I've never taken his seminars or read his books myself. I just love listening to his YouTube videos. Also, I recommend watching his "25-Min Self Healing Meditation For Emotional & Physical Healing" in YouTube. His official website is drjoedispenza.com if you want to take his seminars to learn more about the natural healing of our body parts at the invisible spiritual energy level, called the quantum field.

Also, I recommend viewing scientist, Dr. Bruce Lipton's podcast, "Healing Without Medication". He says: "STRESS is responsible for over the 90% of the health crisis on this planet. Genes are responsible for less than 1% of the disease on this planet. Then he says: "Scientific fact: There is NO GENE that causes cancer... Everything, he says is energy."

Buddhist Beliefs

All living beings have the same basic wish to be happy and avoid suffering, but very few people understand the real causes of happiness and suffering.

We generally believe that external conditions such as food, friends, cars, and money are the real causes of happiness, and as a result we devote nearly all our time and energy to acquiring these. Superficially it seems that these things can make us happy, but if we look more deeply we shall see that they also bring us a lot of suffering and problems.

Happiness and suffering are opposites, so if something is a real cause of happiness it cannot give rise to suffering. If food, money, and so forth really are causes of happiness, they can never be causes of suffering; yet we know from our own experience that they often do cause suffering. For example, one of our main interests is food, but the food we eat is also the principal cause of most of our ill health and sickness.

In the process of producing the things we feel will make us happy, we have polluted our environment to such an extent that the very air we breathe and the water we drink now threaten our health and well-being. We love the freedom and independence a car can give us, but the cost in accidents and environmental destruction is enormous.

We feel that money is essential for us to enjoy life, but the pursuit of money also causes immense problems and anxiety. Even our family and friends, with whom we enjoy so many happy moments, can also bring us a lot of worry and heartache.

In recent years our understanding and control of the external world have increased considerably, and as a result we have witnessed remarkable material progress; but there has not been a corresponding increase in human happiness.

There is no less suffering in the world today, and there are no fewer problems. Indeed, it could be said that there are now more problems and greater unhappiness than ever before. This shows that the solution to our problems, and to those of society as a whole, does not lie in knowledge or control of the external world.

Why is this? Happiness and suffering are states of mind, and so their main causes cannot be found outside the mind. The real source of happiness is inner peace. If our mind is peaceful, we shall be happy all the time, regardless of external conditions, but if it is disturbed or troubled in any way, we shall never be happy, no matter how good our external conditions may be.

External conditions can only make us happy if our mind is peaceful. We can understand this through our own experience. For instance, even if we are in the most beautiful surroundings and have everything we need, the moment we get angry any happiness we may have disappears. This is because anger has destroyed our inner peace.

We can see from this that if we want true, lasting happiness we need to develop and maintain a special experience of inner peace. The only way to do this is by training our mind through spiritual practice – gradually reducing and eliminating our negative, disturbed states of mind and replacing them with positive, peaceful states.

Eventually, through continuing to improve our inner peace we shall experience permanent inner peace, or 'nirvana'. Once we have attained nirvana we shall be happy throughout our life, and in life after life. We shall have solved all our problems and accomplished the true meaning of our human life.

Extracted from Transform Your Life by Venerable Geshe Kelsang Gyatso.

PART III

(+) Body

"Taking Action in Creating Miracles"

7

Working Toward Your Purpose and Goals

And the LORD God took the man, and put him into the Garden of Eden to dress it and to keep it.
—Genesis 2:15, KJV

*Whatever you do, **work heartily, as for the Lord and not for men,** knowing that from the Lord you will receive the inheritance as your reward. You are serving the Lord Christ.*
—Colossians 3:2, ESV

Whether you think you can or think you can't. You're Right.
—Henry Ford

*I [God] have said, **Ye are gods** [we are all mini-gods, not big God, here to co-create with Father God our own mental reality, our own unique perspective of our own Garden of Eden]; and all of you are children of the most High [as His children, we all inherited his power to create and to heal since he is inside us as eternal spiritual energy].*
–Psalm 82:6, KJV

*Verily, verily, I say unto you, **He** that **believeth** on me **(Jesus teachings)**, the works that I do shall he do also **(you can do what I do)**; and greater works **(teaching, healing, creating)** than these shall he do **(you can do better)**; because I go unto my Father.*
–John 14:12, KJV

God put us on this earth, in His Garden of Eden the physical world of objects that we can see and touch, so that we keep it and maintain it; so that we make it better by managing it and taking care of it. This is our purpose. This is where our partnership with Him comes into play; He created it **(the ONE physical world),** and our job is to make it better by dressing it up the way we want it, without destroying it—just as in the story about my mother and the plant bulb. God created the flower bulb; my mother just helped it along by creating an environment where it would grow and prosper by taking care of it, planting it, watering it, and fertilizing it. And it flourished as a result. This is God's purpose for us— here, to help manage His garden and be His gardeners. It's teamwork!

As I said earlier, we were not put here to destroy God's Garden of Eden, the physical world of objects. We are here to help manage and make the world, the next generation, a better place to live for everybody. This is so that we can all evolve together to our next better version generation of who we all are as humans, not just to benefit ourselves or just for a few in the here and now because that's just greed.

What Is It Exactly that We Are All Supposed to Create?
(*PHYSICAL* Universe *vs.* the *MENTAL* Universe)

"A fundamental conclusion of the new physics also acknowledges that the **observer [you] creates the reality. As observers, we are personally involved with the creation of our own reality.**" *Physicists are being forced to admit that the universe is a "mental" construction. Pioneering physicist Sir James Jeans writes, "The stream of knowledge is heading toward a non-mechanical reality; the universe begins to look more like a great* **thought** *than like a great machine. Mind no longer appears to be an accidental intruder into the realm of matter, we ought rather hail it as* **the creator and governor of the realm of matter**"

(R. C. Henry, "**The Mental Universe,**" Nature 436:29, 2005; https://www.collective-evolution.com/2014/09/27/this-is-the-world-of-quantum-physics-nothing-is-solid-and-everything-is-energy/).

Did you know that **no two people think exactly alike**? Not even identical twins. I know because I dated an identical twin, and he was always fighting with his brother. This is why so many people fight. This is also why we have wars, why so many people are divorced, and why siblings fight. Even experts disagree on a lot of issues, just watch the show called Mystery Diagnosis, where a patient goes to multiple doctors, and all the expert doctors give different diagnoses. Why? We are all taught in school and by mainstream scientists *that there is only one universe.* **Then why aren't we all, almost eight billion people in the world, seeing and believing the same thing at the object level? Why do we fight with each other and have wars?**

When I was twenty-one years old, I was with a friend who slipped on oil that was on the ground while he was getting gas at a gas station, and as he was falling, he hit his shoulder against the gas pump. Afterward, he was in a lot of pain and he could not move his arm, so I took him to emergency. The emergency doctor wanted to amputate his arm immediately, and my friend left the hospital room so fast it scared him. The next day he went to a neurologist, and after doing X-rays, that doctor told him he had severed his nerve, but it was still attached. He just needed to put his arm in a sling for a few months to give the nerve time to regenerate itself. He ended up following the second doctor's recommendations, and it worked! He didn't have to amputate his arm after all.

The point is, **at the object level, there is no such thing as one truth in the universe for everybody, even though we are taught in school that there is only one universe,** which is false teaching. This is because there could only be *mental perspectives or views* in the world of objects for people because of the almost eight billion individual human brains. This is why they say when you are very sick and in need of a doctor, make sure you get at least two or three or more other opinions before doing anything invasive.

The only place that there is **ONE UNIVERSAL TRUTH is in the INVISIBLE spiritual energy level** that everything is made of inside all objects because everything at this level is **invisible**, so there are no objects to see, nothing is separate, and nothing to judge. Since physicists say energy can never be created or destroyed, this means it has always existed and, therefore, eternal—as religion has been teaching for centuries, so they are actually in agreement. This means that the invisible spiritual energy level of God the Universe, has always been the same forever and ever. It never changes because it's invisible, and it can never be created or destroyed; it just is.

However, if in the **VISIBLE object level** you have a rose, and you ask people what they think about the rose, then you'll probably get different viewpoints about the rose. One might say, "I love roses." Somebody else might say, "I hate roses." Another might say, "I like the smell of roses." Yet another might say, "I hate the thorns." In other words, even though there is only *one physical universe that God created, his Garden of Eden*, there are actually almost eight **billion different perspectives or viewpoints of the same physical universe called,** *the Mental Universe.* That's the number of people in the world today because of our individual brains, where we get to create our own individual mental reality or perspective of the universe. This is just another example of God's intelligent design of abundance (8 billion perspective viewpoints) at work. This is why the Bible says, *"Ye are gods,"* (*Psalm 82:6*), **here to create our very own Garden of Eden, our own mental perspective of our own universal reality.**

But most of us fight against each other because most of us think there is only one world perspective out there, and our own perspective is the only right perspective, and everybody else is wrong. This is why so many of us suffer mentally and physically, and why we fight with each other. This is another one of the false teachings in our educational system because we were all taught in school that there is only one universe and one reality and that they are the same, but they're not. This is why we are all walking around thinking our own version of the universe must be the only **right** universe. However, because we humans have our own individual brains, this allows us all to actually **create our own mental perspective** (*almost eight billion versions of reality*) of the one physical universe that God created. This is why most people walk around mentally stuck in the visible object level in their own mental ego of righteousness. And you know, it's mentally draining for the rest of us to be around people like this for very long because we too think our reality is the only one that is right, not theirs.

Not understanding the difference between the ONE-*Physical* universe versus the almost EIGHT BILLION *Mental* universal perspectives we each get to create is one of the greatest problems and headaches for humans today. This is because our mainstream scientists and educators have not yet discovered that there is actually a difference between the one *PHYSICAL* world of objects versus the eight Billion *MENTAL* perspectives of the world, that is why they currently do not teach these concepts in schools. We probably have to wait another 2,000 years for them to discover this difference.

Most of us want everybody to think and act like us, and when they don't, we try to change them by bullying them. This is what husbands try to do with their wives, what wives try to do to their husbands, and what parents try to do to control their children. This is how we try to control each other, but when we can't force the other person to think and act like us, we try to put them down, call them names, and beat them up physically and/or mentally to try to get them to see our world view; but no matter what, we suffer and make others suffer as well. Until we learn to *let people go and allow them and accept them to have their own mental perspective of their own world reality* and we learn to stop trying to force others into our viewpoint, we will never have mental peace or happiness, and we will continue to make ourselves and others miserable and sick along the way because of our limited viewpoint and understanding of this fact.

Even in a business setting, if you are the CEO or management or engineer, where you need to try to convince employees or management to go a particular direction to fix a particular problem, in the end, it's each individual who has to decide to mentally follow your recommendations or not. You'll remember my friend at work who had two heart attacks because he couldn't get everybody to see his viewpoint all the time and would fight and argue with other managers and other engineers. He took everything so personally that he had to take an early retirement just so he wouldn't kill himself from all the mental stress he was creating in his head.

This is why ***each of us is responsible for creating our own perspective of our own reality at the object level.*** So, it's our own free choice or free will to create our own ***positive*** Garden of Eden or ***negative*** hell, since we are the only ones who are in control of our own minds. This is why **we are the only ones who can make us happy without needing to hurt anybody else** along the way by trying to force others to see our views all the time. Such an approach comes from lack, that there is only one reality, as taught in school. This is why **people will always disappoint you if you expect them to read your mind and know what you want to make you happy since nobody is a mind reader.**

Remember *there is no such thing as "one truth" or "the truth" in the material world of objects, there are only eight billion different perspectives or viewpoints.* This is why not everybody is going to believe what you believe in, at 100 percent all the time. In fact, no one does or ever will. It is impossible! This is futile; it's a waste of time and energy to believe this. You can try to **teach** others your beliefs, but please **do not force** them, as this will only cause people to hate you and want to fight you. This is why *it's a waste of time to fight with people because their mental universe is always going to be based on their age, gender, race, culture, history, education, religion, where they live, where they grew up, family, etc.*

Look at the religious extremists who want to kill non-believers or infidels. They use negative thoughts of fear and destruction to try to purposely force others to believe in their religion. Even most Christians are taught that there is only one way to know God, which is wrong because there are unlimited ways to learn and work with God. If that were true, how come there are so many Christian denominations, multiple Bible versions, and so many different interpretations of the Bible?

This is pure madness to believe this! If each of us can just leave people alone, so we can give them freedom to choose what they want to believe, and we learn to accept everybody's different viewpoints, we would have peace. However, some of us are so egotistic and righteous, insisting that our own view is the only possible viewpoint that oftentimes we end up hurting others without even realizing we're doing it. This is because we are so automatic with our thinking and behaving most of the time that our version of our universe is the only right universe. Then we make ourselves mentally and physically sick when we don't get our way and/or when we can't make others believe what we believe and behave the way we want them to behave because we can't control them.

Only you can stop *your* own mental MADNESS because only you are in control of your own mind's negative thinking and all your behaviors that go along with it. Try to forget about other people until you yourself learn to control your own mind to create love, joy, peace, and happiness in your own life, so you can also be an example and teach others how to create the same since we are not taught this in school. This is why we have to forgive others since they don't know either. *"Hypocrite! First, remove the plank from your own eye, and then you will see clearly to remove the speck out of your brother's eye!"* Mathew 7:5-NKJV

For example, if love or more love is what you are seeking in your life, then you need to learn to create your own love scenes in your life. Once you figure out what you want for yourself, then go out and create it, again without needing to hurt anybody else along the way. This is very important because you don't need to! If you feel you need to force others to believe what you believe or do what you want to do, that is coming from a lack of abundance. The thought that there is not enough love, joy, peace, and happiness to go around and that there is only ONE reality in the world of objects as currently being taught in our education today is the reason most of us are struggling in this area.

When my kids were in high school and working all the time, the only time we got to spend with them in their busy schedule was at night after they would come home to rest in the living room in front of the TV. We had a large L-shape sofa and all of us most of the time slept together in the living room. We just let them watch whatever they wanted because I hated fighting over who got to control the remote because all my husband and I really cared about was being physically near them. So this was our way of creating a win-win for us. They got to relax and watch what they wanted, and we got to be physically be with them, which is what we wanted. This was our family love scene, but now that they are on their own, I text them at random times just to tell them I love them and am thinking of them. I think the most powerful words a parent can tell their children is **"I love you."** This is healing because most of us never hear this from our parents and we wonder sometimes if they love us.

After my friend committed suicide from lack of love from his parents thinking he was a "mistake" and my own negative trauma experience with my abusive father, I wanted to make sure my kids always knew that I loved them. This is how I help create love and mental peace for them and for me, by creating and building a strong loving relationship with them, even when they are far away. With all the negative bullying at school and work and the mental stress that most of our children experience today, the last thing they need is their parents yelling and bullying them too. As a parent, at least I know I can control what I say and how I treat them, and I choose to be loving with my kids all the time.

My favorite love scene with my husband is holding hands whenever we are out doing errands or just snuggling with him while watching TV in the living room without fighting for the remote. I always let him watch whatever he wants, which is usually military shows, and all I want is to always just cuddle, so this is how I create a win-win love scene for us and how I create an abundance of love in our life, by making sure we all get what we want.

We can all create abundance in our lives with our families and friends when we start looking at the world of objects, not from "there is only one right viewpoint, and that's mine," to realize that *there are abundant viewpoints out there, almost eight billion.* We all need to stop fighting with each other like the reality shows on TV that some of us watch, which are really fake scenes anyway just to create drama. So let's stop creating fight scenes in our lives that make us and everybody around us miserable and sick. Instead replace them with love scenes, so we can all stop the generational curse in our families! So, I ask you:

What are your love scenes?

God's Three-Step Process Plan for Creation

According to John 1:1 (KJV), *"In the beginning was the Word [thoughts], and the Word was with God [invisible energy/spirit]."* Therefore, **everything began with words or thoughts and ideas first**, and then the work to create change that brought about the manifestation of the ideas followed afterward. The following is part of Genesis 1, as an example of God's plan using a three-step process plan in how we are to manifest our own ideas and plans in creating our own Garden of Eden perspective reality. The order of priority was obviously important since He created light first before the plants, otherwise the plants would die without sunlight first being created. Then He just created and **worked** His priorities one by one until they changed and evolved and materialized to where we are now, which took time, from the beginning to now. Work in physics is defined as a change in energy. This is where processing time or change via growth/evolution took over (one day=1000 years, 2 Peter 3:8). Much like in any garden after planting a seed, all plants take time to change, grow, and evolve to maturity.

Genesis 1, KJV:

1: In the beginning God created the heaven and the earth.

2: And the earth was without form, and void; and darkness was upon the face of the deep. And the Spirit of God moved upon the face of the waters.

*3: And God said [**thoughts/ideas**], Let there be light: and there was light. [**He worked it**].*

*6: And God said [**thoughts/ideas**], Let there be a firmament in the midst of the waters, and let it divide the waters from the waters, and it was so. [**He worked it**].*

*9: And God said [**thoughts/ideas**], Let the waters under the heaven be gathered together unto one place, and let the dry land appear: and it was so. [**He worked it**].*

*11: And God said [**thoughts/ideas**], Let the earth bring forth grass, the herb yielding seed, and the fruit tree yielding fruit after his kind, whose seed is in itself, upon the earth: and it was so. [**He worked it**].*

*14: And God said [**thoughts/ideas**], Let there be lights in the firmament of the heaven to divide the day from the night; and let them be for signs, and for seasons, and for days, and years:*

*15: and it was so [**He worked it**].*

God basically knew what He wanted to create. He had a plan of ideas and prioritized them, then He executed the plan, and this is how we are to manifest our own ideas and plans in our own Garden of Eden too. Business owners are actually better than non-business people in creating and formalizing their ideas. They are good at planning and prioritizing which steps need to be done first, then working on each step until their goals are met. The problem with a lot of people is that they often don't know what they want to make them happy, or they expect others to know what they want without expressing what they want, but they expect others to read their minds to make them happy. ***Remember, people are not mind readers, so they can't make you happy, since they don't know what you want.***

This is the problem with a lot of couples, that is one of the reasons why we have 50 percent divorced couples in the US. We all need to get out of the mind-reading business because it does not work well; nobody can read our minds. ***We are all responsible for making ourselves happy because we are the only ones in control of our own minds; nobody else is in control but us.*** For example, I love getting flowers, especially from my husband, but most of the time he only gives me flowers during holidays, my birthday, and our anniversary, so when I'm in the mood for flowers outside those days, I just go buy them myself for me. The other thing I did was plant lots of flowering plants outside around our house so that we always had flowers all year round, and I always kept real or fake flowers inside the house, which made me happy. I stopped waiting for the next holiday, birthday, or anniversary to get flowers from him because he couldn't read my mind when I wanted to receive flowers beyond those days.

So to create your own Garden of Eden, ***know what you want to make you happy***, and set plans and priorities as to which task needs to be done first, then go do each task one at a time until you meet all your happiness goals. If you need help in creating or manifesting your goals, ask God to help you, ask family or friends, or hire somebody who is an expert in the domain you are seeking, or search the internet for free information to get ideas on your projects.

When my oldest daughter was praying about losing weight, a personal trainer came into her life somehow. Now she has set a goal to lose fifty pounds, so she hired him and he's helping her lose weight by working out two-to-three hours a day and doing meal preps by following his recommended food meals. She's only been in the program for three weeks, and already she's lost more than fifteen pounds. She takes weekly pictures of herself to monitor the changes in her body. He even encouraged her to compete in the next women's bodybuilding competition, which is his training expertise. So now she set a goal of winning the competition in six months. The competition encourages her to be serious and diligent with her workout. She loves it! She's so happy, even with just going through the process of losing weight, especially since she gets to buy a new smaller bikini every month. She figures that even if she doesn't win, her ultimate goal is just to lose fifty pounds to feel better about herself and be healthier at the same time. So she wins no matter what the results are of the competition. This is one of her happiness goals. **What are your happiness goals?**

Creating and Serving

Remember, **thoughts** are invisible energy. Because your mind works like a magnet, you have the power to attract things toward yourself based on the thoughts you generate. Some examples of energy are gravity, magnets, and electricity. Whatever thoughts you focus on and put in your mind, whether positive or negative, will be similar objects that are attracted to you whenever you try to manifest your thoughts. You also need to learn to control your thoughts and minimize the number of thoughts you generate so you can avoid going mentally crazy and stressed. That way you can reduce the need to get drunk, take drugs, or fight every time you get depressed, stressed, or angry.

Creation and serving others go hand in hand. If you want to be successful, you need to learn how to master both. All successful companies create and serve people something—some kind of product or service. The more people you are able to help and serve, the more help and servitude will be returned to you. Serving others means giving yourself to others. You can give yourself in the form of your time, your money, your love, your help, your forgiveness, your gifts, your products, or your services. This is especially true in relationships. I think some people forget that you can't just keep taking from the other person in the relationship. You also have to give your time and love to the other person, however that might show up. Don't just take, take, take to the point where the other person wants to leave you.

Here's an example. When my sister started working at a new job, her new boss noticed she was giving up her own time after work, so he gave her a $4,000 pay raise she wasn't even expecting. Here's another example. When I started loving all the people at my job, I was able to do more for them even when the task was not part of my job. As a result, I had four job offers, and it was all because I was giving even though I wasn't expecting anything in return.

> ***But this I say, He which soweth sparingly shall reap***
> ***also sparingly; and he which soweth bountifully shall***
> ***reap also bountifully.***
> –2 Corinthians 9:6, KJV

However, it helps not to attach yourself too much to individual people and things, like money, at the object level. It's okay to love people; however, put your main focus and dependence on God and the big picture. This is more effective because some people can be really mean, and they often disappoint you since they will always have a different belief system and different goals than you because they have a different brain than you. Love all, not just a few. God is in all people, so when you serve the God of all, you will be serving a greater population than just a few individuals because the more people you can give and serve, the more you will receive. All big businesses have to have a "think big" philosophy if they want to grow big and be successful in the global market.

When you think big, then big results will be returned to you; when you think small, small results will be returned to you. If, for example, you want peace and love wherever you go in the world, then you will have to learn to love all, so you can have peace wherever you go. When I used to hate all men, I couldn't go anywhere without being scared and stressed all the time and having a mental breakdown. I thought they might hit me the way my dad did, but as I said, once I learned to love them all, I was at peace wherever I went. Now all I want to do is laugh and mess around with people in a funny way like a kid again. Not laughing at them, but with them, so there's a big difference.

One time my brother and I went to a hardware store, and I saw a man full of tattoos all over his arms and even his face. I said to this total stranger, "Oops you missed a spot," while pointing behind his neck. The guy mumbled something that I had forgotten. He was smiling, so he couldn't have been that mad, but my brother looked at me with eyes popping out, got me out of the store so fast, and scolded me. He was so scared of this guy who looked like a gang member. My brother said, "Are you kidding me? You shouldn't be talking to people like that. I can't protect you!" Oh my gosh, my brother was so mad at me.

A lot of us walk around in fear of people like my brother, but I'm done being like that. I can't help and serve people if I'm afraid of everybody, so the more I learn to love people, the more I can help serve others in abundance. **Negative thoughts of fear of people does not work and does not heal; only positive thoughts and feelings of love, happiness, and forgiveness, can create mental peace in us.**

> *Whatever it is that you fear, take your mind away from it and leave it to God. Have faith in Him. Much suffering is due simply to worry. Why suffer now when the malady has not yet come? Since most of our ills come through fear, if you give up fear you will be free at once. The healing will be instant. Every night, before you sleep, affirm: "The Heavenly Father is with me; I am protected." Mentally surround yourself with Spirit....You will feel His wonderful protection.*
> - Paramahansa Yogananda, *Living Fearlessly*

> *Whatever the mind of man can conceive and feel as true, the subconscious can and must objectify. Your feelings [thoughts] create the pattern from which your world is fashioned, and a change in feeling is a change in pattern.*
> —Neville Goddard, *Feeling Is the Secret*

TIME MANAGEMENT of Future & Present – (Write Goals Down & Create a List of What You Want)

> *In the hand of God is the prosperity of man: and upon the person of the scribe shall he lay his honour.*
> –Sirach [Apocrypha] 10:5, KJV

> *Every thought has a tendency to reproduce itself in physical form. Some thoughts are too weak, some too complicated to ever reach the physical stage, but a clear thought repeated again and again is almost certain to create a replica of itself sooner or later. Sometimes there is a long interval, but a clear non-competitive thought, well visualized and repeated often, will always manifest physically.*
> –Joseph J. Weed, *Wisdom of the Mystic Masters*

In my investment class, I learned about a study that found if you *write down all your goals and work consistently toward them, you will succeed in meeting 97 percent of all your goals.* Isn't that powerful? That's why written goals on calendars or lists or typed on your cell phone are so important in being a successful creator of your happiness goals. A written goal does two important things:

1.   It frees your mind from having to remember all that data, and therefore, keeps you from being mentally stressed so that you have mental peace, which is healing,

2.   It helps keep you mentally focused only on what you need to do that day so that you are always working toward your project goals on a daily basis, once you learn to break it down to a Daily-To-Do-List. This keeps your mind in the moment so that you are not easily distracted, and it keeps your mind focused only on what you need to do now, so you can do more in a shorter amount of time while always working towards your goals without going mentally crazy or getting stressed.

When I was an engineer for McDonnell Douglas Space and Defense in the 80's, they made everybody in the company take a time management course and learn how to use this new tool at the time called Day Planner. The Day Planner was basically a notebook made up of a monthly calendar with a whole bunch of blank lined pages for writing notes and for managing tasks and activities; like future goals, daily-to-do task lists, meeting minutes, grocery lists, class assignments, etc. This was the best time management course I ever took because the tool helped us keep track of all the projects, tasks, and meetings we had to work on—without going mentally crazy with all that data kept in our heads. The goal was to learn to mentally destress ourselves by reducing the number of thoughts we keep in our minds so that we can control our thoughts and have mental peace. The Day Planners helps us to do that. It was a great tool because at the time I was working full time during the week, going to school at night to work on my second degree in interior design, had a second job working on the weekends, and had a family to take care of. The Day Planner helped me manage not only all my work activities that needed to be done, but also my school assignments and projects, and my daughters' activities, without all the mental stress. So with a Day Planner and calendar, you could do more in less time and with less mental stress.

Once you figure out what you want to do and create for others and yourself, make sure to write these things down on your goals list. If you could be and have anything you wanted, what would you dream about being, having, and doing? Goal setting is simply listing what you want. What is it that you want to create in your life that would make you happy? Goal setting helps direct your mind and body as to what needs to be done now to get to where you want to be in the future. Goal setting is a great tool for creating what you want in your life. Read your goals once in a while so you know where you are going, and update your list as necessary. Then break your goals down into smaller tasks by creating a daily to-do list every day from the goal list. Once this is done, keep your daily focus on completing the daily to-do list, not the goal list. Update your list as needed. Cross out those items that you have already met, and add new ones as needed. So be very specific about what you want and when you want it. If you have problems in this area, my next book will be a Day Planner and calendar guide that will provide you with templates for setting goals and breaking them down into doable steps to help you stay on track so you can create miracles in your life and at the same time have mental peace from the stress of having too much information floating in your mind.

There Are Three Parts to Goal Setting

1. Make a list of your goals and be able to visualize what you want.
2. Add due dates to your goals.
3. Create a daily to-do list, so you're always working towards your goals.

To have an abundant life, you need to set goals in all areas of your life that you feel need improvement. Learn to visualize your goals so that your energy pull is strengthened. Here are some examples of goals:

- changing your beliefs about God, love, or peace
- changing behaviors such as smoking or overeating
- improving your marriage
- securing a better job
- creating more money
- getting an education in a specific area
- developing your spirituality

Whatever they are, write them down on your goal lists.

In one of the seminars I attended, I heard about a millionaire who had written over 120 goals, things that he wanted to see, do, and accomplish before he died, and he had already completed over 100 of the items. For me, I have multiple goals that are all on different time frames. I have one-month, six-month, three-year, five-year, and ten-year goals. So to push myself, I purposely push the dates up. If I miss the date, I don't get frustrated or angry, and I don't give up or think I've failed. I simply reschedule because I know that the schedule is aggressive. Even when I don't achieve some of the things that I want,

I don't get frustrated. For some reason, it's always because God has something better for me, and I simply change my plans accordingly, going with the flow. I'll take something better from God any day.

Writing down your goals in a list frees your mind from churning them in your head, and you are more likely to accomplish your goals. Also, regularly visualizing your goals as if you have already met them helps you move toward your goals. What I do when I want something is to cut out pictures of what I want and look at them daily to make me think about the goal. For example, I printed out a color copy of the house I wanted to buy and pinned it to the wall in my office so that I could look at it daily until I actually finally bought it. Also, I made a vision board as my computer background so I would see it every day. My husband cut out pictures from magazines and brochures of the things he wanted and pasted them on a poster board that he hung in his office so he could look at them on a regular basis. My teenage daughter cut out pictures of things she wanted and made a collage and put them on the front and back side of her folder so she could look at them regularly. Visualization helps you to create and be clear about what you want to happen faster.

YOUR ACTIONS – Creating and Working on your Daily To-Do List

Once you've listed your goals on paper, PC, or phone, it is easy to decide what you can do to help you get closer to where you want to go. Always ask yourself, "What can I do today to help me get closer to my goals?" You can then break your goals down into smaller, bite-size steps that you can do each day until the entire goal is met. Every day, write a daily to-do list of small steps that help you meet your goals. Cross out items from the list as they are completed.

> *Always focus your mind only on what you want to create at the present moment on your daily to-do list to keep from being easily distracted.*

Writing a daily to-do list helps you focus on what needs to be done on a daily basis, and at the same time, it keeps you directed toward your ultimate goals by having you do a little bit at a time. When you focus on your daily to-do list, your mind acts like a magnet. It's like taking a magnetic bar and pointing it at paper clips. By pointing the magnet toward the paper clips, you focus all its energy on attracting the paper clips toward it. Because we are made of energy, like a magnet, when we focus our minds on anything, we attract to us whatever it is we are putting our attention to in our minds. So, for example, if your mind is focused on negative thoughts, then negative things will be attracted to you because this is what your mental focus is on. However, when you put your focus on positive thoughts, then that will be reflected in what shows up for you. **So be conscious of your thoughts to see if you are being negative or positive.** Updating this list daily will help you focus on what is important for you to do each day to achieve your ultimate goals. You will feel good as each step is accomplished because you will be that much closer to meeting your goals.

When writing a daily to-do list, make the list as long as you can, but don't just write what you think you can do. You will be amazed at how much you can accomplish in a day when you have a list to focus on. Prioritize your list if necessary. It's all right if you can't get all of your tasks done in one day; leave the leftover ones for the next day's list. But don't stress out if you still have leftovers; again, save them for the next day. That is why I want you to make the list as long as possible, just to push you toward completing as much of them as you can. Figure out ways to accomplish your list efficiently. If certain tasks can be done sequentially, do them then even though some of the items may not have high priority. For example, on days that I needed to go to my mailbox to pick up our mail, I always did it in the morning after I dropped my daughter off at school, and then went to work. By doing this, I accomplished two or three things in that hour before work.

Multitasking is grouping items that can be done together. This is another great time-saving trick that I do all the time. For example, part of my regimen for losing weight is going to the gym during my lunch break. I always accomplish two things on my to-do list by going to the gym: I'm working out, and I'm always reading things that are on my to-do list while on the treadmill or reading a positive-thinking book.

When Solving Problems

With God all things are possible.
– Mark 10:27, KJV

Consider what's best for the whole, not just the parts. Think big, not small. Another thing you can do to create abundance in your life is to try to eliminate the word ***or*** from your vocabulary and replace it instead with the word ***and***. The word *or* is a limiting word. If you have a family, as I do, using the word *or* would mean somebody would be sacrificed in their activities; but by using the word *and* instead, it is more likely that the entire family's desired activities can be all met, or at least most of them, which helps to create abundance in the family as a whole.

For example, when my daughter got sick when she was in high school, and my husband thought his only choices were either to take my daughter to school to pick up her books so she could start her homework, take her to the doctor, and get her homework from the teachers, ***or*** meet a couple of appointments he had previously scheduled. I could see that he was frustrated because he had made these appointments weeks before, and to him, the only solution was to cancel them. To give him mental peace, I provided a different solution that allowed him to take her to all her activities **and** at the same time allowed him to keep his appointments, and he was able to do them all successfully. I asked him to call the school and have the teachers call him or e-mail him with her assignments, and I scheduled an afternoon appointment for him to take my daughter to the doctor. He then took her to school first thing in the morning to pick up her books, and he was able to get back home in time to make it to his two appointments. So, by eliminating the word **or** in your conversation and replacing it with the word **and**, you can actually do more and be at peace. In other words, you can do it all!

When I was initially doing my research work on this book, I wanted to create a miracle to test out what I was saying in this book as an example of what you can do. So I posed a question to God to help me on a big project that I was working on at that time. I asked, "How can I purchase this house and buy this facility and still keep all my cash and still be able to make all the payments work?" The answer I got back was, "Get a zero-down loan for the house, transfer your equity temporarily from your apartment buildings to the facility by refinancing them, and keep your cash. To pay for it all, pay your mortgage with your cash until you own the facility. This can generate more income later." The next day, I met with my loan broker and told her my plan (which was really God's plan), and she said it was all doable. During the next few days, she got bank preapprovals for all the loans that I needed. This project cost over $13 million altogether to fund, and God made it all work for me. The entire time, I was at peace and in love with it all, and life for me is good! In other words, I wasn't stressed at all because I knew I had the best partner of all. Please try to learn to use God as your life partner in everything you do. Let Him do all the hard thinking and lifting. He always has a better and easier way of doing things than you can imagine when you learn the proper process of working with Him.

This is what I mean by being able to create miracles with body, mind, and spiritual energy alignment working together as one unit. With my body, I took real estate classes to learn about the subject matter from experts, then I set goals for my own projects, and I followed through with them. I cleansed my mind and learned not to think so much (so I could hear God's voice) and kept it positive, and I opened it to allow God's spiritual energy to work and flow through me so that together we could co-create my and His projects together. So learn to keep all three of these areas (body, mind, energy/spirit) in positive alignment and going in the same direction to help you get to where you want to go faster. Before this, there would have been no way for me to put this big project together by myself. My negative state of mind and my limited understanding of how God's universe worked at the time, along with my body's low energy level, would not have allowed me to make it all work together on my own. I mostly sat on the sofa feeling sorry for myself. I was angry at the world, depressed, and vindictive. That's where I was at the time, at the bottom of my energy flow.

Ask God to help you come up with a solution, but don't get stressed out about it because being stressed only causes you to be negative, which then causes you to mentally close up. Be at peace, keep your mind silent, and surrender your concerns to Him. This keeps your bubble clear so that when God does answer your questions or prayers, you will be open to accepting and receiving His answer through your magnified intuition. He'll answer through a strong feeling you might get in your stomach or your mind, or He might send you some kind of a symbol or people you need to help you with your project. However He responds to your questions or prayers, you need to be open to His response and recognize it. This can only be done when you are calm and mentally at peace, not thinking so much. And learn to meditate, like the Buddhist monks, so you can hear God's voice come to you faster. There's a whole bunch of free meditation topics like weight loss, healing, and manifesting on YouTube.

When you do think, be positive. Think of Him as your parent or your partner in all your projects and issues by asking Him questions to help you with whatever it is that you need help with. So next time you are stuck on a problem, ask Him for His help. And even if you can do it yourself, ask Him to bless your projects, your relationships, your children, your health, etc. He is better, more powerful, and more creative than people, and he loves you no matter what.

Don't try to do everything on your own, as this can be very stressful when you think you are all alone and have to do everything yourself. Instead, make Him your silent partner in everything you do. Trust that He will answer you and help you solve your problems. It doesn't matter how big or small the problem is; He will help you. I notice that even when I lose things, like my keys, I just ask him, "God, please help me find my keys," and symbols of locations come into my mind to try. I notice I find things faster when I call upon Him for help when I'm calm than when I try to do it on my own and I'm angry at the same time.

Whenever I practice letting go and letting God handle my problems, I get solutions faster, and often they are actually better than they would be if I handled the issues myself. So use God and hand Him your problems like a business partner, or ask Him for a solution as a child might ask a parent. Surrendering means sharing all your problems with God and letting Him help you solve them. You have to trust that He can help you. If you give your problems to God, but you are still stressing out, that means you don't trust Him to help you. So when He does answer your problems, you will not be able to receive His answer because you will not be able to see or hear Him through your negativity. That's why you should not feel stressed about your problems after you give them to God; rather, you should try to be at peace. This is where meditation, by quieting the mind, becomes important. Trust that He will answer, and trust that you will be able to make it work once He answers you. Like a parent, God will give you answers, that is why He is called Father. You still have to do what you must do and follow through though. Some people believe that God will solve their problems for them, but that's not the way God works. God only gives you answers to your questions or directions so you know how to proceed with your problems and issues when you are stuck. You still have to do the actual work. Remember, God only helps those who help themselves. It has to be a partnership between you and God. It's about doing things together with Him as one, better and faster, to reduce your cycle time in creating whatever it is you are trying to create.

There's a joke about a guy who kept praying to God about wanting to win the lottery. For days he kept asking God to help him win the lottery. After days of praying, he became frustrated with God for not helping him. Finally, God said to him, "It would help if you got off the sofa and actually bought a ticket."

So when you are stuck or have problems, be calm, be positive, and ask God to help you. When He answers, it is up to you to take the next step. Whenever you want to be successful at anything, you have to follow through. You do your part, and He will just guide you along the way when you ask for help. He might bring people to you that you need, and when He does, you need to be open to it, or you will miss it; or He might give you clues through your intuition as to what to do.

A couple of my happiness goals for my children are for them to be happy and be successful in their work and school projects. To keep from being negative and worried and stressed for them, every day I pray for my kids instead, and I surrender my thoughts to God to give them mental peace, to help them with their projects, and I thank Him for surrounding them with His love and protection, and He answers my prayers. This gives me mental peace.

> Ask, and it shall be given you; seek, and ye shall find; knock, and it shall be opened unto you. For every one that asketh receiveth; and he that seeketh findeth; and to him that knocketh it shall be opened.
> -Matthew 7:7-8, KJV

8

Working in Your Environment

*We know that in all things **God works for the good of those who love him,** who have been called according to his [God's] purpose.*
—Romans 8:28, NIV

A man reaps what he sows.
—Galatians 6:7, NIV

When It Comes to People

You need to give and share your love, your peace, your time, your knowledge and your talents to others in order to receive. The more you can give and help others, the more you receive.

Once you have listed your goals, ask yourself, "Who do I need to work with in order to achieve my goals?" Then surround yourself with the people who come to mind. For example, as a real estate investor, I work with a wonderful team of people whom I regularly work with when I buy properties. I have a real estate broker, a loan broker, an insurance broker, a CPA, and lawyers on my team. Together they help me meet my investment goals. Always hire the best people you can afford in your area of study. For example, when I wanted to learn about love and forgiveness, I turned to Dr. Dyer's books and tapes as my starting point.

When you learn to love God at 100 percent with all your heart and soul, **He will work for you** to help you meet your goals by bringing you the right people that will help you meet your goals faster, especially if the project you're working on is His calling for you. You just have to make sure you are listening to His voice when He is talking to you. This is why we all need to learn to focus our minds on Him when we need to and balance with the world of objects as we work towards our projects and problems because He can help us work through them faster if we allow Him.

Accept the fact that you need people to help you get to where you want to be because you can't do it alone. God created us all for a reason. We are all here to serve God and each other not through force but through love for one another since He gave each of us different gifts and talents to be shared with others who may not have your particular talent. *(Remember, God's spiritual energy is inside all people, even your enemies. That is why we need to love them regardless, especially if they don't know God themselves.)* After all, not all of us could be preachers, doctors, nurses, lawyers, engineers, police, fireman, accountants, mechanics, plumbers, electricians, or teachers all at the same time, which is why we all need each other. We are all here to help elevate each other to our highest energy levels. We're all here to help each other grow in love, in peace, in spirit, in marriage, in money, in health, etc. Working with people is a give-and-take relationship. Remember, give and you shall receive. Learn to love all people and be in a constant state of cooperation so that working with them becomes easy. For example, whenever I get an oil change for my car, I always manage to get a discount because I treat the employees with love, kindness, and respect. Smiling helps a lot too.

Remember, do not take people for granted and just take, take, take, and use people; otherwise, they won't want to play and work with you. Instead, love them, cooperate with them, and provide them what you can with what they need that you are good at. In return, you can get what you need from them to meet your goals also; it's a win for both sides. When you share or give your talents to others, you are at the same time giving them peace of mind. For example, if my toilet is clogged, I'll call a plumber to fix the toilet so that I have peace of mind. If my dog is sick, I'll take him to the veterinarian so I won't worry about him being sick. Every year when my taxes are due, I need my accountant to do my taxes, and he gives me peace of mind once it's done. When I get into a car accident, I may need a lawyer. By helping others solve their problems, by being of service to them, not only are we helping them solve their problems, but at the same time, we give them peace of mind, which is why we all need each other.

> *Jesus said, "Peace I leave with you [his teachings of God]; my peace I give to you. Not as the world gives do I give to you. Let not your hearts be troubled, neither let them be afraid."*
> –John 14:27, ESV

Training and Education

Reduce your cycle time in meeting your happiness goals, by copying the success of others in your field of choice so that you know how to think and use your body properly, which will give you mental peace by doing what you love.

Some goals require training and education, so invest in yourself by getting the proper training you need from the best people you can afford in the area of your focus. I highly recommend training if you need it. Getting trained by the right people can save you time and money in the long run. If, for example, you want to improve your spiritual level, then copy Jesus, Andrew Harvey, Dr. Dyer, or Mother Teresa, etc. If you want to be an Olympic skater, don't go to your next-door neighbor, who is perhaps a nurse. A better choice for this situation would probably be somebody who's an Olympian ice skater as your teacher. So make sure to pick the right teacher or coach for the projects you are trying to manifest to help you get there faster.

Seeing God's Light & Talking to God

Seeing God's Light and Love: Once I understood God at 100 percent, and I was able to consolidate both science and religion in my mind in a way that made sense to me, peace took over chaos. I was walking around surrounded by the brightest light I have ever seen all around me and everywhere for two whole weeks, and all I could feel was just pure unconditional love around me. I was able to see through people as they truly are, as nothing but pure light, peace, and love, for all of us connected as one, as spiritual energy. All my tendencies of anger, hate, and guilt were replaced with pure love and peace. It was indescribable! I hope and pray that everybody experiences God's light and unconditional love during their lifetime. It's just the most incredible feeling of peace and euphoria. You don't have to go through a near-death experience (NDE) in order to experience and see God's light and feelings of pure unconditional love. *(NDEs are the hundreds of people around the world who were pronounced dead by their doctors, but only to come back to life after minutes, hours, or days like Jesus. See YouTube for NDE interviews.)*

You just have to get to know and understand God, until you get it, at 100 percent knowingness of his ONENESS in all or everything as invisible energy. This is the level of what religious people call enlightenment—the seeing of the light and the feeling of nothing but unconditional love. This is experiencing heaven on earth, or nirvana as some religions call it. It's a natural high, no drugs! This is a natural phenomenon that all enlightened people have experienced, and I was blessed enough to experience it. This is why some people choose to be monks, to live away from all the people's drama and chaos, and just meditate and focus on being mentally one with God's unconditional love and peace. But you can do this from anywhere and at any time, once you get God at 100 percent.

It's sad that a lot of people who do not understand God, therefore, cannot see and imagine Him in the invisible realm. They will often dismiss Him as not existing just because they do not know or understand Him and simply give up learning such a big part of their own life and who they are in relation to it. So they remain in darkness. He is real folks! He's waiting for you to open your mind's door and to put your mental focus on Him, in the invisible realm, where there are no objects, no drama, and no chaos to judge. This is the only place where you can find the unconditional love and peace you're searching for. Once you have learned to build a strong relationship with the light that resides inside you and all around you, you can then ask Him to help you co-create love scenes in your own Garden of Eden. Remember, this is your own responsibility since you are the only one in control of your own mind and the only one who knows what you want to make you happy.

Hearing God's Voice: As if seeing God's bright light and love wasn't strange enough, what's even stranger was hearing His voice. Up until the time I actually heard the voice myself, which I call God's voice, I really did not believe in God at 100 percent. This is one of the reasons why I, and most religious people, was only a 50 percent God-believing Christian; the other 50 percent was science. This is also one of the reasons I was a very sickly person, both mentally and physically, because I really never understood Him at 100 percent, and I didn't understand the process of communicating and working with Him, even though I prayed a lot. I thought that was enough. I went to church sometimes, but I never heard the voice like the people in the Bible. I thought that the stories in the Bible about people talking to God and hearing Him talk were only reserved for special people like Moses or Jesus, the upper echelons of the enlightened ones. You know, the few chosen ones.

The reason why we can all hear God's voice when we learn to quiet our minds is that our mind acts as a form of a receiver, much like a radio receiver that can receive sound waves (a form of energy that is eternal) from say, China, even though we may live thousands of miles away in the USA. You just have to adjust your mind to the right frequency, like a radio. If you want to hear God's voice, you need to be tuned into His love channel. Because like attracts like. If you are a negative thinker, stuck in your ego and only on the object level, then you will attract negative thoughts. But if you are a positive thinker, you will attract positive thoughts. This is the Law of Attraction.

To Hear God's Voice, Three Things Must Happen in Your Mind

1.   You must believe and understand God at 100 percent, that He exists in you as His spiritual energy. Anything less than 100 percent won't work to heal your mental and spiritual disconnection with Him.

2.   You have to learn to quiet your mind by controlling and reducing the number of thoughts you generate in your mind, as suggested in chapters 5 and 6, so you can actually hear God's voice. You see, He's always trying to talk to ALL of us, but because we're too noisy in our heads, chattering 12,000 to 60,000 thoughts a day, we cannot hear His voice when He is trying to talk to us. Effective communication between two people, as you know, is a two-way street. One has to be quiet and be the listener so they can hear the other person speak. Learning to speak to God works the same way. When you pray, that is your turn to talk to God. However, to actually hear God talk back, you need to learn to quiet your mind by reducing the number of thoughts you generate. So be quiet and silence your mind so you can hear Him.

3.   Learn to meditate like the Buddhist monks to quiet the mind so that God's voice frequency can get through to you so you can hear His voice. Just listen to the free meditations on YouTube. They have one for every topic, like a peaceful mind, improving your concentration, improving your health, losing weight, etc.

> *Tremble, and do not sin; **meditate** in*
> *your heart upon your bed, and **be still**.*
> –Psalm 4:4 KJV

You see, *once I corrected what I was doing wrong in the process*, like believing and understanding what God was at 100 percent and improving my relationship with Him by loving Him and putting Him first in my life, learning to be a positive thinker, learning to think less to quiet my mind, and doing nightly meditations before going to bed—this was when I started hearing the voice. It was this *voice* that was telling me to write this book, and He guided me through it all, just like the authors of the book *A Course In Miracles* by Helen Schucman and William Thetford, Professors of Medical Psychology at Columbia University's College of Physicians and Surgeons in New York. It was Helen Schucman (an ex-atheist) who heard the voice, and the entire book was actually channeled or given to her. Likewise, Dr. Dwayne Dyer had similar experiences where he would meditate and hear God talking to him, and all his books were, according to him, channeled to him this way also. You too can learn to hear God's voice. It's all a natural phenomenon, and it works because it's all invisible energy connecting us all as one. However, you have to learn the process and universal laws on how we are to work with the universe's spiritual energy level as your source to help you create your happiness goals faster.

It's all **thought** energy in vibration, but it's more like a sound you could hear in a dream state. This is why it's not audible to others and why religious monks meditate, so they can quiet their minds and hear God's voice come through to them. But you can do the same, just by learning to meditate to quiet your mind so you think less, so that you can hear His voice. This is what it means to "**be still**" in the Bible. Seeing God's light and love, and hearing His voice by today's standards are considered a supernatural phenomenon because they are uncommon. It's only labeled as supernatural because not too many people today know Him at 100 percent, and few know how to work with God's invisible spiritual energy level. However, once everybody gets this natural phenomenon as just a normal process, it will no longer be so mysterious and supernatural. It will just be something we all do and experience naturally on a daily basis, as it should be. I think once our scientists and educators discover that all these are just a natural part of who we all are and that we should all learn to master how our body parts (body, mind, spiritual energy) work best together when they are in sync as ONE whole unit—this is when this will stop being so mysterious and miraculous. This is so we can all stop fighting over nomenclature, so we can progress to the next natural human evolution of our ONENESS with God the Universe.

Praying and Meditating (asking God to help you find answers when you are stuck)

In the movie *Phenomenon*, which is one of my favorite movies with John Travolta, there is a scene where Travolta's character is telepathically moving a pencil, and the FBI investigator asks him how he is able to do it. John's character replies, *"It's energy. We are all made of energy, but you have to ask it—you can't demand it."*

> *Be ye not afraid neither doubt; for God is your guide.*
> –2 Esdras [Apocrypha] 16:75, KJV

> *Ask [questions], and it shall be given you [answers]; seek, and ye shall find; knock, and it shall be opened unto you."*
> –Matthew 7:7, KJV

> *In the past you may have been disappointed that your prayers were not answered. But do not lose faith....God is not a mute unfeeling Being. He is love itself. If you know how to meditate to make contact with Him, He will respond to your loving demands.*
> -Sri Sri Paramahansa Yogananda, Journey to Self-realization

I've found that the most powerful way to talk to God is to ask Him questions both big and small. When you talk to God, He always answers by giving you signs through books or through a feeling or by talking directly to you in a voice. This is called your intuition. It's the voice within. It's your inner guidance system—your navigator.

As you develop your spirituality and clean up your attitude within your bubble, your intuition intensifies and becomes stronger, so that most of your energy is focused on Him. Previously, even though I used to pray, at times it seemed He would never answer my prayers. I finally realized that for the most part, because I was operating at a negative energy level, my bubble was dirty and cloudy. As a result, I could not see or hear Him answer through all the anger and hate that clouded my mind. But once I changed my attitude from negative to positive and learned not to think too much, and to quiet my mind, I was able to see clearly through my mental bubble the signs that God was sending me in answer to my prayers. Remember, the negativity and darkness of not knowing Him at 100 percent blind you so that you cannot hear or see His messages come to you because you are too focused on the temporary physical object level of chaos that's always changing—the illusion.

Prayers are extremely powerful when you need understanding or when you are unsure of how to proceed with your goals. I used to not pray as much because I thought I could do my life on my own and didn't need Him or anybody. I didn't really know how to communicate with God. However, once I changed my perspective and learned how to talk to God, everything I'd always wanted started to show up for me. *Make God your life partner. When you are stuck with a problem, ask God to help you in the form of a question so that He can answer.*

> *I am the vine, ye are the branches: He that abideth in me,*
> *and I in him, the same bringeth forth much fruit:*
> *for without me [spiritual energy] ye can do nothing.*
> –John 15:5, KJV

My sister told me about the time she almost drowned in the ocean in the middle of a large bed of kelp. She noticed that the more she struggled and panicked in trying to fight it while trying to free herself from the kelp, the more the kelp held on to her and pulled her down. But as soon as she prayed for help and stopped struggling, she started to relax and be at peace. The kelp also loosened its grip on her, and she just swam up with the ocean to get back to the surface.

If you can think of the ocean as part of the universal God, you can do the same thing with your personal problems and goals. You can change your negative attitude to positive. You can learn to pray and make God your partner in everything you do so that you don't struggle and drown yourself in your life's vomit, which you have created in your mind. You need to learn to work with God by loving all, and you need to trust Him so that you live not in fear and panic, but in love, peace, and happiness. Start by forgiving and loving everybody. Change your attitudes, and be positive in everything you do and with everybody you interact with. Forgive all and love all, since everybody is just doing their best and since we are not taught how to think positively in school, since science and education have not figured out the importance of learning God's natural process yet, and have not yet discovered that thoughts even exist. Until then, we have to forgive them—everybody!

To remind myself that God is my life partner, I have a mantra that I repeat to myself over and over again. My mantra is: "I love you, God. I love you, God. I love you, God. I love you, God. I love you, God. I love you, God. I love you, God. I love you, God. I love you, God." I say it in the morning and at night, wherever I am. I repeat it in my car (I stopped listening to music and negative news), at work, at home while washing dishes, or when I'm jogging. This mantra helps me to focus on God. It reminds me to accept and love all because we are all part of God's universe as His spiritual energy. This mantra helps me avoid negative thoughts, and it helps me from being swayed by negative people. This mantra helps me to have a peaceful, loving day when I silently repeat it all day long. I let this mantra fill my mind all day long so that all I think about is God, not my problems that only create stress in my mind. This helps me focus on the big picture so I don't sweat the small stuff. This is how I stay focused in the moment and in love with all so that even if I do get negative, I don't get stuck in negativity for long because this mantra won't allow me to fill my mind with anything else but love. So create your own affirmation or prayer that is short and easy to remember and reminds you of God's unconditional love that you can repeat easily. This is so that you can change your state of mind quickly from negative thinking in a second, if you need to, by repeating your mantra.

Meditation

> *I remember you [God] on my bed, and meditate on you in*
> *the watches of the night.*
> –Psalm 63:6, NIV

When the turbulence of distracting thoughts subsides and our mind becomes still, a deep happiness and contentment naturally arise from within. This feeling of contentment and well-being helps us cope with the busyness and difficulties of daily life. So much of the stress and tension we normally experience comes from our mind, and many of the problems we experience, including poor health, are caused or aggravated by this stress. Just by doing breathing meditation for ten or fifteen minutes each day, we will be able to reduce this stress. We will experience a calm, spacious feeling in the mind, and many of our usual problems will disappear.

–Introduction to Buddhism

What also helps in achieving mental peace is meditation. There are many meditation topics (*e.g., healing, manifesting, losing weight, etc.*) on YouTube available for you to help you learn this process. Spending quiet time alone with God at night or in the morning when everybody else is asleep is very powerful because you can have clearer communication with Him. If we remember that God is mostly space, which is nothing, we can try to match this higher vibration by reducing the number of thoughts in our minds by quieting our minds. I've already mentioned two other ways to reduce the thoughts from your mind. One is by removing **past** and **future thoughts** from your mind, and the other is by removing **negative thoughts** from your mind. A third way is by **meditating daily**. All three together help to quiet your mind so that your communication with God is stronger and clearer. In addition, this process helps to magnify your intuition.

Your intuition is the voice within; it's your heart telling you what feels right—this is your internal guidance system. Meditation opens up your mental link to the invisible part of God's universal energy; this really helps to calm and quiet you down. After your meditation, the quiet time helps you become more creative; it helps you find solutions to your problems sooner, and it energizes you so you become more effective and are able to do more in a shorter amount of time. This happens because when you are silent and in the silence, you create space between thoughts in your mind so that you are in alignment with God's invisible spiritual energy level that is inside you and all around you.

It is this practice that allows you to access God's divine wisdom and inspiration—your creative genius. So you need to learn to listen to that inner voice because it guides you as to what you need to take care of and focus on. When you learn to take care of what's important in your mind, that voice—that constant nagging—will disappear, and you will have mental peace.

The difference between your voice and God's voice is that your thoughts tend to be selfish or negative. Your thoughts are in terms of limits, boundaries, and how solutions to your problems can benefit only you or a small group of people such as a religion or a club. God's voice will always benefit the greater good of the whole universe because He is about the union of everybody through unconditional love. He works for the good of all, not just the good of some. This is because He is everything and everywhere as invisible spiritual energy. This is why it's important to learn to silence your mind's thoughts by learning to stop judging everything on the object-level chaos and drama, and to refocus your mind's eye on God's invisible level instead, where there is nothing to judge. Judging is not necessary. It will drive you crazy if you don't learn to control your mind. That's why God can't help you when you are chattering—because you can't hear Him answer your prayers when your own internal voice is louder than His. You will always win the fight inside of you, but I assure you, you will lose the war. How good is that? Meditation is a way to mentally focus away from the chaotic physical world of objects to the God within, internally at your invisible energy level, by connecting to the universe of limitless love, happiness, peace, and joy that is inside you already.

Before I meditate, I pray and take all my issues and thoughts—whatever is in my mind—and surrender them to God and ask for His help. Essentially, I do a data dump prior to the actual mediation by praying first. This is how I empty out my mind so that I get rid of any and all mental stress and concerns and give them to Him to take care of. Then I close my eyes so that I don't see objects or boundaries. I relax and I do my slow breathing, and I focus inside of myself on the invisible level and I pray for Him to help me meet my goals because He does that so well.

A calling is when God asks you to create something for Him, even when you don't want to or don't think you can, that will be for the greater good of all. God's calling for me showed up when I asked the question, "Why isn't there just one easy book to explain all this stuff?" I got God at 100 percent after reading hundreds of books, attending different churches, and going to expensive seminars. Then I heard His voice, and He said, "I want you to create this book." As I heard the voice, I became like Moses. I told him, "No, I'm not good enough. Pick somebody who is a devout Christian, a writer, a preacher, or somebody with a fancy title. But please don't pick me because I can't do justice to Your book." These kinds of conversations went on for several months, and I tried to ignore this inner voice until I could no longer keep it quiet. He would not even let me concentrate on the things that were important to me, like my investments. His voice was very loud and clear. I finally answered His request for several reasons. I wanted inner peace for one, and because when I asked Him, "Why don't you pick somebody who has memorized Bible verses or somebody who at least reads the Bible?" He said to me, "I want you because you are open to loving all, which is what I want you to teach. You don't have an agenda to want to control them, and you are willing to question tradition. If I pick somebody else, they will want to control the conversation with only Christ as the focus. That's not all that I'm about. I'm more than that. This is what I want you to teach." So, this is why I am writing this book . . . or rather, His book.

Listen to your inner voice and address those important personal issues that you may have first so that you silence your mind. Maybe it's family, maybe it's creating more money to pay the bills, maybe it's work, maybe it's losing weight, maybe it's to stop smoking or drinking or drugs—whatever it is, take care of your personal issues first. Until you can take care of yourself and all the things God has already given you; He will not call you to help others because how can you? When you get God and understand Him at 100 percent, and you've learned to take care of all areas of your concerns, then don't be surprised when God whispers to you to help Him help others: "I've got something better for you to do. This is my purpose for you." What is it that God is asking you to do for the good of <u>all</u>? When you get a calling, you'll know it. That's when God reveals to you His purpose for you.

State of Mind of High-Energy People

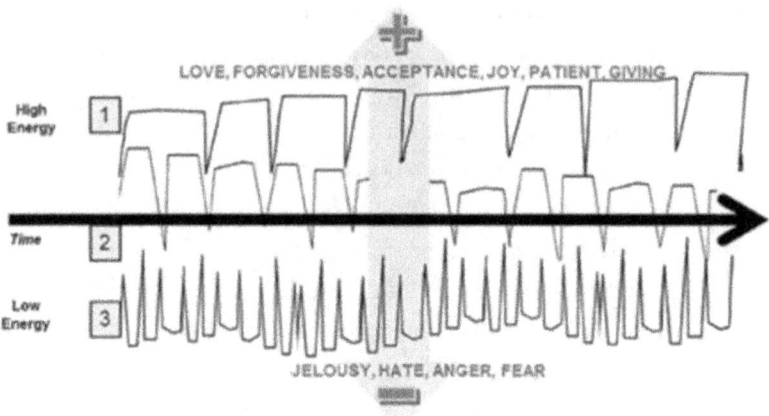

Characteristics of people who have high energy levels—the upper range in the diagram above—are people who choose to be consistently positive in their daily lives. They focus on solutions, not problems. They focus on creating big, not complaining big. This is their norm, their habit. They still have down days, but they are rare, and they can pop back up easily and quickly because that is what they choose to be. Being stuck, depressed, or sad for too long, is not their choice of being.

People who are in alignment in the three areas of mind, body, and spirit/energy operate at a higher energy frequency level than most people, which allows them to easily create and manifest things by simply focusing their thought energy through visualization and meditation. These people are not easily distracted or pulled down to negative thoughts and feelings. Or as I said before, if they do, it's very brief. If they are not getting the results they want, they don't get upset; they simply make adjustments by trying different ways of doing and thinking until they get the results they want by focusing on what they want. They are experts in streamlining. They don't like to waste their time on bad moods, depression, and gossip because these take up mental real estate and pull them down to lower energy levels, which is a waste of time. These people love what they do and enjoy life while doing it.

They are extremely active in creating their unique perspective of their own life. They have the same amount of time and mental space as everybody else. However, because they fill theirs with mostly love and passion to create, they appear as if they can just about manifest anything and everything they want in a short amount of time. They know and are clear on what they want, and they just go for it. To an outsider, these people seem to be able to create miracles.

To reach this level is the ultimate goal. Through conscious practice, this level is attainable for everyone. It's nothing unique because it's just the natural way God's universe works. Once we all learn this natural process, since we're not taught in school, and our educators and scientists haven't figured this out yet, it won't be so miraculous or supernatural anymore. The more open-minded a person is to God and learning the laws of working in the invisible energy/spiritual level, the easier and faster that person can reach this level.

State of Mind of Low to Middle – Energy People

Most people fall into levels 2 and 3, and people can be between levels too. The goal is to reach a level that is higher than the one you are at, and it doesn't matter where you start from. You are where you are; accept it so you may have mental peace. For me, I started from level 3 and lifted myself up to level 2; but sometimes, I'm between 2 and 1. And very rarely, I still find myself between level 2 and level 3. None of this really matters. My only point to you is that because **this is just a process of learning**, as you are evolving and growing to the new you, don't get frustrated if you find yourself fluctuating between the stages because it's all natural. Whatever you do, never give up on yourself. You need to be okay with where you are and not worry about where you think everybody else is. If this is difficult for you, then you still have an issue with acceptance of yourself and of others. You only need to think about and focus on where you want to be next, what you want to learn, where you want to go, what you want to do, and what you want to create in your own life for the sake of the people you love. The more people you love, the more people you can serve, and the more prosperity you will have. That's why it's important to learn to love all if an abundance of happiness, peace, and love is what you want to create in your life.

For those of us who are not experts at creation, we are like people who use those bumper rails they have at the bowling alley to help guide the ball away from the gutter; we too need a little bit of help until we no longer need the guide. The best tool for guiding our thoughts so that we stay focused is goal writing and writing out daily to-do lists to go along with visualization and meditation. These all help to guide us in creating whatever it is we want to manifest, whether it be learning about our spirituality, improving our relationships, improving our careers, creating more money, or whatever our desires might be. And don't forget God. He is the light that guides us through our problems and goals.

The above is not an exact science. It's just to illustrate the different levels of our state of mind. It's kind of like the different phases of water—solid, liquid, and gas—how the different vibrational speeds of electrons manifest differently in form for the same matter, such as H_2O. I hope you remember this from fourth-grade science. Like matter that is fluid and constantly changing, so are our minds always changing and creating new thoughts mixed with old thoughts, what scientists say is about 12,000 to 60,000 thoughts a day. We all need to be extremely mindful of the thoughts we generate because they affect our bodies, and we all need to learn to control them so we can all live longer, happier, and healthier lives.

9

Observing Yourself
(Monitoring Your Thoughts and Actions)

Ask yourself, *"Is it working or not working?*
Am I getting the results I want?"

If things are not working for you, work on them until you get the results you want. As long as you don't give up and keep adjusting your strategy until it's working, you will eventually become successful in meeting all or most of your goals. The problem with most people is that they give up after one or two tries, or they get so negative that they don't even bother. That is why most remain where they are, and even after five or ten years, they still have the same job or a similar one because they have stopped trying to be better at work even though they are miserable, or they are divorced because they have stopped trying to make their relationship work.

It is important to observe yourself as you are making changes in your life. Be aware of both the thoughts that are coming out of your mind and the actions of your body. What you want to watch for are negative thoughts and behaviors. When you notice that you are negative, quickly change the direction by being positive again. If you practice this enough, the duration of negativity between incidents will become longer and longer intervals until positive thinking becomes your norm.

Remember, what you want to avoid is being stuck in negativity for too long because you don't want that to be your norm. Positive people still get negative once in a while, but they don't allow themselves to remain on that negative energy level for too long. They practice being in control of their thoughts. When they notice themselves going off track, they immediately correct the problem and get back on the positive track.

Take a rocket that has just been launched, for example. From far away, it appears to be following its intended trajectory; however, in actuality, it's continuously going off track. But its inner guidance system, a computer system that monitors its trajectory, is preprogrammed to allow it to go off track within a specified range, and when the rocket hits either the upper or lower limits of the software program, the system automatically corrects its direction so that it is within the acceptable range until it hits its target. This is what makes it appear like it's following a smooth trajectory from far away, even though close up, in reality, it isn't. The system is continuously adjusting itself.

Don't worry if you mess up. Just notice when you do, stop yourself, and go back on track. Eventually, the changes will become new habits. As you repeat the process enough, you won't need to watch yourself as much because these new habits will become automatic for you. Remember, when you observe yourself thinking about your problems, that means you are thinking too small, at the object level. If you start getting overwhelmed, relax and breathe slowly, scale up, and enlarge your scope by refocusing your thoughts toward the love of God. Believe that God loves you as you are, no matter what, and that He can help you through whatever it is you are going through. You just need to ask Him for help. We all need help sometimes.

Do not bother trying to be a perfect person at the object level, since being perfect is a judgment call. You'll never be able to please all the 8 billion different perspectives of perfection in the world; it's impossible. It's better to just try to be a loving person towards everyone—by understanding and accepting that everybody else will probably have a different viewpoint than you. That's why it never makes sense to try to fight and argue or force others to believe and act as you act, since there is never only ONE truth that everybody can believe in at the object level, only different viewpoints. The only place where there is **ONE truth** is in the invisible spiritual energy level that is eternal, since everything there is invisible and nothing to judge, nothing is separate, and everything is the same. God doesn't care if you are not perfect at the object level either, because He only sees himself in you, as already perfect invisible spiritual energy.

Redesigning Yourself

Now you are ready to redesign yourself. Redesigning yourself is simply recreating yourself by changing the conversations or stories you tell yourself about yourself by rewriting how you view yourself, the people you are in contact with, your environment, and your world. As I said earlier, everybody has his or her own individual perspective of the world. That is why people fight, and that is why we have wars. Actually, fights and wars are due to thoughts of being righteous: We're right, you're wrong, our way is better than your way, we are better than you are, etc. There are no two worldviews that are exactly the same, because what you see as your world is an illusion created by your mind. You can change that illusion by redesigning your own perspective of the world you live in so that it works better for you. It's similar to redesigning a room in your house. Go ahead and move things around, change the color, get new furnishings if the old ones are not useful anymore, get rid of all the clutter, and get organized. In your mind—your world—you can do the same thing by simply changing your perspective and getting rid of your belief systems that no longer work for you. What is it that you want to be? Do you want to be a loving, caring, forgiving, creative person? If so, rewrite your conversation or story about yourself in this positive light.

If you have any negative thoughts about yourself or of others prior to reading this book, then you can take those negative words and simply change them to positive words. In the beginning, you will feel awkward, but as you repeat and practice the positive thoughts or words you use, they will eventually become more and more natural. If you are persistent in your quest for love and peace in your life, like anything new, your habits will eventually become automatic.

In my own experience, it took about six months of conscious focus and determination before the awkwardness disappeared and positive thinking became the norm for me. You can do the same thing. If I can, you can. So, if you are sick and tired of being lonely, fighting with people, struggling every day, and being unhappy at home or at work, then choose today to stop that craziness. Consciously choose instead to be mentally ONE with God and to be positive during every moment of your life from here on. Every morning when you first look in the mirror, hug yourself and tell yourself, "I love me. I am special because God made me like Him, in His image. I just have to choose to be like Him, to be loved, to be peaceful, to be trusting, to be forgiving, to be creative, and to be positive during every moment of my life with myself, with everybody, and with everything. I choose to work with God as my lifelong partner by surrendering to Him and trusting that He has my back, that He will answer my prayers, and that I will be at peace. He is the source of all the love and peace that I need, and He is the source of all that I create. I choose to make my life easy by loving everything and everybody unconditionally, especially me. I'm going to keep my bubble positive and clean every moment of my life at the object level, by keeping my mind focused on the invisible spiritual energy level of God where there is absolutely nothing for me to judge. This is how I choose to live my life, that: **"From here on out, I'm going to take full responsibility for creating my own HAPPINESS and I'm going to be positive and loving to ALL, which is God."**

In God is my salvation and my glory:
the rock of my strength, and my refuge, is in God.
–Psalm 62:7, KJV

Evaluating Your Commitment Level For Change

Below is a matrix you can use to evaluate your level of commitment to change the various domains of your life. You don't have to use the -3 to +3 scale. I am just trying to simplify it. You can also use -10 to +10 scale or -100% to +100% scale. Use whichever is easier for you, as long as you are consistent in using the same scale in the three areas of mind, body, and energy when evaluating a specific area of improvement. The result just gives you a quick glance at where you are when you are assessing your performance level in a specific area, whether you are mainly negative or mostly positive, or somewhere in the middle. Just make sure you are honest with your self-assessments; that way you'll know where you can work on improving.

MIND, BODY, and ENERGY.

COMMITMENT EVALUATION LEVEL								
AREA >								NOTES
MIND	-3	-2	-1	NEUTRAL	+1	+2	+3	
BODY	-3	-2	-1	NEUTRAL	+1	+2	+3	
ENERGY	-3	-2	-1	NEUTRAL	+1	+2	+3	

For example, in the area of weight loss for me, I failed drastically because you can tell from the matrix below that I'm really not ready for change since I'm clearly not very committed to changing how I think about food and my behavior. We have to remember that to change successfully, we have to be in positive alignment in all three areas and that the stronger all three of these areas are (body, mind, energy), the faster we can meet our happiness goals:

COMMITMENT EVALUATION LEVEL								
AREA >	Weight Loss							NOTES
MIND	(-3)	-2	-1	NEUTRAL	+1	+2	+3	Not commited. My conversation goes something like "I need to eat this or I will waste it" and "it's FREE!".
BODY	-3	-2	-1	NEUTRAL	(+1)	+2	+3	A little bit commited. Willing to take NO EXERCISE DIET PILLS and eat salads once in a while.
ENERGY	-3	-2	-1	(NEUTRAL)	+1	+2	+3	Neutral. My conversation goes something like: "God, I got this! Don't need you."

Our Calling to Exercise Self-Control

Thou shalt love the Lord thy God with all thy heart,
and with all thy soul, and with all thy strength, and
with all thy mind; and thy neighbour as thyself.
 –Luke 10:27, KJV

In the Bible, we are all called to be followers of God and called to teach others about God and loving one another as ourselves and others unconditionally as God loves us unconditionally so that we can all help reduce evil and darkness (*not knowing God*) in the world of objects (*Matthew 28:19–20*). After all, we can only control ourselves and not others willingly. The Bible and all other self-help books like this book are really all trying to teach us self-control (*e.g., Ten Commandments*) because we all have the propensity to be and do evil or be hurtful to ourselves and to others.

However, because God gave us all **free will** to choose to decide for ourselves whether to be loving or not, to be godly or not, to believe in Him or not, to be evil or not; then, there will always be those few people who will choose evil as an option because they do not know God and don't understand how to work with His invisible spiritual energy level at 100 percent. Although most of us are sinners, believing we do not need God in our lives, evil people are even worse. Evil doers are people who are intent on choosing to purposely destroy and hurt others to show themselves and others how powerful they are, for example, raping and murdering innocent people: ISIS, 9/11 Al Qaeda Terrorist (2,977 killed), the KKK, Hitler's Holocaust (11 million killed), Stalin (more than 20 million killed), and Mao Zedong (45 million killed) are just a few examples. These people are often control freaks, out to control others outside themselves, justifying their mental craziness since they themselves are mentally out of control and have no self-control. This is why learning self-control for all of us is so important because most of us are mentally out of control as a result of schools failing to teach our kids self-control, self-love, and the importance of loving others. That some of our kids are acting out their anger on others or themselves or later as adults. I'm talking about bullying, suicide among kids being on the rise, and illegal drug use on school campuses being on the rise. Even doctors and pharmaceutical companies are getting on the bandwagon and making billions in our society's mental madness, prescribing happy pills that are not only addictive but also cause suicidal tendencies to be magnified in their patients who are usually seeking help. The sickness of depression is getting younger and younger.

This is where religion becomes important, but only when they are being careful not to teach their followers to be evil themselves—to hate and/or kill nonbelievers in the name of God as some do! Even public schools do a great job teaching our kids the history of evil people, with the likes of Hitler and the KKK, where these evil people are immortalized. In history classes, teachers teach evilness, and their perpetuation is the focus. But they refuse to teach and give equal importance to God's love and learning, who we really all are as spirit/energy, so kids themselves can learn self-control from being evil. I believe learning to love one another, forgiveness, acceptance, and tolerance of each other's beliefs and practices is the greatest life lesson, and yet our educational system fails to teach any of this to our children. If we are to help the next generation of kids from this form of hell, the generational curse, we must all work together and do our part in helping stop the madness! The question for you is,

How are you going to help stop the madness?

Light up the World by Sharing Your Knowledge

This then is the message which we have heard of him, and declare unto you, that God is light, and in him is no darkness at all.
–1 John 1:5, KJV

According to *Merriam-Webster's Dictionary*, darkness is nothing more than *"the absence of light"* or the absence of God's light (since God is Light) and His unconditional love for all. It's the absence of the knowledge of our own divinity, our realization of our oneness with God the Universe and how to work with it, that creates our darkest moments and suffering in life. But, we can all learn to stop our mental stress and suffering caused by our inability to control our own thoughts by learning to control them so we can get out of the darkness. If we can just remember not to think so much, and when we do think, to try to think positively by bringing God's ***thought*** energy of unconditional love, peace, joy, happiness, forgiveness, patience, and acceptance out of darkness into our awareness, so that we can then bring God's light out to others as well, through us, by our example. In other words, don't think so much, and just be ***loving*** to everybody. Because if we can do this, one person at a time, I believe world peace is possible.

> *"Come, follow me [my teachings]," Jesus said, "and*
> *I will send you out to fish for people [to help others]."*
> –Matthew 4:19, NIV

If this book has inspired you in any way, I invite you to take my challenge to help me fish for people, by buying at least ten copies of this book to gift away to your loved ones, friends, or strangers. Let's all help others wake up, so that they too can get out of their darkness and mental madness. Once they've read this book, you can then share what you have learned, how you have implemented it in your life, and what positive changes have happened in your life as a result. Then read other books together and discuss them similarly with friends and family to keep growing in God's spiritual energy level. I highly suggest watching the movie *The Secret* as a must. When you are in a changing mode, you need to keep the momentum going; otherwise, like a rubber band, you will revert back to your old ways. That's why it's necessary to keep reading these types of books or join a spiritual center, your local church, or a spiritual group that discusses these topics to help you with your own spiritual growth and oneness with God. Always aim to reach your highest energy level of unconditional love.

Thank you!
May God Bless you and all your loved ones,
NAMASTE!

Who Are God's Superheroes?

There are those whom God calls to **"serve and protect"** people from evil, with their lives if need be. They are our police officers, fire and rescue fighters, our military, and anyone else who hears and answers the call. These are God's chosen few, the 5 percent or so elite group that I lovingly call God's superheroes. Their act of selfless love goes above and beyond that of a good Samaritan (*Luke 10:25–37*). According to the Bible, this is the greatest and highest form of love, are those that are willing to die for another.

Greater love hath no man than this, that
a man lay down his life for his friends.
– John 15:13, KJV

To all of God's superheroes,
Thank you for serving!

You're ALL the greatest!

Summary

GOD = 1) VISIBLE + 2) INVISIBLE
(UNIVERSE) (Objects/Matter) (Spirit/Energy)

$$GOD = O + \infty$$

(1)   Infinite
(▲ Cycles)   (Eternal)

SIMILAR beliefs & teachings...

SCIENCE – conservation of energy in quantum physics states that:
1) <u>EVERYTHING</u> in the *Universe* is made of out of
2) *INVISIBLE* energy, that can
3) <u>NEVER be CREATED or DESTROYED</u> *(∴eternal)*

RELIGION states that:
1) <u>EVERYTHING</u> is made out of *God's*
2) *INVISIBLE spirit,* that is
3) <u>ETERNAL</u> *(no beginning, no ending)*

DISSIMILAR Conclusion, in beliefs & teachings ...

SCIENCE – conservation of energy in quantum physics states that:
1) EVERYTHING *(except thoughts or words)* in the *Universe* is <u>made out of</u>
2) *INVISIBLE* energy, that can
3) <u>NEVER be CREATED or DESTROYED</u> *(∴eternal)*
∴OUR BODY & MIND are **NOT** CONNECTED to Universes' invisible ENERGY
force field that everything, including our Bodies, is made of

RELIGION states that:
1) EVERYTHING *(**including** thoughts or words)* is <u>made out of</u> *God's*
2) INVISIBLE *spirit,* that is
3) <u>ETERNAL</u> *(no beginning, no ending)*
∴OUR BODY, MIND, SPIRIT/ENERGY <u>are</u> all CONNECTED as ONE with
God's Universe, since everything is made of invisible SPIRIT or ENERGY

SOLUTION TO SOCIETIES MENTAL CRISIS

<u>SCIENCE, EDUCATORS & Dr's.</u> – Take DRUGS to control your thoughts,
since thoughts do not exist, they are not real
<u>RELIGION</u> – Learn to mentally control your own THOUGHT Energy & learn
how your BODY, MIND, & SPIRIT/ENERGY work best together in POSITIVE
ALIGNMENT as ONE with God's Universe, so you can mentally & physically
be more efficient and live longer healthier lives in Love, Peace, & Joy.

https://www.collective-evolution.com/2014/09/27/this-is-the-world-of-quantum-physics-nothing-is-solid-and-everything-is-energy/

Nothing Is Solid & Everything Is Energy – Scientists Explain The World of Quantum Physics

Published 4 years ago on September 27, 2014
By Arjun Walia

It has been written about before, over and over again, but cannot be emphasized enough. The world of quantum physics is an eerie one, one that sheds light on the truth about our world in ways that challenge the existing framework of accepted knowledge.

What we perceive as our physical material world, is really not physical or material at all, in fact, it is far from it. This has been proven time and time again by multiple Nobel Prize (among many other scientists around the world) winning physicists, one of them being Niels Bohr, a Danish Physicist who made significant contributions to understanding atomic structure and quantum theory.

"If quantum mechanics hasn't profoundly shocked you, you haven't understood it yet. **Everything we call real is made of things that cannot be regarded as real."** – Niels Bohr

At the turn of the nineteenth century, physicists started to explore the relationship between energy and the structure of matter. In doing so, the belief that a physical, Newtonian material universe that was at the very heart of scientific knowing was dropped, and the realization that matter is nothing but an illusion replaced it. Scientists began to recognize that everything in the Universe is made out of energy.

"Despite the unrivaled empirical success of quantum theory, the very suggestion that it may be literally true as a description of nature is still greeted with cynicism, incomprehension and even anger." (T. Folger, "Quantum Shmantum"; Discover 22:37-43, 2001)

Quantum physicists discovered that physical atoms are made up of vortices of energy that are constantly spinning and vibrating, each one radiating its own unique energy signature. Therefore, if we really want to observe ourselves and find out what we are, we are really beings of energy and vibration, radiating our own unique energy signature -this is fact and is what quantum physics has shown us time and time again. We are much more than what we perceive ourselves to be, and it's time we begin to see ourselves in that light. If you observed the composition of an atom with a microscope you would see a small, invisible tornado-like vortex, with a number of infinitely small energy vortices called quarks and photons. These are what make up the structure of the atom. As you focused in closer and closer on the structure of the atom, you would see nothing, you would observe a physical void. The atom has no physical structure, we have no physical structure, physical things really don't have any physical structure! Atoms are made out of invisible energy, not tangible matter.

"Get over it, and accept the inarguable conclusion. The universe is immaterial-mental and spiritual" (1) – Richard Conn Henry, Professor of Physics and Astronomy at Johns Hopkins University (quote taken from "the mental universe)

It's quite the conundrum, isn't it? Our experience tells us that our reality is made up of physical material things, and that our world is an independently existing objective one. The revelation that the universe is not an assembly of physical parts, suggested by Newtonian physics, and instead comes from a holistic entanglement of immaterial energy waves stems from the work of Albert Einstein, Max Planck and Werner Heisenberg, among others. (0)

The Role of Consciousness in Quantum Mechanics

What does it mean that our physical material reality isn't really physical at all? It could mean a number of things, and concepts such as this cannot be explored if scientists remain within the boundaries of the only perceived world existing, the world we see. As Nikola Tesla supposedly said:

"The day science begins to study non-physical phenomena, it will make more progress in one decade than in all the previous centuries of its existence."

Fortunately, many scientists have already taken the leap, and have already questioned the meaning and implications of what we've discovered with quantum physics. One of these potential revelations is that "the observer creates the reality."

A fundamental conclusion of the new physics also acknowledges that the observer creates the reality. As observers, we are personally involved with the creation of our own reality. Physicists are being forced to admit that the universe is a "mental" construction. Pioneering physicist Sir James Jeans wrote: "The stream of knowledge is heading toward a non-mechanical reality; the universe begins to look more like a great thought than like a great machine. Mind no longer appears to be an accidental intruder into the realm of matter, we ought rather hail it as the creator and governor of the realm of matter. (R. C. Henry, "The Mental Universe"; Nature 436:29, 2005)

One great example that illustrates the role of consciousness within the physical material world (which we know not to be so physical) is the double slit experiment. This experiment has been used multiple times to explore the role of consciousness in shaping the nature of physical reality. (2)

A double-slit optical system was used to test the possible role of consciousness in the collapse of the quantum wave-function. The ratio of the interference pattern's double-slit spectral power to its single-slit spectral power was predicted to decrease when attention was focused toward the double-slit as compared to away from it. The study found that factors associated with consciousness, such as meditation, experience, electrocortical markers of focused attention and psychological factors such as openness and absorption, significantly correlated in predicted ways with perturbations in the double-slit interference pattern.(2)

This is just the beginning. I wrote another article earlier this year that has much more, sourced information with regards to the role of consciousness and our physical material world:

10 Scientific Studies That Prove Consciousness Can Alter Our Physical Material World.

What's The Significance?

The significance of this information is for us to wake up, and realize that we are all energy, radiating our own unique energy signature. Feelings, thoughts and emotions play a vital role, quantum physics helps us see the significance of how we all feel. If all of us are in a peaceful loving state inside, it will no doubt impact the external world around us, and influence how others feel as well.

> *"If you want to know the secrets of the universe, think in terms of energy, frequency and vibration."* – Nikola Tesla.

Studies have shown that positive emotions and operating from a place of peace within oneself can lead to a very different experience for the person emitting those emotions and for those around them. At our subatomic level, does the vibrational frequency change the manifestation of physical reality? If so, in what way? We know that when an atom changes its state, it absorbs or emits electromagnetic frequencies, which are responsible for changing its state. Do different states of emotion, perception and feelings result in different electromagnetic frequencies? Yes! This has been proven. (3)

HERE is a great video that touches on what I am trying to get across here. We are all connected.

> *"Space is just a construct that gives the illusion that there are separate objects"* Dr. Quantum (source)

Sources:

(1) http://henry.pha.jhu.edu/The.mental.Universe.pdf

(2) http://media.noetic.org/uploads/files/PhysicsEssays-Radin-DoubleSlit-2012.pdf

(3)http://www.heartmath.org/research/research-publications/energetic-heart-bioelectromagnetic-communication-within-and-between-people.html

communities.washinghttp://media.noetic.org/uploads/files/PhysicsEssays-Radin-DoubleSlit-2012.pdftontimes.com/neighborhood/energy-harnassed/2012/sep/30/secrets-universe-unlocked/

Antidepressant Use Jumps 65 Percent in 15 Years

Women nearly twice as likely to use the drugs as men, CDC report finds

By E.J. Mundell

HealthDay Reporter

TUESDAY, Aug. 15, 2017 (HealthDay News) -- The number of Americans who say they've taken an antidepressant over the past month rose by 65 percent between 1999 and 2014, a new government survey finds.

By 2014, about one in every eight Americans over the age of 12 reported recent antidepressant use, according to a report released Tuesday from the U.S. Centers for Disease Control and Prevention.

Women are nearly twice as likely as men to be taking the medications, the report found, with antidepressants used by 16.5 percent of females compared to just under 9 percent of males.

Also, "long-term antidepressant use was common," said a team led by Laura Pratt of the CDC's National Center for Health Statistics (NCHS).

The researchers noted that "one-fourth of all people [surveyed] who took antidepressants over the past month reported having taken them for 10 years or more."

Why the steep rise in antidepressant use? Two psychiatrists offered up possible theories.

"Keeping in mind that antidepressants are used for a multitude of reasons -- not simply depression -- we should expect to see increased use of these medications as the FDA approves more indications for their use," said Dr. Ami Baxi, director of inpatient psychiatry at Lenox Hill Hospital in New York City.

But Baxi also credited the rise in use of the drugs as "a sign of decreasing mental health stigma," where more people feel comfortable asking for help against depression and anxiety.

Another expert believes Americans could simply be living more stress-filled lives.

"People have become increasing stressed and depressed in our society," said Dr. Seth Mandel, who directs psychiatry at Northwell Health's Huntington Hospital in Huntington, N.Y.

"Social media continues to paradoxically cause people to be more isolated and out of touch with their feelings," he said.

"In addition, direct-to-consumer advertising, coupled with an evolving societal mindset to just take a pill to make things better, both contributed to the growth in antidepressant use over this time period," Mandel said.

The new report is based on replies by more than 14,000 Americans, aged 12 and older, to a federal government health survey conducted between 2011 and 2014. Results were compared to those from prior surveys stretching back to 1999.

Besides the notable gender gap in antidepressant use, the survey also found that whites were much more likely than blacks, Hispanics or Asian-Americans to avail themselves of the drugs. For example, while 16.5 percent of whites took an antidepressant over the past 30 days, that was true for just 5.6 percent of blacks, 5 percent of Hispanics and 3.3 percent of Asians, the study found.

According to Mandel, "there are two factors at play here, one being that whites tend to have greater access to psychiatric services than do minority groups. The other is cultural -- it is often considered more OK culturally for whites to take antidepressants than for blacks or Hispanics, especially for men."

The fact that women are twice as likely as men to take an antidepressant may also have cultural roots, Mandel said.

"Despite our society being progressive, there are still ongoing gender stigma related to seeking treatment for depression ⬡. It is more 'OK' for a woman to be depressed and seek out treatment for this, whereas men are supposed to be tough, suck it up and move on," Mandel noted.

"One other possible confounder is that males, in my experience, are more upset by the sexual side effects associated with antidepressants -- such as erectile dysfunction and delayed ejaculation -- and could make them more reluctant to take these medications," he explained.

And while some people with chronic depression may need to stay on the drug for years, in many cases long-term therapy may not be warranted. "I always re-evaluate whether these medications should be continued on at least a yearly basis," Mandel said.

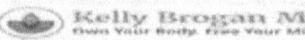

Kelly Brogan MD
Own Your Body. Free Your Mind

Start Here   Health Topics   Read The Book

Recent Study Confirms That Antidepressants Increase Suicide Risk

By Kelly Brogan, MD

Robin Williams, Chris Cornell, and Chester Bennington all revealed details of their struggles with depression and anxiety before they made the tragic decisions to end their lives. You're probably not surprised that people diagnosed with a psychiatric disorder, such as depression or anxiety, have an increased risk of suicide; in fact, a recent study estimates that 80% of people who attempt suicide have a psychiatric diagnosis associated with suicidal ideation. The startling news comes from the science that supports the causal role of antidepressants in the actual completion of suicide.

If depression leads to suicide and antidepressants like SSRIs resolve depression, we could decrease suicide rates by increasing the number of antidepressant prescriptions, right? That's the pharmaceutical argument for medicating people who are "at risk".

Yet, the evidence reveals some inconvenient truths, demonstrating that antidepressants actually increase the risk of suicide. Furthermore, just as the serotonin model of depression has never been scientifically validated, there is no evidence that antidepressants meaningfully and statistically significantly resolve depression – but, instead, we are confronting a growing signal of harm, including live-streamed suicides and school shootings committed by those recently prescribed. And a new study from Sweden that examines antidepressants in the context of suicide suggests that **antidepressants are pushing people towards, not away from, suicide.**

Swedish researchers analyzed data in a timespan in which antidepressant prescriptions rose steadily; the percentage of young women who were prescribed antidepressants increased from 1.4% to 5%. Approximately 500 young women committed suicide during this time period, and because toxicological analyses were performed postmortem, researchers could determine if these women were on antidepressants at the time that they made the decision to end their lives.

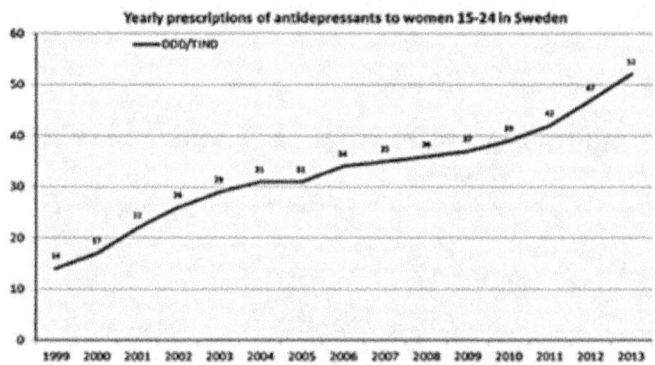

Yearly prescriptions of antidepressants to women 15-24 in Sweden

From 1999 to 2013, antidepressant prescriptions increased 270%. In 2013, about 5% of Swedish young women (36,345) were prescribed antidepressants.

If antidepressants indeed resolve depression and prevent suicide, those who committed suicide, would be the unmedicated ones right? Also, suicide rates would decrease as antidepressant prescriptions increased.

Yet, researchers found the opposite. As antidepressant prescriptions increased 270% over 15 years, suicide rates also increased. Strikingly, more than half of the young women who committed suicide (52%) were prescribed antidepressants within a year of committing suicide. And antidepressants were detected in 41% of the women who committed suicide, showing that they were under the influence of antidepressants at the time of death. In the remaining subjects, it is also important to know whether they had recently discontinued psychotropic medication. As many who have done so would tell you, abrupt (or sometimes even cautious) tapering of medication can lead to suicidality and homicidality with associated impulsivity (long after the medication itself is undetectable).

We are a culture that believes that force is necessary for change and progress (rather than natural momentum and emergent processes). But maybe we shouldn't be surprised when we learn that throwing more of the same failed medicine at the very problem created by the failed medicine – well, it doesn't actually work. Herein lies the thinly-veiled agenda of the industry – use the shortcomings of the intervention (in this case, continued and worsened depressive symptoms) to justify further interventions (more medications for all). This is like calling for more and more barricades to cover up any visual evidence of a forest fire while the fire blazes behind the facade. What is needed, at the first sign of risk outweighing benefit, is true informed consent – and thankfully, each and every prospective patient can now be empowered with a fuller version of the truth than they might receive from media, the government, or their prescribing doctor.

For more information on this topic, click here.

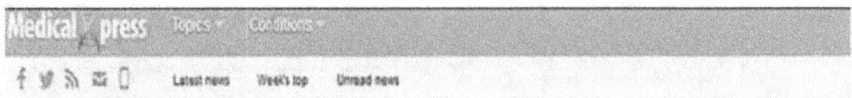

US antidepressant use jumps 65 percent in 15 years

August 15, 2017 by E.j. Mundell, Healthday Reporter

https://medicalxpress.com/news/2017-08-antidepressant-percent-years.html

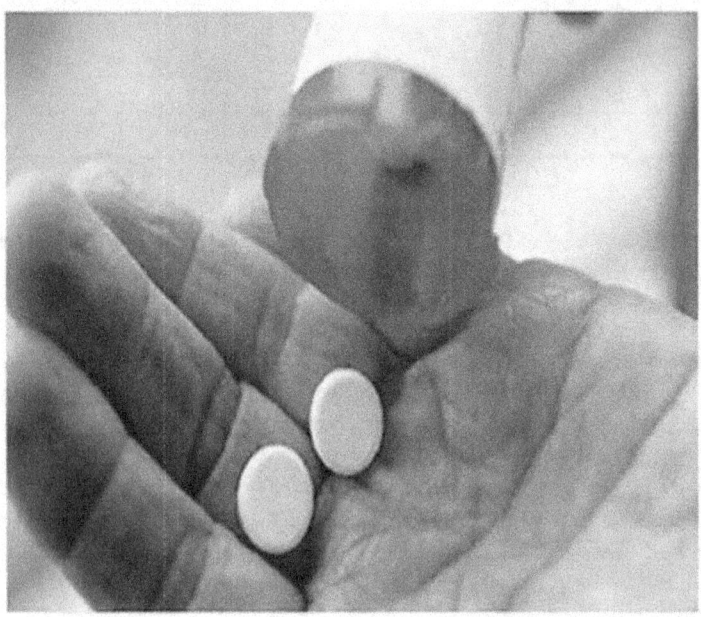

(HealthDay)—The number of Americans who say they've taken an antidepressant over the past month rose by 65 percent between 1999 and 2014, a new government survey finds.

By 2014, about one in every eight Americans over the age of 12 reported recent antidepressant use, according to a report released Tuesday from the U.S. Centers for Disease Control and Prevention.

Women are nearly twice as likely as men to be taking the medications, the report found, with antidepressants used by 16.5 percent of females compared to just under 9 percent of males.

Also, "long-term antidepressant use was common," said a team led by Laura Pratt of the CDC's National Center for Health Statistics (NCHS).

The researchers noted that "one-fourth of all people [surveyed] who took antidepressants over the past month reported having taken them for 10 years or more."

Why the steep rise in antidepressant use? Two psychiatrists offered up possible theories.

"Keeping in mind that antidepressants are used for a multitude of reasons—not simply depression—we should expect to see increased use of these medications as the FDA approves more indications for their use," said Dr. Ami Baxi, director of inpatient psychiatry at Lenox Hill Hospital in New York City.

But Baxi also credited the rise in use of the drugs as "a sign of decreasing mental health stigma," where more people feel comfortable asking for help against depression and anxiety.

Another expert believes Americans could simply be living more stress-filled lives.

"People have become increasing stressed and depressed in our society," said Dr. Seth Mandel, who directs psychiatry at Northwell Health's Huntington Hospital in Huntington, N.Y.

"Social media continues to paradoxically cause people to be more isolated and out of touch with their feelings," he said.

"In addition, direct-to-consumer advertising, coupled with an evolving societal mindset to just take a pill to make things better, both contributed to the growth in antidepressant use over this time period," Mandel said.

The new report is based on replies by more than 14,000 Americans, aged 12 and older, to a federal government health survey conducted between 2011 and 2014. Results were compared to those from prior surveys stretching back to 1999.

Besides the notable gender gap in antidepressant use, the survey also found that whites were much more likely than blacks, Hispanics or Asian-Americans to avail themselves of the drugs. For example, while 16.5 percent of whites took an antidepressant over the past 30 days, that was true for just 5.6 percent of blacks, 5 percent of Hispanics and 3.3 percent of Asians, the study found.

According to Mandel, "there are two factors at play here, one being that whites tend to have greater access to psychiatric services than do minority groups. The other is cultural—it is often considered more OK culturally for whites to take antidepressants than for blacks or Hispanics, especially for men."

The fact that women are twice as likely as men to take an antidepressant may also have cultural roots, Mandel said.

"Despite our society being progressive, there are still ongoing gender stigma related to seeking treatment for depression. It is more 'OK' for a woman to be depressed and seek out treatment for this, whereas men are supposed to be tough, suck it up and move on," Mandel noted.

"One other possible confounder is that males, in my experience, are more upset by the sexual side effects associated with antidepressants—such as erectile dysfunction and delayed ejaculation—and could make them more reluctant to take these medications," he explained.

And while some people with chronic depression may need to stay on the drug for years, in many cases long-term therapy may not be warranted. "I always re-evaluate whether these medications should be continued on at least a yearly basis," Mandel said.

The study was published Aug. 15 as an *NCHS Data Brief*.

○ Explore further: In US, many with severe depression go untreated

Exposed: Our dangerous dependency on antidepressants

A study giving 'happy pills' a clean bill of health is seriously flawed

Angela Patmore

We have become a nation of sad pill-poppers. The British, once Churchill's 'lion-hearted nation', are now among the most depressed people in the developed world. The UK ranks joint seventh out of 25 countries, with double the rates of Poland, Estonia and the Slovak Republic. According to the Children's Society, English children are more miserable than those in 13 other countries such as Ethiopia and Algeria — despite the widespread introduction of 'wellbeing' lessons. One in six workers in England experiences 'symptoms' of mental illness, and around 300,000 people leave their jobs every year because of them. The cost to the economy is put at up to £99 billion.

And the lower we plummet, the more antidepressants we take. Doctors, at a loss for other solutions, dish them out like candy. Last month a study was splashed over the front pages suggesting that we should take more. A million extra NHS patients should be dosed up with them, said the report's lead author, Oxford psychiatrist Professor Andrea Cipriani. He claims this meta-analysis provides 'the final answer' to the controversy over happy pills.

Can that be right? Is the science now complete, all questions answered? Or might Cipriani's advice, and our cavalier attitudes to dosing ourselves with brain chemicals, be seriously misguided? As he says, the answer can be found in the study — although not in the way he thinks. Its findings do not support the hype at all. In fact, the difference between antidepressants and placebos was so marginal that scientific critics who have analysed the results (such as Professor Peter Gotzsche of the Nordic Cochrane Centre) call it clinically negligible.

For a start, the study — hailed by newspaper headlines like 'The drugs do work' — looks only at adults 'with unipolar major depressive disorder'. Depressed young people are excluded. Many depressed adults are also excluded, partly because they are routinely excluded from trials in the first place. People with a medical condition or judged to have 'treatment-resistant depression' were debarred. 'Minor depression', which prompts so many to consult GPs, was deemed not relevant to the review either, so it would be clinically unsound for doctors to treat these patients with antidepressants on the basis of it.

Needless to say, the vast majority of the trials under analysis (78 per cent) were funded by the drug manufacturers. Of the 522 trials included, only 96 (18 per cent) were considered at 'low risk' of bias. Even the authors admitted that the certainty of evidence was 'moderate to very low'. This is not exactly a ringing endorsement of the clinical evidence they were examining — where the cutoff point for analysis was after only eight weeks of treatment.

What about false positives? The study says, for example: 'Depressive symptoms tend to spontaneously improve over time' and that this is why placebos appear to work. What it does not say is that this may also explain why antidepressants appear to work.

Professor Cipriani disputes some reactions to the study and says its focus was intentionally narrow to provide a clear-cut result. The heart of the problem — one that won't appeal to the drugs companies that have managed to acquire a striking amount of influence over our understanding of depression — is this: if depression 'spontaneously improves over time', why are doctors so keen to administer quick-fix chemical solutions? Edition after edition of the *Diagnostic and Statistical Manual*, the western diagnostic textbook, has expanded the number of mental illnesses, driven not by new research but by other considerations. It is an invitation to over-diagnose. Originally there were 16 vague disorders. The latest edition has 374 conditions, doubtless including a 'depression' to fit you.

Little wonder that the number of antidepressant items prescribed has more than doubled in the past decade. The so-called worried well visit the doc with a case of every-day blues, and instead of being told gently that time will heal, or listened to carefully, they're dosed up. GPs have eight to ten minutes per patient. This may not even be enough time for the person to get control of their emotions to speak, let alone explain their troubling circumstances. Chances are the GP will fetch out a questionnaire. The one for depression is called PHQ-9. The one for anxiety is called GAD-7. Both were devised by the pharmaceutical company Pfizer, which happens to market drugs for depression and anxiety.

GPs claim not to be overly reliant on these forms but they are pressed for time and the patient's distressing problems may be complicated. There's not enough time to work out if drugs are the right answer; or, for that matter, which drugs are best.

For all of the ubiquity of the drugs, there is still no proof behind the biological theory of depression as a 'chemical imbalance' of the brain that can be corrected by drugs. Combine this with a 'stress' ideology medicalising people's emotions and you end up with a very serious problem. Distressed patients who might benefit from wise advice instead get an unnecessary chemical coshing.

Some of the world's leading experts are now demanding a review of the whole approach to 'chemical cures' and biological explanations for mental illness. The British Division of Clinical Psychology, part of the British Psychological Society, has called for a paradigm shift away from the 'disease model' of mental health. The Council for Evidence-Based Psychiatry is pushing for radical change. Its eviscerating exposé *The Sedated Society* presents detailed evidence of flaws and fraud in the 'chemical imbalance' research; of rigged and corrupted data, of psychiatry's huge financial indebtedness to the pharmaceutical giants, and of unsuspecting patients being dosed with drugs that they did not need and that have gravely harmed them.

This, then, is the really dark side of sunshine pills: they may actually induce the very symptoms they're taken to alleviate, or worse. Antidepressants and benzo-diazepines or 'minor' tranquillisers may cause both disturbing side-effects and terrifying with-drawal symptoms. When a patient experiences bad reactions to the drugs, his or her GP, instead of tailing off the medication, tends to prescribe additional 'countering' drugs. This happened to my father, who ended up incurably addicted to two dangerous brain drugs, rather than just the one that apparently caused him to beat my mother, hold a breadknife to my throat and smash up everything breakable in our home.

All the drugs work by depressing the brain's central nervous system, and the brain counters this interference with chemicals of its own before it finally succumbs to organic damage. Patients may initially think they are getting better. But while some may find these pharmaceutical fixes help them through crises (rightly or wrongly attributing their emotional healing to the pills rather than themselves), others have seen their lives disintegrate.

Two years ago, the *BMJ* published an analysis of 70 trials involving 18,526 people (the biggest review of its kind) on anti-depressants, suicide and violence. Its findings were alarming. In under-18s the risk of such adverse events was doubled. The review states prominently: 'In the summary trial reports on Eli Lilly's website, almost all deaths were noted, but all suicidal ideation events [moments when patients form the idea of killing themselves] were missing.' A review of 142 trials of three antipsychotics, two antidepressants and the ADHD drug atomoxetine showed that most deaths (62 per cent) and suicides (53 per cent) reported in summaries did not appear in crucial articles about the trials.

A lot of patients on antidepressants experience a potentially dangerous side-effect called akathisia, or violent mental agitation. Symptoms include 'severe anxiety and restlessness', floor-pacing, sleeplessness and violent jerking of extremities. Says the reforming psychiatrist Professor Peter Breggin: 'Akathisia can become the equivalent of biochemical torture and could possibly tip someone over the edge into self-destructive or violent behaviour.'

In June 2012, James Holmes walked into a cinema in Colorado armed with an assault rifle, handguns and a canister of tear gas and shot 12 people dead, wounding 70 others. In March 2015, German airline pilot Andreas Lubitz deliberately flew his plane into the French Alps, killing all 150 on board. In May 2016, investment banker Sanjay Nijhawan killed his wife Sonita in a frenzied axe and knife attack at their Weybridge home, inflicting 124 wounds.

In June 2016, jobless gardener Thomas Mair of Birstall, West Yorkshire, a reader of far-right literature but 'mild-mannered' and 'kind' according to neighbours, walked into the Wellbeing Centre in Birstall run by Rebecca Walker and asked for help. He said his medication for depression wasn't working and 'seemed agitated and treading from side to side'. He was asked to come back the next day when the centre reopened. Instead he shot and stabbed to death the MP Jo Cox.

In October last year, Stephen Paddock opened fire on a Las Vegas music festival from the 32nd floor of the Mandalay Bay hotel, killing 59 and injuring 489. In November, Devin Patrick Kelley opened fire with an assault rifle, killing 26 at a church in Texas. All of these killers had been taking prescription medication for depression. You'd think it might have helped.

I asked the Office for National Statistics about antidepressants involved in suicides registered in England and Wales. It said: 'The main issue we have in monitoring suicides relating to specific drugs is that the information we require is not always on the death certificate... I'm sorry that we can't be of more help.' A recent statistic report was bad enough. It reported 3,346 registered drug-poisoning deaths (involving both legal and illegal drugs) in England and Wales in one year and added: 'There were 517 deaths involving antidepressants, the highest number since 1999.' And all trends are up. Deaths involving antidepressants between 2012 and 2016 numbered 2,358.

The obvious question is: would these people have committed suicide anyway, or did they do so because of the effects of the drug — or in despair at the failure of the drug to help them; a sense that there was no way out? The pharmaceutical manufacturers have always argued the former. Scientific and medical critics argue the latter. If you are about to swallow antidepressants, you are the line-judge.

Warning: A patient should never just stop taking the pills. Most authorities agree this is dangerous.

Appendix A

Book List

A Course in Miracles by Foundation for Inner Peace
Access the Power of Your Higher Self by Elizabeth Clare Prophet
Ask and It Is Given by Esther and Jerry Hicks
Bringers of the Light by Neale Donald Walsch
Creative Abundance by Elizabeth Prophet and Mark L. Prophet
Creative Mind and Success by Ernest Holmes
Creative Visualization by Shakti Gawain
Freedom the Courage to Be Yourself OSHO
Getting in the Gap by Dr. Wayne Dyer
Higher Self by Elizabeth Clare Prophet
Holistic Living by Neale Donald Walsch
How to Heal Your Body With Your Mind, by Dr. Joseph Murphy
Lucid Living by Timothy Freke
Manifest Your Destiny by Wayne W. Dyer
Meditations, James Van Praagh
Nothing Is Too Good to Be True by John Randolph Price
Re-Creating Your Self by Neale Donald Walsch
Secrets of the Millionaire Mind by T. Harv Eker
The Abundance Book by John Randolph Price
The Disappearance of the Universe by Gary R. Renard
The Force by Stuart Wilde
The Little Money Bible by Stuart Wilde
The Laws of Spirit by Dan Millman
The New Revelation: A Conversation with God by Neale Donald Walsch
The Power of Intention by Dr. Wayne Dyer
The Power of Now by Eckhart Tolle
The Power of Positive Thinking by Norman Vincent Peale
The Secret by Rhonda Byrne
The Seven Spiritual Laws of Success by Deepak Chopra
The Success Principles by Jack Canfield
The Toltec, the Four Agreements, Wisdom Book by Don Miguel Ruiz

Tomorrow's God: Our Greatest Spiritual Challenge by Neale Donald Walsch
Wisdom of the Mystic Masters by Joseph J. Weed
Your Erroneous Zones by Dr. Wayne W. Dyer

Notes

About the Author

Aura McClain is a Certified Life Coach specializing in spiritual and relationship healing. She was past president and member of the Orange County Youth Motivation Task Force, helping motivate at-risk kids and imparting the importance of education. She was an aerospace engineer for twenty-five years, working for Hughes Helicopter,  McDonnell Douglas, and Boeing Space and Defense, supporting different programs in various engineering capacities. Her first job as an engineer involved doing research work in artificial intelligence when the technology was in its infancy and was one of the first engineers to develop a working expert system. Most of her work as an engineer involved analyzing systems and processes to improve their quality and reduce their cycle times by incorporating best practices in the industry. She incorporates what she had learned as an engineer in improving systems and processes by analyzing how our body parts *(mind, body, and energy/ spirit)* are actually connected and work together best, when they are in positive alignment, as one unit. She teaches how to mentally reconnect to our own energy level *(that physicists say everything is made of)* so that we can all be more efficient in creating happiness, love, and peace in our own lives; thereby, helping to improve our human effectiveness by ending the generational curse of mental stress in us naturally.

www.ingramcontent.com/pod-product-compliance
Lightning Source LLC
Chambersburg PA
CBHW060759120626
46557CB00001B/32